For the Love of Dogs

My Life in Dog Years

by
Jory Ames

Copyright © 2014 Wordsworth LLC Publishing
All rights reserved.
ISBN: 9780990582816

Publisher: Wordsworth LLC Publishing
PO Box 2397, Palmer, AK 99645
www.wordsworthwriting.net
To contact the author, e-mail jory@joryames.com

For links to other books by Jory Ames, please see www.joryames.com

Selections from this book have been previously published in *Chicken Soup for the Cat and Dog Lover's Soul* and *Alaska Pet News*.

Portions of this book sales support STOP the Overpopulation of Pets' spay/neuter program (see www.alaskastop.org). Thank you for purchasing!

FOURTH EDITION

DEDICATION

If you live with dogs, you'll never run out of things to write about.
—Sharon Delarose

I have been so blessed to be able to share most of my 54 years with incredible dog companions.

Most of my dogs were "rescues," but I believe they rescued me more than me them, as I hope their stories will show you.

So this book is dedicated to, first, my dogs, and second, to those who know and love dogs as I have.

I also want to express my gratitude to those people who have tried to find some purpose in life by volunteering to help animals. Anything we can do, whether it be rescue a dog, donate to humane societies, push for spaying and neutering, walk a shelter dog, or just sit down with and pet your own dog, has so much meaning for the beautiful creatures who give so much to us, and yet ask so little in return.

Thank you to my proofreader, Gregory Drummond, and my editor, Eva Nagy, for all your wonderful suggestions. Thank you to David Jensen for allowing me to use some of his photographs of my dogs. You are a wonderful friend, DJ. Thank you to Michael Walker, for providing tough editing suggestions

And thank you to my son, Winston, for helping me raise, train, and clean up after the latest puppies, as well as for making my life especially wonderful. I am so lucky to have a kind son like you. I love you, and I'm so proud of you and your love for animals.

The author, Jory, and Buddy, in Washington.

TABLE OF CONTENTS

INTRODUCTION 1

CHILDHOOD IN ALASKA (1960-1982): POOCHIE & SNOOPY 3

1.   Poochie: First Lost Love 4
   - The Painting...7
   - Anchorage..8
   - Lessons Learned from Poochie......................................9
2.   Snoopy: Childhood Best Friend...................................10
   - Jealousy...12
   - Sleeping with Dogs..14
   - Biting...15
   - Teenager 19
   - A Purpose 20
   - Sacramento 21
   - Missing..22
   - Giving..26
   - Lessons Learned from Snoopy 28

MY TWENTIES IN CALIFORNIA, ALASKA, & OREGON (1978-1990): BOBBIE, DANE, & BEAR..........................29

3.   Bobbie: Two Lives Saved 30
   - Sacramento 30
   - The American River...36
   - Fears and Comfort 38
   - The Bite 38
   - Alaska Rental...40
   - Humane Societies and Animal Controls....................41
   - What Matters Most 42
   - Moving to Oregon 43
   - The Ending 46
   - Remembrances...49
   - Lessons Learned from Bobbie....................................51
4.   Saint Dane 52
   - Naming 55
   - Attention Must Be Paid 56
   - Centering 56
   - The Dane Effect on Bobbie 57
   - When Dog Love Seemed Not Enough 58

	The Train Ride	60
	Moving to "the States"	61
	Wild Dog	62
	Dog Memory	63
	Patience	64
	Aging	65
	Our Last Walk	65
	Forget-Me-Not	71
	Lessons Learned from Dane	73
5	Bear, Who Waited by the Road	74
	Lessons Learned from Bear	78

MY THIRTIES IN OREGON, ALASKA, & WASHINGTON (1988-1999): WOODY, EB, & BOOTS 79

6	Woody: My Transition Dog	80
	Transition Dog	81
	The Miracle	87
	The Abuser	88
	Going Home to Alaska	94
	Losing Mom	94
	Language	98
	Woody Love	99
	Washington	100
	My Mistake	103
	Just a Dog	107
	Lessons Learned from Woody	107
7	Eb: Woody's Best Friend	109
	The Meeting	109
	Best Friends	112
	Nights in Oregon	114
	Alaska	115
	The Moose Kick	117
	Losing Woody	118
	Dogs Grow Old	120
	Lessons Learned from Ebony	126
8	Boots: My Father's Dog	127
	Lesson Learned from Boots	130

MY LATE THIRTIES TO FORTIES IN WASHINGTON AND ALASKA (1997-2012): BUDDY & SCHATZY 131

9	Buddy: Woody's Replacement	132

	"Free Puppies"	132
	Living in Washington	135
	The Gun	136
	Schatzy: And the Pack Is Born…	137
	Leaving Washington	138
	The Last Hurrah	140
	The Baby	142
	The Sickness	143
	Lessons Learned from Buddy	146
10	Schatzy: My Treasure	148
	Lessons Learned from Schatzy	156

MY FORTIES IN ALASKA (1999-2010): NEWT, BAILEY, BLUE, CHEWIE, & STRAYS 159

11	Bailey and Newt: Not My Dogs	160
	Bailey: Chained Dog	161
	Lessons Learned from Bailey	166
	Newt: The Accused and Sometimes Guilty	167
	Lessons Learned from Newt	175
12	Blue-Chew	176
	Fostering	177
	Veterinarians	181
	Dog Parks	187
	Cars and Communication	191
	Weighty Issues	193
	Satisfaction	194
	Lessons Learned from Blue and Chewie	196
13	"Dog": The Seeker	197
	Lessons Learned from Dog	200
14	Lessons from Louisiana Puppies	201
	Lessons Learned from Louisiana Puppies	204

INTO THE FIFTIES IN ALASKA (2009-2014): MIZA & THE FOSTER PUPS 205

15	Miza: A Very Bad Dog	206
	How I Chose This Particular Piece of Trouble	207
	He's Got Personality…	208
	The $10,000 Accident	211
	Car Rides	212
	About His Name	213
	The Trauma of Life with Miza	214

Marked for Death	219
All God's Creatures	225
"A" Stands for…	226
Lessons Learned from Miza	228
16　Foster Puppies	229
Lessons Learned from Foster Puppies	238

WHAT THE FUTURE HOLDS **239**

INTRODUCTION

Sometimes I think I like dogs more than I like humans. The only time a dog has ever betrayed me...was by dying.
—*José N. Harris, Mi Vida*

"Are boy dogs different than girl dogs?" my graduate school friend Nick once asked me, 25 years ago in Oregon.

"What do you mean?" I asked, confused.

"Well, you have two boy dogs now, and you used to have two girl dogs. Are they different?"

Nick has never had a dog. I thought, he really, I suppose, wants to know, and is not just making conversation, but he doesn't realize that the question itself makes no sense to me.

"The thing is," I tried to explain, "I can say some things about male and female dogs, I suppose, and there might be some differences based on that. But what's hard about your question is that they are all individuals. Every dog I've known is unique, just like people are."

Eleven dogs have given me their love and attention, were my guides and teachers through my decades, devoted their too-short precious lives to me, moved to and traveled through various states with me, helped me through failed relationships and the deaths of family and friends, let me cry into their warm fur when I needed to, wrestled and played and walked with me in our happy moments, and cuddled up with me at night. Three more, who weren't really mine, were also a significant part of my life, and I of theirs. Two stray dogs and four stray puppies, who stayed with me briefly, left their imprints on my life. Two puppies have just arrived, ready to begin sharing our own amazing years together, until, ultimately, the heartbreak will come.

The only regret I have in my life with dogs is that they have shorter lives than mine, and so I must miss them. Still, I try to take comfort in the memories of each of them, especially, the special ways they told me they loved me.

Looking back, I realize, I have been a very lucky person to be so loved.

In this book, I describe, I hope, the beauty of dog love as I tell the individual stories of the dogs I've known. But remember that I am limited to using those things that dogs don't need to use: words. I have done my best to tell their stories, and mine, but it's best if you can read it while your hand is stroking the head of an old Labrador, a tightly curled poodle, a grateful mongrel, or even a grinning beagle, one kind of like Poochie, my first dog, and first heartbreak.

Blue in 2014 (Photo by David Jensen)

CHILDHOOD IN ALASKA (1960-1982): POOCHIE & SNOOPY

1 Poochie: First Lost Love

When was the last time someone was so overjoyed to see you, so brimming with love and affection that they literally ran to greet you? A dog will do that for you—ten, twenty, thirty times a day.
—Lionel Fisher

If dogs could talk, it would take a lot of fun out of owning one.
—Andrew A. Rooney

Photo by David Jensen of a beagle that looks similar to Poochie.

I was four years old when the Great Alaska Earthquake hit Anchorage on Good Friday 1964 and when my mother took Poochie away. My memories of both days are almost the same—yelling, chaos, excitement, then silence.

FOR THE LOVE OF DOGS: MY LIFE IN DOG YEARS

What was Poochie to me so young, and how do I remember him so well? Mostly I remember the feelings. The sensation of being connected to someone else so perfectly. Neither of us spoke much, but we spoke to each other in that perfect nonverbal way that humans and animals are capable of, or, as I learned years later, that lovers can do: when you look someone else in the eyes and you can read all the love inside those orbs.

Poochie was a beagle, the first of two beagles and the only dogs my family had during my childhood. The space between them was four dogless years.

I call Poochie "my dog," even though I wasn't old enough to possess anything, because he quickly became attached to me. My days were full and happy, with Poochie following me everywhere, as dogs in love do. My earliest years were spent exploring my parents' big two-story house with him; maybe when I started talking, I told him about everything we found, while he gave me his beagle grin, panting in encouragement. Maybe when I played with toys, I shared them with my best friend and always companion.

At night, I'd sneak down the stairs, Poochie always following me, and we'd go out the front door, down the street, then still dirt and gravel, looking for woods to explore. The way my mother told it, Poochie and I we used to run away together, naked and free, in the cold early mornings down the street in Anchorage, and my father's business partner used to find us happily trotting down the street as he drove to our house in the mornings.

The way I saw it, we weren't running away, but running to the woods. My dog and I exploring the world together, that's how it's always been for the fifty years since, and it started with Poochie, even though he was with me for such a short time.

Most of my memories of Poochie are feelings...the love and happiness I felt being around him. Those are still strong, all these years later.

But my most vivid, specific memory of him is when I was just-turned five, just before he disappeared from my life.

I am standing in the living room, and my mother is frantically running toward the door, yelling. Poochie comes up the stairs, proud and wagging his beagle tail, his tongue hanging out as he seems to laugh.

He knows he's done a Very Good Thing. He has protected the home, his family, us. I try to understand the details of what has happened as the turmoil grows around me. Poochie has bit someone who opened our front door. He was just doing a dog's job; I understood the dog's point of view even then. So what if the intruder happened to be the mailman?

It was bad, whatever it was, and I backed up tight against the wall, starting to feel frightened and helpless, because even though I didn't know that it was called "love" at the time, that is what I felt for him. Pure unashamed adoring love, and he felt the same for me. Everything about him made me happy; everything about me made him happy. We were partners, and he was just mine.

But now all I knew was that there were loud angry noises and running back and forth in front of me by my mother and my older siblings, and there was Poochie, grinning at me as he ran back and forth too, wagging his tail, proud that he'd warded off that awful intruder trying to break into our house.

I kept my place at the wall, confused, scared, knowing it all involved my best pal.

To my mom, there was only one solution.

Poochie was gone.

Forever.

She told us it was to a farm in Eagle River, but no matter how many times we asked over the coming years, she said we couldn't visit. Sometimes I wondered if there really was a "farm." My mother is gone now, so I can't confirm this, but she wouldn't ever discuss him with me anyway. Not once. No matter how much I tried to find him, to see him again, or to just talk of him. I imagine she felt guilty about it, now, but as a child, I didn't know how she felt. I never saw the best friend of my toddler years again.

It was my first loss in life, and it hurt, and it never did stop hurting. I missed him; I yearned for him; I ached for him; I didn't understand why my parents would take him away.

After Poochie disappeared, for the first time, I felt lonely. It wasn't a feeling I understood or could express to anyone, but I remember feeling a vast hole of missing him, and nothing seemed to help or make it go away.

Although I had two brothers and two sisters, I was the odd one out, the loner. They bunked together, played and fought together, and all slept downstairs together while I stayed in the sole bedroom upstairs other than my parents'. My mother was busy running the household. My father, like many Alaskan dads, was often gone to the "bush" working or hunting.

It would be four years until another dog, Snoopy, came into my life, until that loneliness ended.

Thirty years later the whole episode with Poochie all came back to me in full force, and I was filled with fury at my sister Ellen because she did the same thing to her dog. Not because the little black cocker spaniel-terrier had bitten the mailman, but because she bought a new house and didn't want dog hair in it.

"Where's Cassidy?" I asked when I went to see her house.

"Oh, we found him a home in the country."

That's exactly what my mother said she did with Poochie, but I never saw him again; I never saw the home in the country; what I did see, not too many years later, was the dog pound, and I sometimes wondered if Poochie ended up in the oven.

"A home in the country? If you really did find your dog a home in the country, then you'd better take your kids out there to visit him," I told Ellen, after I said a lot of other things that I don't regret. Such as never get a dog again; this is at least the second time you've done this to a dog; you always have an excuse: your husband's allergic, the kids are allergic, or the furniture gets dog hairs on it. You have no right to have a dog.

Of course, she has every legal right to get and get rid of as many dogs as she wants. But in my view, she has no ethical right to have one.

Losing Poochie was my first loss, but not my last. And ever since, most losses of loved ones, dog or human, have made me feel that same way—helpless and backed up against the wall and no one is able to understand and no one bothers to explain.

The ones I love just disappear and then I'm supposed to keep living somehow.

The Painting

A year or two after Poochie was gone, a babysitter came over one night. She said she could paint, and we begged her to paint us a picture of Poochie. We showed her a similar beagle in a book, and she created a beautiful head drawing of Poochie in oils for us. It looked just like him.

It was decided that the picture would hang in my room; I am certain I begged for it to be there. I stared at the painting as I fell asleep. Hours later, I woke up screaming. I ran to my parents' bedroom and crawled in their bed, crying.

Every night it was the same.

I wanted the picture of Poochie, but every night that his picture hung on my wall, I woke up screaming and screaming.

Every night I'd crawl in my parents' bed, where my mother would get angry at me for kicking her during the night.

After a week, the picture came down, to be shoved into the clutter in her room, behind her door (I'd sneak a look at it sometimes), and where it eventually disappeared forever.

My nightmares stopped.

I'm not sure I yet understand why this picture would create such nightmares in my mind, but I do know that even though I am now 54, I can still remember the agony I felt over missing him and the inability to express that loss to anyone. I was alone alone alone and nothing—not even a picture—could end the terror of that realization.

Poochie gave me the purest love. Perhaps at that age my mother and father represented pure love too, but somehow, after they took him away, I didn't see them quite the same anymore. How could they get rid of Poochie? He was family. Could they get rid of me too if I did something wrong? Why can't I just see Poochie one more time? Please? No, you cannot. Poochie is fine, she'd say.

Poochie was not fine.

I'm sure he died, alone, at animal control. Or perhaps a vet's office, but that would have been too personal for my mother. Better to drop him and not think about it.

But the child still remembers.

After my parents died, I searched for Poochie's painting in their room, but it was gone. I always knew it was there, and I thought maybe now I was ready to hang it up again, somewhere away from where I dreamed. Perhaps my sister Ellen, who came to Alaska to take everything she could because every little thing was precious to her suddenly, took it home and it sits in one of the hundreds of boxes she took away. It was silly to want it anyway. It wasn't

Poochie, it could never be Poochie. Perhaps that is why the picture tormented me, after all.

Anchorage

Growing up in Alaska was a treasure; I knew I was especially blessed, the luckiest of all children, just for this reason. That is, until the pipeline came. The pipeline would eventually make my family, as it did many families in Alaska, rich, but that didn't matter to a child. The only difference I saw was that my precious woods would disappear, seemingly overnight, into the noise and dust of construction. But until that happened, in my preteen years, I had hundreds of acres of wilderness to explore. The joy of going to school was the joy of slipping away, during recess or lunch, out into the woods, and not returning for an hour or more, sneaking back through a gym door or an empty art room window.

Our neighborhood, College Village, was a special wonderland, new houses interrupted by undeveloped lots to explore, and what few houses there were contained young families, my human entertainment. Decades later, several of the neighborhood boys these houses contained are still my dear friends.

I left College Village the day after I graduated from high school in 1978, and I was happy to escape. Anchorage had "boomed" during my childhood, thanks to the discovery of oil in the North Slope fields, and every precious parcel of woods I explored and thought of as mine was quickly turned to houses, schools, colleges, and shopping centers.

Years later, I would return to the old neighborhood: in 1994 while my father was dying, and then again in 2007, oddly forced back by my own son's "special needs"; the only school that had a "highly gifted" program in Alaska sat in the old neighborhood. I thought it would be fun for my son to live in a neighborhood and make lifelong friends there like I did, but I didn't realize the old neighborhood was in fact old. The young couples who had populated College Village in the early 1960s had stayed, aging grandparents and great-grandparents now, but their children, as most Anchorage children do, had moved out of state during college years and most never returned.

I was one of those children, who never thought I would move back to Alaska, but life's circumstances brought me back twice: 1994-96 and 1998 to today. The first move home was because of my father's illness and the need to escape an abusive relationship; the second return was because of the death of another beloved dog, as explained later.

Although I love Alaska, I sometimes find myself pining for another place, a place that is dying instead of growing, a place where the wilderness is taking over instead of buildings daily taking over the wilderness. Escaping into the woods with my dogs, wherever I live, is my favorite time of the day, and has been ever since Poochie.

There was another difference in Anchorage by the late 1990s compared to the 1960s, something permanently and sadly changed. It had to do with dogs.

When I was a child, after Poochie was no more, I still had the company of dogs. Every day, I would sit on the lawn, and every day, some dozen or so neighborhood dogs would come, one by one, to visit with me. I gave them my own names since I didn't know their true ones. I sat on the lawn and played with them—sometimes one, sometimes three or more—for hours. I was on their daily stops as they roamed the nearly empty streets.

How I loved those dogs! There were the Labradors, the huskies, the Great Pyrenees, the German shepherds and collies and various unrecognizable breeds. The gold, gray, white, black, and mottled sparks of life and fun came to see me, and it was a gift to me to see them.

As the neighborhood grew, of course, and especially after oil was discovered far up in the northernmost fields of Alaska, the streets were paved and became a steady stream of cars, fences went up, and the dogs disappeared into their now treeless lawned yards.

Anchorage became a leash town, and then, years later, came another citywide shift for those who walk with their dogs. In the late 1990s, became more athletic, sporty, filled with semiprofessional bicyclists and runners and skiers, all of whom wanted the trails for their own use. "No dogs allowed" signs began to pop up on all the public trails that the skiers groomed. "Dogs must be on leash" signs appeared in every park—city, state, federal. Title 17, the municipal code, was rewritten to forbid off-leash dogs anywhere in the municipality, which encompasses 1,969 square miles of not just city, but mountains, lakes, rivers, woods, parks, and wild trails, from Girdwood to Chugiak.

I left Anchorage for the Matanuska-Susitna Borough ("Mat-Su"), 50 miles north and still-shared trails, where a horseback rider and a bicyclist could still pass each other with a smile instead of an argument, and a dog could run freely alongside his human companion without angry threats from a skier who screamed that the holes made by paws were ruining his groomed adventure.

"I will never move back to Anchorage," I would say, upset at its antidog sentiments, exhausted from trying to get dog owners to stand up for their rights, and I never would have predicted that 10 years later I'd be back, forced to move again to do the right thing for my child, back in the old neighborhood with four large rescued dogs in a tiny yard. In the decade since I left, though, the dog owners had won some sort of concession for the brutal leash laws. Five off-leash parks were scattered throughout the city where dog owners conglomerated, happy to still have a few areas to let the dogs run, play, swim, and just be dogs.

But I get ahead of myself. Decades ahead.

Lessons Learned from Poochie

Stay close to the one you love. Explore the world together. Protect your family, but be careful who you bite.

2 Snoopy: Childhood Best Friend

> *The great pleasure of a dog is that you may make a fool of yourself with him and not only will he not scold you, but he will make a fool of himself too.*
> —*Samuel Butler*

> *The only creatures that are evolved enough to convey pure love are dogs and infants.*
> —*Johnny Depp*

In 1968, when I was eight, my mother decided that the family could have another dog. Once again, she was determined it was to be a beagle, perhaps thinking that Poochie and his protective bite was an anomaly, and so one day she drove us out to a breeder's farm on the outskirts of Anchorage (which within a few short years would be a bustling part of midtown as Anchorage sprawled into the barricades of the Chugach Mountains and down to Cook Inlet, even on the steep mountain slopes behind Potter's Marsh).

FOR THE LOVE OF DOGS: MY LIFE IN DOG YEARS

How does one pick a puppy out of a litter of perfect little joys? Somehow, one came to us, and I knew he was to be my best friend, even before he got in the car of five children fighting over who got to hold him. A beagle, of course, had to be named Snoopy, the children (who all read Charlie Brown) agreed, although my father tried to get us to name him Sniffy, perhaps just to torment us.

All my life, dogs have bonded with me, and I with them. You know how some people just "get" babies, or toddlers, and vice versa? I was never one of those people. But I "got" dogs, and they knew it. We are drawn to each other, dogs and me. Snoopy, from almost the moment we came home, chose me.

Even with five children in the family, it soon became clear that Snoopy was my dog. At night he would sleep in my room; all day he would follow me around the house, never letting me out of his sight. When I did leave the house, he would wait for me. Walking home from school each day I'd give a loud, special whistle to let him know I was coming, and he would answer from a block away with those eager howls that only beagles have. When I rounded the corner and would see him at the side gate, waiting for me, I would cry, "To the back door!" and he would rush to it joyously, as I ran inside to let him in.

Yes, he was my best friend. Snoopy was the kind of true friend that only a dog can be—unrelentingly faithful, tolerant, and loving.

This drew some ire from my siblings. A few months after Snoopy came home with us, my brother Aaron challenged me to a contest to see who Snoopy liked the best. It was such a ridiculous idea. I knew; we all knew. So with complete confidence, I stood in a line with my siblings, and we all called him.

"Snoopy, come here!" I called, knowing he would come straight to me. After all, I was the one he slept with, followed, played with. I was the one who trained him to sit, to stay, to come...all the lessons we were using now to play this silly game.

Snoopy started coming, looking right at me, as I knew he would, but then suddenly veered off to Aaron. I was stunned. It made no sense. He was mine! All mine! Why?

Perhaps seeing I was really hurt by my dog preferring someone else, or that I looked confused, wondering if I had misunderstood the close relationship between Snoopy and me, Aaron finally laughingly fessed up to the treats in his pocket, which he'd showed our little beagle just before the contest started. It was a cheat! Snoopy ate his treats, and then *my* dog came to me.

I was nine, and Snoopy was one, when this photo was taken in 1969. He is giving me his "love bite."

Jealousy

In the late 1980s, scientists actually began to debate and study whether animals have sentience, or emotions, a debate Charles Darwin's writings had inspired almost a hundred years before. Back then, writers such as Jack London and Ernest Thompson Seton, two of my childhood favorites, were accused (including by Theodore Roosevelt) of being "nature fakers" for suggesting that animals could think or feel.

But to me, and I am sure to anyone who has shared their life with a dog, there was no question.

The first time I learned about jealousy, for example, was from Snoopy. There were to be other times in life I would relearn this lesson, and how jealousy could make a dangerous man much more dangerous, but a dog, whose love was pure and complete, dealt out punishment in a way not physical but certainly clear.

I was always finding strays and desperately trying to find their homes, even as a child, and still today. But my parents made it clear early on that I was not to bring them home. The father of one of my classmates was a veterinarian in the neighborhood, so I would sometimes take them to Dr. S.'s house, sure at that time that veterinarians loved all creatures and would take fine care of them. (Years later, when I was in high school, Dr. S. would lead the collective, powerful veterinarian battle against the spay clinic I was trying to get built, and so my view of veterinarians as all animal-loving saints began to change.)

FOR THE LOVE OF DOGS: MY LIFE IN DOG YEARS

One day, when I was about 11, I found a cat in the neighborhood. She was black, hungry, and lonely. She mewed to me desperately, and as soon as I knelt to pet her and talk to her, she decided I could help and followed me home, as so many animals did. I built a box in the front yard for her since my parents hated cats. Both of them had been raised in rural Washington, and both saw cats as barn creatures only, with one purpose: to catch mice. They were never to be allowed indoors.

I gave my little black cat food and petted and played with her in the front yard. Snoopy watched me miserably from inside the fence prison. He howled hatefully and pitifully. When he was a puppy, a neighbor cat liked to torment him by leaping in the yard and scratching him, then leaping back to the top of the fence and hissing at him. He could not reach her there, no matter how high he jumped or how loud he protested. He detested cats, but this was even worse. I—the love of his life—was playing with this cat right in front of him! How dare I! Why would I? Did I not understand that I belonged to him?

That night, inside the house, Snoopy did something he had never done before in our years together. He wouldn't let me near him. When I tried to pet him, he rose up and moved away. He stared at me from behind the rocking chairs, then under the table, with angry, hurting eyes. I realized then and never forgot a lesson of jealously like no person ever could teach me. Snoopy was so hurt by my attention and affection lavished on that stray cat that he insisted I know about it in a very—well, perhaps I should say humanlike—way.

He had been jealous of me before, when he smelled that I had petted another dog, for instance. He would inspect me carefully every day when I got home from school, and if I had stopped and played with another dog, Snoopy would grumble about it until I washed the smell away. But he had never treated me like this. I had caused him to feel the deep, vicious pain of rejection.

Not until I was finally suffering, hurting, and crying in my shame, begging him to let me pet him, and kneeling on the ground in front of him, did Snoopy allow me to touch him again. We made up.

A few days later, our neighbors adopted the cat, which upset me at the time, but now I know that her life in their home was much better than the life I offered her in a cardboard box in the front yard.

And the rest of my life, when someone tried to say or when my various school textbooks proclaimed that nonhuman animals aren't capable of "feeling" emotions, I would just think of Snoopy, and know better.

Snoopy was three, in 1971, when this photo was taken.

Sleeping with Dogs

As I said, Snoopy slept in my room, but that wasn't enough for me, for us. He was my best friend, and oftentimes my only friend. Always an insomniac, the only way I could happily fall asleep was to call him up to my bed and snuggle with him till sleep came.

But my father, in particular, forbade this.

I respected and somewhat feared my father, mainly because of how enraged he was when he caught Snoopy sleeping with me. He was always, to me, a gentle, kind man, except when it came to this.

I would be deep in sleep, and suddenly I would hear shouting, and Snoopy was literally being picked up and thrown off my bed, and then kicked outside, winter or summer.

I would always end up crying, sobbing for my poor Snoopy, wanting to go let him back in, but afraid to. Sleep would not come those nights.

But it didn't stop me and Snoopy from sleeping together. Every night I'd call him on the bed, and fall asleep hugging him. I had no interest in dolls or stuffed animals; I just wanted my best friend Snoopy.

At one point, my mother even switched my bed to a bunk bed, but I taught Snoopy to climb the ladder, and so we would snuggle again, although always fearing the creaking open of the door and the consequences.

Just like my mother's getting rid of Poochie, I could never understand my father's anger when it came to Snoopy sleeping with me. I imagine it had something to do with growing up on a farm, and animals were utilitarian things, not family. Perhaps, I assume, in his childhood, any dogs, like cats, were prohibited from the house. He never told me why.

(Years later, in my early 20s, I was back living in Anchorage but at a rental with no fenced yard, so Snoopy stayed at my parents' house. I had met and briefly married a man, Bert, who also forbade me from having dogs on the bed. He would actually sniff the bed to see if I'd had my dogs on it. I thought he looked ridiculous, and of course I had my dogs on the bed as often as I could. One night I brought Snoopy over to visit me; he was now 12 years old, weak, and obese, so could no longer crawl up on a bed. Bert actually lifted him and put him on the bed next to me. That was definitely the kindest thing Bert ever did for me.)

I have always loved sleeping with dogs. They snuggle and hug me and snore happily next to me. It is the best and least-lonely time of my day. Before I fall asleep, I take this time to "baby talk" to my dogs (how they love this) and scratch their ears and tell them what good dogs they are. I give them toys and we play together. We watch a show. We fall asleep, happy to be together.

My biggest fear about growing old is not disease or suffering, but being stuck in some "home" where I can't sleep with my dogs.

Snoopy and me in 1973.

Biting

So, dogs sometimes bite. This has never concerned me to the level it does the law, animal controls, dog haters, or my mother. (Of course, these years spent with Poochie and Snoopy were long before the popularity of beating and breeding dogs to fight that created stocky little creatures designed to kill and before horror stories of pit bull attacks on innocents filled the news.)

I figured, they don't have fingers or hands or the ability to communicate through human language, but their mouths are certainly a powerful and clear way to communicate and accomplish necessary matters. (Even having fingers, hands, and human language has not stopped humans from committing atrocities against each other, though.)

Some dogs will "love bite." Snoopy was one of the two dogs in my life who liked to do this. Jack London describes this perfectly (although it was never "akin to hurt" in my experience) in *The Call of the Wild*:

> Buck had a trick of love expression that was akin to hurt. He would often seize Thornton's hand in his mouth and close so fiercely that the flesh bore the impress of his teeth for some time afterward. And as Buck understood the oaths to be love words, so the man understood this feigned bite for a caress.

But there's another reason dogs bite. They bite to protect, either themselves or their loved ones.

So, when Snoopy bit, I always looked at it from his perspective, and saw it clearly. Maybe once it was uncalled for, and he was certainly very sorry about that one.

Twice, he was sleeping, and someone fell on him, and he woke up with a snap. One was Irene, neighborhood drunk who, like so many women and children of our neighborhood, sought out my mother for their daily complaints or concerns (my mother, it turns out, was the focal point of our neighborhood; I often wish I had her skill with making people feel comfortable, but as a loner, I do not). It was late afternoon, Snoopy was sleeping on the floor, and Mrs. I., furious and typically drunk, tumbled and fell on top of him. In his perspective, he was under attack, and he awoke with a start and with a snap at whatever was assaulting him. Just one snap; he came to his conscious senses and understood this was a human, and an accident, and so he tried to escape my mother's screams, tail down sorrowfully.

The second time he was asleep, it was the next-door neighbors' grandchild, a boy I babysat sometimes, who fell on the sleeping dog, and that was when Snoopy truly looked sorry. He woke, snapped, and regretted instantly.

But my mother's punishment, each time (even though I think sometimes she wanted to bite Mrs. I. herself), was to take him to the pound.

Nowadays my dear friend Dave says I shouldn't call such places "dog pounds," but animal controls or animal care centers, as they lately like to be called.

But I had, by the time of these bites, being about 10 years old and 12 years old for each respective one, outgrown the innocent age when I came running home from school telling my mother how the animal control people who talked to our class told us how they "send the dogs to Heaven" and how wonderful that is. In fact, they described it in such glorious terms to the class of second graders that I suggested we should take Snoopy there. (And after I learned the truth, ever since, I've avoided the terms "put to sleep" and even "euthanize" when telling children what happens there. They are "killed," I say, because there are too many and not enough homes. So spay and neuter, don't breed, and adopt your pet for life, I tell them. None of those kids are running home begging for their dogs to be sent to the wonderful pound.)

In any case, Snoopy was punished each time for biting by being driven to the dog pound. I believe it was three times, because, like Poochie, he also managed to clamp down on the mailman, who finally decided to stop just walking into our house anytime he pleased after that incident.

FOR THE LOVE OF DOGS: MY LIFE IN DOG YEARS

Each time my beloved Snoopy disappeared, for a few days, once for almost two weeks. The last time, animal control called my mother and said he was going to be killed. A man had tried to adopt him, and Snoopy had bitten him at the checkout counter.

So my mother retrieved him each time.

The only other time Snoopy bit anyone was when I made him do it, and I enjoyed it thoroughly.

"Hit me," I told my parents one night, both of them comfortable in their rocking chairs, enjoying a rare evening when my father was home and not working or hunting in the Alaska bush.

"What?"

"I just want to see what Snoopy will do," I said. Snoopy, as always, was at my side.

"What do you think he'll do?" my mother asked.

"He'll protect me," I answered.

So they each took a turn playfully punching me, and he immediately jumped up on them in turn, growling and frantic, snapping just over their hands to force them to quit.

Snoopy was fearful of my father, in particular, but he had no choice but to protect his true love. It irritated my parents, of course, but I was so proud of my dog.

"Mon chien," I'd call him ("my dog" in French, my brother taught me). "You're my love dog!"

He'd grin at me, wagging his beagle tail, so proud and happy to have protected me. Then we'd jog happily back to my room, and climb into bed and play, another forbidden act, which my parents had eventually given up on fighting, I suppose.

Years later, when I was a teenager, Snoopy almost bit again, but I was proud of him, as he was once again protecting me, protecting mine.

I had a girlfriend over, in my room, and when I left to go to the bathroom, she decided to sneak a peak in my diary. She opened my bedside drawer and grabbed it, and Snoopy jumped on her where she was sitting on my bed, and stood on top of her, furious. I found them there, diary in her hand, him snapping the air over her face and growling, her screaming. I patted him and thanked him, and took my diary back. She never tried to do that again.

Unfortunately, there was another very troubling consequence of Snoopy's bites. My mother forbade him from ever leaving our fenced yard again. He was no longer allowed to run alongside me on my bike rides or go on walks with me again. He couldn't go explore the Alaska woods with me. He couldn't even go on leash and jump the plywood jumps I'd set up out front and trained him to go over.

This I found too horrible of a punishment, so I would "forget" and leave the gate open many times, and say, "Run, Snoopy!" And he'd take off for a grand adventure for a day, coming back tired and happy that evening. My mother would be furious every time. This was before the pipeline hit, of course, and before Anchorage became a huge bustling city of cars and dangers to a dog running the neighborhood, and before the patches of woods all disappeared.

But back when I was still allowed to walk him, there was one house in our neighborhood that I feared passing, for this is where Snoopy's mortal enemy lived: Scamper. And sometimes Scamper was out. And when Scamper was out, he headed right toward Snoopy, and Snoopy jerked the leash out of my hands and they tumbled together into a ferocious fight.

There is nothing I hate more than a dog fight. I hated reading about them in *The Call of the Wild* and *White Fang*, but I much more hated seeing Scamper and Snoopy tearing chunks of each other's flesh off one another.

The other neighbor kids—all boys—would come running and watch but would do nothing. I think they rather enjoyed it, cheering on Snoopy. Nobody liked Scamper. But I would pound on the closest house doors, begging for help breaking up the fight.

One time Scamper's owner came running down with salt and pepper and poured it on their open wounds, and the fight immediately ended, both dogs whimpering miserably. I thought that was a brilliant solution.

Interestingly, I was told by a neighbor boy that when I let Snoopy out of the fence "accidentally," he had seen Scamper and Snoopy touch noses and ignore each other.

So I learned another lesson. The leashed dog is a protective, aggressive dog. When he was connected to me by leash, Snoopy was on defense. When he was off leash, he never once got in a fight.

I've seen this behavior at dog parks. Fifty dogs can be running free, but bring a leashed dog into the mix, and the dogs all run toward it, its owner screams, the leashed dog begins barking a challenge, and the play can suddenly turn serious.

For most of my life, I have only rarely used a leash, then; only in cities. I try instead to find places to walk where my dogs can run free, around me or ahead of me.

All my dogs have always stayed right with me on such walks, except one. That was Snoopy. Especially in the dark winter days, as I got older and convinced my mother to let me walk him once in a while, I would take him to a huge acreage of woods near my house that is now the University of Alaska Anchorage and Alaska Pacific University. I would strap on cross-country skis and let him go. He'd be off, deep into the woods, and I'd hear his howls as he trailed some snowshoe hare, never catching one, but loving the chase.

I would usually spend a couple of hours in the woods that way, skiing the beautifully silent winter woods, listening to his bays, and then be ready to return.

"Snoopy!" I'd call, often several times, as I headed back toward home, and always, by the time I reached the edge of the woods, he'd be there, waiting for his leash and our walk back.

My father built a cabin on a lake some 70 miles north of Anchorage. Back then, before the pipeline and money and people and subdivisions came to the Mat-Su Borough, we had to snowshoe or boat across the lake to get to our one-room cabin. It was my absolute favorite place in the world. We didn't just own seven acres; we owned thousands, it seemed, as no one else lived anywhere near us. Snoopy would usually get to come, and so there we could spend the whole day out exploring the woods and lakes and marshes together. On those walks, he stayed close to me. There were no people, no dogs, no streets. There were bears and moose; perhaps that's why he stayed so close. For whatever reason, he knew that at the cabin, we were to walk as one.

Teenager

All through my teenage years, when dating took priority in my interests, and I spent fewer and fewer moments paying attention to him, Snoopy continued to adore me, follow me, wait for me. It seems he had to wait years for me to pay attention to him again. Or perhaps I never could. Not the way a child can understand and love a dog so fully and unashamedly.

When I was very young I was unashamed of the friendship I shared with "my old hound dog," "mon chien," or "my love dog," all terms I liked to use. I hugged, played with, petted, trained, and talked to him endlessly.

One game we liked to play involved food. I'd tell Snoopy to stay, then I'd take a piece of bologna from the fridge, and make a trail of it, around the living room, behind chairs, through the dining room, back to the living room, and then hide the meat at the end.

"Go get it, Snoop!" I'd say, and he'd get busy, his superb beagle nose sniffing the trail out quickly, following it loop after loop, till he found his prize.

Snoopy had my full attention for hours every day. What adult can do that? I pet my dogs now, often, but for minutes at a time. And often I am doing something else while I pet them—watching TV, talking on the telephone. Adults are much too busy to focus on dogs. But even so, our dogs wait for us to finish being busy and take full joy when we design to give our attention to them.

Snoopy and I loved each other as only a child and dog can love each other—and as only someone who's known such a love can understand.

I grew up and away from him.

It hurt him terribly.

Of course I wasn't physically abusive to him. But perhaps it is just as painful to a dog when the child he loves ignores him, a certain truth illustrated by the song, "Puff the Magic Dragon":

> *A dragon lives forever but not so little boys*
> *Painted wings and giant's rings make way for other toys.*
> *One grey night it happened, Jackie Paper came no more*
> *and Puff that mighty dragon, he ceased his fearless roar.*

I remember those large brown eyes following me continually for attention, for the love and warmth shared before, but I was too busy and too caught up in the misery of falling in love with boys to reassure him.

I regret it now, of course.

He always remembered me, though.

One summer I went to visit my sister in California and was gone for three weeks. When I returned, I ran through the house to the backyard, flung open the door, and my hound dog howled and wailed like I had never heard him, plunging into my arms, telling me loudly and fiercely how much he missed me. I wept for the intensity of his love. I hugged him as he howled for a full 15 minutes. I said I was so sorry I left him and never would again.

Such promises a child can't keep, but wants to.

I had, generally, a miserable teenage existence. I fought with my mother constantly, I had lost respect for my father when he returned from Africa with a game room full of heads and bodies, including an elephant ear coffee table, and I had discovered that I wasn't pretty enough to be popular, but just enough to be used.

Because of my miserable fights with my mother, something that is probably a fairly normal part of weaning but certainly didn't feel normal at the time, I often dreamed of running away from home. But my plans always fell through because of Snoopy. I knew I couldn't leave him, and how would I take him, when I didn't even know where I was going or how I would get there? So I stayed.

I worked long hours at various restaurants so I could buy a horse, and when I finally got one, she was bitter and detested people and lived to fling me off her back. Cherokee taught me, in her fury, that everything I'd been raised to believe about horses was wrong. All she wanted was to be back in the herd, not with me on her back. But still, I was now responsible for her hefty monthly boarding fees for the next eight years, so I always worked.

Snoopy at the trees I called "The Three Musketeers," where I buried my parakeets, guinea pigs, and turtles who passed on. These were back in the woods that the University of Alaska Anchorage now resides on, where I would ski while Snoopy chased snowshoe hares through the woods.

A Purpose

In 1977, I came home from another long night working at a restaurant, and found myself, per usual, unable to sleep at 11 p.m., even though I had school the next day.

I had recently scored a little TV set for my room, so I turned it on low volume, so as not to wake my parents. I called Snoopy up on bed with me, and there I sat, horrified.

It was the local PBS station, and they had made a documentary about pet overpopulation in Anchorage. I only saw the end, but it changed my life.

The end was a silent, tortuous filming of two dogs (one a puppy or small dog) being shoved into a decompression chamber and slowly dying. It took them at least 10 minutes to die.

My tears wouldn't stop; I turned off the TV and sat in horror, thinking about my life, my purpose.

I always knew there was an animal control. I knew, vaguely, that there was a problem.

What I didn't know was nearly 9,500 beautiful souls were being killed every year just in Anchorage, Alaska. And killed in torture, from the looks of it.

I always knew something else. I knew I'd be an "old lady in tennis shoes" fighting for animals, after life had happened, after school, and college, and perhaps a marriage, and work, and retirement.

But now, suddenly, I knew I was going to be a young lady in tennis shoes.

The next three days, without telling my mother, I skipped school and headed down to animal control, to do something, anything, to stop this.

And so I started a drive to build a spay clinic in Anchorage. (I also, a few years later, was able to get the decompression chamber outlawed in the state of Alaska for killing dogs and cats.)

I had a purpose, and that purpose was to end pet overpopulation, in every way possible. It wasn't as sudden as I hoped it would be, but I have seen, over my life, a dramatic reduction in the numbers killed, from 30 to 40 million dogs and cats killed annually in the United States in the 1970s to 3 to 5 million a year in the 2010s (many humane societies and animal controls don't report, so numbers are estimates). I attribute the drop to spay clinics and education, but still there are breeding mills (puppy mills) and backyard breeders. I won't be satisfied until the number is zero, and all dogs and cats are valued as the individuals they are.

All pets deserve a good home and someone to love, like Snoopy had, I believed, and so that night in eleventh grade, I made that my life's mission.

Sacramento

At high school graduation, my father gave me a one-way ticket to Sacramento to stay with my sister. They were as ready for me to move on as I was. I leased out my "mean ole mare," as I called her, for a year, and I flew away from Alaska. I didn't come back for eight months.

My only regret was leaving my dear Snoopy. He was the one I missed most, as I couldn't call or write to him, and I felt terrible about this, remembering my earlier promise to him.

He was old, it had been eight months, would he remember?

I ran to the backyard that December night as soon as I got home, just as I had four years earlier when I returned from my previous California trip.

It was dark, I called his name, and he stared at me in disbelief this time, sniffed me in the dark.

"Snoopy, don't you remember me?" I said, hugging him, tightly, afraid.

Slowly, softly, then louder and louder, my dear old friend began his joyous howling.

The old love howl just for me was much weaker now, and he couldn't stand very long, but fell to a sit. His eyes were glazed. My long leaving had taken much from him and had aged him permanently.

I took him in my arms and cried. "Snoopy, Snoopy. I'm home. I'm so sorry I left you again."

Snoopy, beginning to age.

Missing

In the winter of 1982, my dear old dog and childhood companion Snoopy disappeared. He was now 14 years old (I was 22), and I knew he probably only had another year or two left in him, but his disappearance I was completely unprepared for. His disappearance had nothing to do with irresponsibility. He was more than secure in my parents' backyard the morning it happened. The gates were iced shut and partially buried in the snow. The possibility of him climbing or jumping the 5-foot fence was nil—my beloved old beagle was obese and arthritic, barely able to walk, let alone climb a chain link fence.

I wasn't allowed to live at my parents' house after I'd returned from California, because I had brought my dog Bobbie with me. My parents, instead, in what they thought was punishment but was in fact just what an 18-year-old girl wanted, put me and Bobbie in their one-bedroom rental house. But I still went by to visit my parents, and, of course, Snoopy.

One night I stopped by, heard Snoopy scratching to get in, and went to open the door until my father called, "Leave him out." I remember thinking, "I should take Snoopy home with me tonight." But I was already late for my college class. The class lasted three hours till 10 p.m. And my small rental had no fenced yard and sat near a busy intersection, so it was too dangerous for Snoopy.

How could I know that the most dangerous place for him to be would be his home of 14 years in one of the nicest neighborhoods in Anchorage?

I was working hard to earn money and finish college. One of the main reasons was that I wanted my own home in the woods, so I could bring Snoopy home to me.

"Someday I will bring you home to live with me," I promised him. Once I was out of my parents' rental, with their "no more dogs" rules and no fence.

But even more important, I only brought Snoopy over once in a while because I was afraid he would realize that the dog I had brought home with me from California, Bobbie, was mine. That I had replaced him, betrayed his love. So far, on the few brief times over, he seemed confused by the new surroundings, and had not yet realized Bobbie was my dog, and I wanted him to keep thinking that. There was no need to crush his heart. Perhaps he thought she belonged to Bert, who was living there within a year of my return to Alaska.

Bobbie, my new dog, was young and could see well and was obedient. She stayed close and never strayed from the unfenced yard. Snoopy had always been in a fenced yard, and any chance he got to escape it, he had wandered. He was not a dog to stay close to a house just because it's a house. At his age, and with his failing eyesight and strength, I was afraid he'd get lost, stumble into the traffic roaring by my house.

Finally, the neighbors had a large male dog, Sam, who controlled the yard we shared, and Sam tried to fight Snoopy every time I brought him over. Snoopy, ever the fighter, would not survive a fight with young, strong, tall Sam.

So after my Poetry class that night, I went home, without stopping to get Snoopy.

The next morning, I got a call from my brother Robbie. "Do you have Snoopy?" he asked.

"No, why?"

"I can't find him."

"What? I'll be right over!"

We both searched the yard. We knew my father always let him out before he left for work; this morning he had had to fly to Kodiak, so he'd left about 5:00. My mother was down in Washington caring for her mother. Robbie was the only one home, and when he got up, he went to let Snoopy in. He was gone.

I was suspicious that my father had made a decision, taking the old, failing dog to a vet to be put down, so I called every veterinary office in Anchorage. None of them had seen him. I called animal control and filed a report. No, no beagle had been brought in. I finally tracked down my father in Kodiak. No, he hadn't taken Snoopy.

By now, it was light out, so Robbie and I checked the yard again. This time we saw it. Tracks. Human tracks.

We checked the outside of the fence. Yes. Someone had walked up through the snow through the side yard to the fence. There, they had climbed the fence. Then they had climbed back over.

Someone had taken our old obese dog.

It was too unbelievable. And too terrible. Despite what I saw, what I knew, when I saw those tracks, I still remember searching the yard in tears, over and over, all winter long. Often, after the many ads offering rewards received no response, after every vet in town again told me they'd seen no such dog, after the pound's Dead on Arrival and Hit by Car files and cages turned up empty of a beagle day after day, I began to pray that he was under the snow. Peacefully dead.

It was clear that Snoopy's body was not in the yard.

And he hadn't escaped.

He had been taken.

And my heart has been torn with prayers ever since I finally realized that someone had taken my dog—I prayed that he died quickly and without pain.

For who could want an old, arthritic, obese beagle? Who could want the best friend I ever had, the truest love, a child's joy?

I had three suspicions.

My husband and I were now divorcing. It was ugly, as these things are. There was no fight over money. I had none, but I certainly didn't want anything of his. A child of the '60s and '70s, I never believed in alimony. I just wanted to be free of his sometimes-terrifying jealousy and madness. On the divorce papers I had listed that I wanted my "dogs, cat, birds, horse, and flute." On his he had listed that he wanted his bank accounts, motor home, airplane, cars, truck, camper, tools, equipment, and various other items. Could he have taken Snoopy in punishment, or in thinking that I would take him back in my trauma and tears? I demanded and begged of him to tell me the truth. I believed him that he had not.

Second, by now I was running a humane society, on the board of another, and serving on the Municipality of Anchorage's first animal control advisory board. Through my volunteer work, I learned that dogs were being purchased, as well as being taken from animal control, for trauma experiments at Providence Hospital. Our neighborhood vet, the vet we'd always taken Snoopy to, was in charge. The dogs were forced into trauma, the physicians flown from Alaska's villages were to resuscitate them, then the dogs were "humanely" killed. I didn't find this out till months later, and I fought long and hard to stop it. I believe I won the case to stop the taking of dogs from animal control for this, at least. I argued that nowhere in Title 17 was animal control given the authority to sell or give animals for vivisection.

I was afraid to ask my family's veterinarian, the only one I could think of who would know, if Snoopy was one of those dogs. Perhaps someone had made a few dollars by selling him to them. But my anger toward her was too deep, my loss was too great, my suspicions against her were forever. What if she requested him, as a perfect example of an old, fat being for their trauma experiments? I was afraid of the fury I would have against her.

The only other possibility was also a terrible one, and one I would have never considered but for the calls I received as a humane society director. A woman called one day, terribly upset. She was working a cannery in southeast Alaska. She said a lot of Filipinos worked there, and they were killing and eating people's dogs.

"What?" I couldn't believe it. Absolutely positively not.

She explained what she witnessed. She said they would steal them from people's yards.

I didn't know what to do for her or for those dogs. I didn't know how to battle an entire culture that sees dogs as food, much like Americans see cows and pigs. I couldn't fathom how someone else could see my beloved best friend and family member as food, and actually kill him for food. (Years later I met someone who lived in Hawaii, and said this had happened to his dog, and it was a "real problem" there.)

But why else would someone trudge through the snow, climb over a chain link fence, and lift out an old, obese beagle and steal him?

It couldn't be good.

One of the last pictures I have with Snoopy, the summer before he disappeared.

When someone you love disappears, you never stop looking for him. Someone says they saw a beagle roaming a neighborhood a year later, and you go knock on every door.

You look, and you look, and you hope, and you hope.

You just want his death to be a kind, humane one.

When you think that it probably was not, you go crazy inside, deep inside, in pain and worry and regret. You cry so much you think your eyes will bleed; you are so sorry for not taking him home that night after class, so sorry, so sorry.

You feel so bad, you don't think about the 14 happy years together.

You just want an answer, you think, and then sometimes you think you don't want an answer.

You want to tell yourself, "Someone loved him, and wanted to care for him, and thought, why is that poor old dog outside in Alaska in the winter at 5:00 in the morning? I will just take him home and love him."

But of course, that didn't happen.

They would have seen my advertisements; they would have known he was loved. Kind people don't steal; they ask to help. Dog people would have known he was loved by his size, demeanor, age, and huge fenced yard.

But still, you want to tell yourself such a lie so that madness doesn't take over your mind and your soul.

You want to remember the many happy years and not be looking for him the rest of your life, even though you know in dog years he is long, long gone.

When someone goes missing, there is a hole in you forever that can never be healed.

It turns out, my mother had the same feelings about Snoopy's disappearance. My mother, whom I had probably lost some trust in when she took my first love, Poochie, away. When she returned from Washington, I demanded from her whether my father would have taken Snoopy somewhere to get rid of him.

"He would never do that," she insisted, her eyes starting to fill with water, till, as always, she fought them back, replacing them with an angry scowl. I realized, suddenly, that she had shared 14 years of her life with him too, her home, and indeed, her love. His disappearance hurt her too. I was instantly closer to her than I had been in years, bonded by the love and loss of a poor old dog.

That next spring, she told me something strange happened. She looked out the kitchen window, and saw the gas meter man in the back yard.

Opening the window, she shouted, "What are you doing back here? We have a dangerous dog, and that's why you made us install a meter out front!" (She was right; I remember when they maced Snoopy because he was threatening them for coming into the backyard, so at great expense my parents installed a second meter outside the gate.)

"Oh," he insisted, "we have a note here that your dog disappeared."

She shut the window after telling him to use the meter out front and to never come into the yard again.

But it was another mystery. How would they know? Why would they know? Why would they care? Why would they want to go to the back yard?

Giving

Sometimes I think I'd like to have another beagle, and sometimes I'm sure I never will. Both Poochie and Snoopy were so dedicated to me, to only me. Both those dogs were my best friends. Both those dogs disappeared. And I, I am just left living.

FOR THE LOVE OF DOGS: MY LIFE IN DOG YEARS

Some say that children should have pets because it teaches them about death. But what does it teach them? I learned the pain of losing love, the tears that seem they'll never stop, the desire to stay inside and never go out where it snows and suns again, the guilt of feeling I should have covered my aquariums so my bird wouldn't drown, or cleaned my guinea pig cages more, or never should have taken that frog from the wild in the first place.

But then I think of the love that Poochie and Snoopy gave me, so fully, so completely. Have I ever known such pure love from another, except a dog? Decades later, I was to have a child, and only the love of a toddler toward his mother can I compare to the love my dogs gave me. They give and give and give.

Snoopy, Snoopy, mon chien, my hound dog, my love dog. You gave me the best years of your life; you got me through some of my worst.

Despite the risks of severe punishment, you slept with me because I needed you. Many nights I cried into your white, brown, and black fur as the trauma of teenage years left me emotionally bruised. No matter how much boys hurt me or girls ignored me, you were there for me. Even when my interests strayed to boys and band and work, you waited for me, for my strokes and my acknowledgement. Even when I left you for extended stays in California, you waited for me, hoped for my return, remembered me and forgave me instantly when I finally did.

You, more than anyone perhaps, taught a lonely young girl about true love, friendship, and faithfulness. I hope there is a Heaven, so I can hold you again, and call you "my love dog," and make everything, even the end, all better for you, and for me.

Snoopy, 14, his last year, in his backyard.

Snoopy at six years old, looking over his backyard.

Lessons Learned from Snoopy

Sometimes its worth the risk to sleep next to the one you love. If your true love leaves on vacation, wait for her…she'll return someday. Teenagers aren't as much fun as children, but love them fully, and give it time. They'll come around and pay full attention to you again. If someone falls on you while you're sleeping, wait to make sure it's a real attack before biting. Jealousy doesn't feel good and isn't worth the misery.

MY TWENTIES IN CALIFORNIA, ALASKA, & OREGON (1978-1990): BOBBIE, DANE, & BEAR

3 Bobbie: Two Lives Saved

He is your friend, your partner, your defender, your dog. You are his life, his love, his leader. He will be yours, faithful and true, to the last beat of his heart. You owe it to him to be worthy of such devotion.
— Unknown

The opportunity to love a dog and treat it with kindness was an opportunity for a lost and selfish human heart to be redeemed. They are powerless and innocent, and it is how we treat the humblest among us that surely determines the fate of our souls.
—Dean Koontz, The Darkest Evening of the Year

Sacramento

I met Bobbie in 1978 in the Sacramento, California, "dog pound." It was merely a death chamber designed to hide and efficiently destroy a human-created problem—the problem of pet overpopulation. (Thirty years later, many of these places have indeed changed to trying to find homes for the animals instead of killing them as quickly and cheaply as possible, but I encountered one recently in rural Louisiana that took me back to Anchorage and Sacramento of the '70s;

in this tiny town in the 21st century, the animal control was killing over 700 a week, including the four beautiful puppies—now souls—my friend and I and my son found. I didn't blame them as much as the people who were too cheap to spay and neuter, of course, and the pet mill breeders who spun out thousands of unwanted animals while breeding the females to death in tiny cages. Recently, a vet told me he had to kill 600 pets in one day at a shelter in Texas. "How did you not go home and kill yourself?" I asked, shocked, and immediately regretful. But I was curious.)

When I met Bobbie, I was 18 years old, just graduated from high school, and recently moved to the "lower 48 states" from a childhood in Alaska, to live with my sister Corrine.

Loneliness was my life there, but I didn't mind so much, because I had a bicycle. Then it got stolen. So I borrowed my brother-in-law's bicycle, and continued my ten-hour-per-day bike rides on the trails and city streets and out into the countryside in and around Sacramento. This was my life: riding my bicycle to cemeteries, malls, movies, flute lessons, Old Sacramento, pastures where horses lived so I could wish and stare, and especially every day to the secret ponds and favorite riverbanks I had discovered.

It was dusk when I pulled into a parking lot one day; I heard dogs barking. There was nothing I missed more than my dog, Snoopy, back home. I wanted to make my own life, wanted to escape my parents' house, but every night I missed the dog I'd slept with since I was eight years old. So when I heard this dog, I rode my bike up to the sound, and there I saw them. Wooden drop-off boxes with locks on them to seal after you put your dog in them, marked "Sacramento Animal Control." Out of convenience, Sacramento had provided dog owners with the perfect way to eliminate their problems without even going to the pound or facing any other human being with their conscience. I petted two beautiful Irish setters through their cages, trying to calm their confusion and fear, trying to find some way to break through the locks that had been attached after proper disposal. I rode away frustrated and ashamed for being human that night.

Then my brother-in-law's bike was stolen. I tried to walk, but summer had by this time become cruel and angry with me, piercing into my Alaskan-born skin with its fury. There was no cool wind of the bicycle speed to protect me.

I took to riding the bus out to the mall to get giant bags of chocolate chip cookies, then back to my sister's to eat them, gaining a tremendous amount of weight quickly, and losing hope about anything while stifling in the air-conditioned house where I was the silent witness to the end of a marriage.

I still had no friends; one day I rode the bus on its route for hours because the bus driver said hi to me, finally ending up at 11:00 p.m. in a parking lot filled with buses that reminded me of where I imagined dinosaurs would go to die. She gave me a ride home in her car.

One day I sat down with myself and made a list of what was important to me, what made me happy and what I felt I had to do in life. One of them was volunteering to help animals. The time when I had started the spay-clinic drive in Anchorage a year before was the most fulfilling time of my life, for I was doing what I felt I was supposed to do. So this day in Sacramento I called up a humane society listed in the phone book, and soon started working at "Pets & Pals" in the office every Friday, while Leslie and Connie went out on field calls.

It took them a long time to bring me into the field with them, and I understand it now. I was an idealist; even with what I'd witnessed in the volunteer work I'd done in Anchorage, I didn't believe in dogs and cats being killed just because people overbred them; I felt there was a cure for pet overpopulation and it was merely that people should get their pets spayed and neutered (and that is true, actually). In Anchorage at the time I left, 26 dogs and cats were killed every day, and I believed that if people just knew what was happening, they would quit breeding their pets.

Connie and Leslie, just like me, got into humane society work because they cared about animals—I don't mean we were blind "animal lovers"—I mean we saw each dog and cat as the individuals they were, with a right and desire for life as strong and meaningful as our own.

But Connie and Leslie had accepted that their role in saving animals was being involved in their destruction. Years of witnessing cruelty and worsening pet overpopulation, despite all their efforts, had taught them that killing was an important part of their work. (Indeed, I remember being shocked—but later in Alaska temporarily agreeing with her after a horrendous day of witnessing animal abuse—when Connie told me, "I wish all animals were dead so there could be no cruelty.") Just as I was later to do (and deeply regret) with the Alaska Humane Society, a good part of their job was to capture feral cats in live traps, take them to the pound, and then wait for their cages to be returned empty. Then they would return to the scene of the captures. At the first house call I went on with them, for example, one referred to them by the local welfare agency, there were over 80 cats to be trapped and destroyed. Why did they destroy them? To prevent the situation from getting worse. Let me explain what that situation was.

Two years before, a stray cat had shown up on the property of this elderly couple. The woman was bedridden; the man was barely able to function himself, and was certainly unable to care for his wife by the time the welfare officer arrived. When I walked into this house, I never stopped looking at the wall, for it was moving. I thought my eyes had given out on me somehow—the wall was black and alive and changing and shimmering before me. Then I realized that it was covered with flies.

They had begun leaving food for the cat; soon she gave birth to a litter of kittens. Within two years, there were over 80 of them, wild about the place, sick with disease and deformities and starvation, but still breeding. It was an easy place to trap because of the inbreeding; smart wild cats will learn from witnessing the capture of one or two; inbred cats stupidly come into the traps one after the other.

During that first trip to the animal shelter ("shelter" being the ironic term when we consider what is done there), I learned something else. I learned that wild cats, unlike tame ones, never make a sound when they are trapped. If you are delivering one in a trap and you hear a "meow," you have someone's pet, recently abandoned or not. The wild-born cat waits silently for its fate.

Its fate is death.

You are waiting for your cage to be returned, and it is as if you love nothing more in the world than children and respect nothing more than the fetus's right to life, but are having an abortion. You got involved in humane society work because you loved animals, and you care, and want to help them, but you are delivering them to the needle that will end their lives. You try not to think, or you try to justify that you didn't cause this situation, and this is the only way to keep it from getting worse, to prevent other cats from being born into this unfair obscenity. You are "killing to save," as I later titled an article which tried to explain this reasoning.

(Years later, I don't believe in "killing to save" at all. It was a myth instilled in me by the animal controls and humane societies I volunteered with from the young age of 17. Now I think there is no justification for killing healthy, adoptable pets. The problem should not be hidden; the dogs and cats should not pay with their lives for the overbreeding of them by stupid people. Instead, people should be educated, laws should be passed, spaying and neutering should be required, no adoption of an "unaltered" pet should be allowed, and pet mills must be shut down now and forever.)

I did something else while we waited for the return of the cat traps.

I walked through the animal shelter, and tried to pet every doomed animal in it, caress it, talk to it, comfort it.

Maybe I felt it was my duty in this purgatory to make amends for what was happening to those cats in the back room.

Maybe it's because I missed my dog Snoopy so much.

Maybe it's because I loved each animal so much.

I knew one thing: it was unfair—what had happened to them, what would happen to them. I looked in each one's eyes, knowing that soon, long before me, they would know what death was, what it meant, what it felt like or didn't feel like.

They would know an answer I wanted to know, long before they should rightfully know it.

There were hundreds of dogs in the shelter this day, the day I met her, and I petted all of them. Except for one.

She wouldn't come to the front of the cage.

All the other eight dogs crammed in there came up to receive my finger strokes through the wires, but she would not move.

"Come here," I said softly, "come here and let me pet you."

Slowly, carefully, slightly, she raised her head, just enough to look me in the eyes with her own caramel-brown ones, and then let it fall back to the cement floor.

I was crying then, because she had communicated more to me in that brief look than any other being—human or non—ever had.

Her eyes told me a life, and it also explained a death.

Her eyes told me that she had been there long enough to know there was no point in coming to the front of the cage anymore. Her eyes explained to me that she knew exactly what was going to happen to her here. Exactly. There was no doubt at all; she knew it and I knew it and she wasn't coming up to see me and pretend to be a dog for me and to comfort my guilt.

It was pointless, that's what they said. You are pointless, they explained. But it was more that she was pointless. There was a broken heart in those eyes, and she gave it all to me with one glance, everything that had happened to her.

So I wasn't surprised when I looked through my watered eyes at her yellow card on the cage to see that her owners of three years had dropped her off and wrote, "Can't afford no room." They also wrote "outdoor dog" and "good with children" (which turned out to be a lie—Bobbie detested children, and this was not a surprise to me either).

I saw her life in that instant: she'd been chained, never allowed in the house, left alone out back for most of her life; there were children who ignored her or kicked at her, it was a filthy yard and a filthy family and one day they'd taken the "goddamn dog" to the pound.

I stumbled away shocked and crying from what I had just experienced, back to Leslie, back to the front of the pound, away from the cages and the victims of human cruelty, into the car, away, trying to think how I could get her.

My sister Corrine hated dogs; she hated all animals, really. I don't know where it came from—the same family, two opposites. I felt it had to be based on fear from somewhere. My childhood experiences with animals had all been good; hers had been, to her, bad. She'd been thrown by a horse and had broken her arm; my brother's escaped hamster ate through the floor in her bedroom; the neighbor's cat had dropped off dead mice outside her window. She had never known the joy of having a pet; she had never wanted one. I hadn't ever once seen her pet Snoopy. He didn't exist to her, I suppose. I could not know her mind, but I knew mine. I knew I had to have this dog.

It was a difficult afternoon, but she finally drove me back, yelling at me all the way, to the shelter to get my dog. She was furious, but I had to have this dog. Her eyes had told me something today; I spent the ride praying I was not too late.

I almost was. She was destined to be killed that night, after fourteen days in the dog pound, which was just about to close when we arrived. I ran back for her, I found someone, I told him to bring her out, I was taking her home.

The kennel worker walked in the cage, and the dogs who'd recently arrived came up to him eagerly and curiously; those that had been there longer pushed themselves back against the walls, watching him intently. Bobbie was still lying in the same place, refusing to move, but she was trembling.

Death was coming, she knew it, oh how I will never God I promise forget those eyes. Those eyes are what have kept me working to help animals when I didn't want to fight anymore; those eyes are what keep me telling people they should spay or neuter their pets when they try to give me free puppies and kittens even though they never are kind or caring when I talk to them. Her eyes looked up at him, though her head flattened more against the floor. I know, they said, exactly why you are here, and it is not right.

Of course dogs know. They can smell death, for one thing. Dogs communicate in amazing ways that we can't even fathom, but one thing we know for certain: their sense of smell, with their 220 million scent receptors, is far superior to humans—scientists estimate anywhere from 10,000 to 100,000 times better than ours. This is why dogs are used to detect drugs such as marijuana and cocaine, bodies under rubble and snow, the trails of missing persons, and even cancer in humans.

Bobbie was wrong about why she was being selected to be pulled out of that cage, but she didn't know it then. She didn't know it when the animal control worker attached the leash and dragged her trembling body out of that cage. She didn't know it when he brought her before me, and still she cowered, and her body shook worse than ever.

He handed the leash to me, and I knelt down to explain to her that she was wrong about what I was here for, and she did something which made me know absolutely that I had made the greatest decision in my life, that I was about to meet one of the most interesting individuals I would ever know.

She growled.

It wasn't a growl at me; I understood that, though the kennel worker's immediate and gruff response was, "You sure you want that one?" He was angry with her for not being a "good dog"; I was proud that she was, with all her acceptance and understanding of her fate, leaving the world with a growl to this creature that had only done her wrong.

The kennel worker would never understand; he spent the next 15 minutes trying to convince me to adopt another dog instead while Bobbie was given a quick health check ("She has a high fever; she might have kennel cough"), her shots, and I was given paperwork (I gladly signed and paid to have her spayed within a few days). But I had never felt so absolutely unashamedly right in my life. I would have taken her if she'd bit me, even if she'd bit me furiously and shredded my arm.

Why? Because she had every right to bite me. I already knew what her life had been for her eyes had told it all to me, but now her paperwork and her body confirmed it. She was completely emaciated; I saw every rib and hardly anything else though she was a Labrador-beagle cross the size of a black Labrador. She cowered and trembled at the bare movement of a human hand, and yelped in pain if her back was touched (injuries I assumed and veterinarians later supported, since she was sensitive in the back and hips the rest of her life, were due to kickings and beatings). Her encounters with humans had been wretched, and I was going to show her that another type of human/animal relationship was possible in her life. But she couldn't know this yet, and if she wanted to growl at me—yes, even if she wanted to bite me—in the transition, I would more than happily accept it.

No one in this world was happier than me, age 18, sitting in the back seat of my sister's car holding a trembling, terrified dog, listening to Corrine scream about what the hell did I have to get a dog for and it damn well never be in her house.

I petted Bobbie and talked softly to her and held her and tried to calm her trembling (how this memory brings back my same actions during her seizures ten years later, bringing her into life, trying to help her through the final passage out—and somehow it allows me to forgive myself a little for that ending that so troubles me), and I noticed she lifted her head two or three times to look out the window during that car ride—the first hopeful gesture I saw her make. Then she quickly put her head back down each time, trembling again.

"In the back yard!" Corrine yelled, slamming the car door, furious that I was changing all of our lives by insisting upon having this dog.

Bobbie didn't have to be pulled or dragged this time, though she still cowered as she followed me through the gate. She cowered still as I took off the leash and said, "This is it! You're home!" She looked up at me, questioning, disbelieving, and I was lucky again to witness hope cross those round caramels. Tentatively she walked, still hunched to the ground, explored, sniffed, looked back at me. I watched her, smiling and crying and so happy with life and the future we would have, ignoring the slamming doors inside Corrine's house.

Then, she saw it. She looked at it, surprised, and turned her head to look back at me.

"Yes, it's yours, go ahead!" I encouraged.

For the first time, Bobbie's tail wagged, just a little, just a half-wag, as she picked up my nephew's Frisbee. I watched her trembles smooth away, and saw her eyes give up their fears and death in an instant, as she brought it to me and raised her paw and placed it into my outstretched hand.

Bobbie with the Frisbee that made her so happy. Even though this is a few weeks after I adopted her, you can still see how starved she had been by her previous owners.

The American River

I was bikeless now, but I had a dog, autumn had come and the killing heat had subsided, so now, when I wasn't in college classes, I was walking my dog. We walked to the tiny Pets & Pals office every Friday, where I'd fill out spay/neuter vouchers, and Bobbie would lie on my feet, happy, sighing, often standing to put her head on my lap in gratitude for her new life.

It was still dark and foggy when we left my sister's house those Friday mornings, and when we came to a giant field to cross, I'd let Bobbie off leash, and she'd run circles around me, enjoying the leaps of jackrabbits from the long grasses. I will always remember those images as magic; Alaska had no jackrabbits, and I loved to see their amazing leaps, obscured by the fog, so it looked like magic creatures all around us in the air.

We only received one actual visitor to the Pets & Pals office those Fridays, and he started to come every Friday. He dressed as a clown and had an actual bird on his shoulder. I don't know why he liked to visit with me, but even though I had no interest in clowns, and perhaps some dread of them, I came to enjoy his chats.

Most of Bobbie's and my Sacramento walks were to the American River, so I could be in woods again, and listen to the bullfrogs and watch great blue herons walk grandly through the water. I have always been most comfortable deep in the woods, whether in Alaska, now in California, or the two times we visited Washington when I was a child.

At age seven, in Washington, I mortified the entire extended family of some three dozen adults by running back into the campground from my explorations in the woods with an armful of snakes, something we didn't have in Alaska.

"Look what I found mom!" I yelled excitedly. As the women jumped screaming on the picnic tables, and the men gruffly grabbed the friendly garter snakes from my hands to throw them in the lake, I heard someone ask, "What's *wrong* with your daughter?"

You see, in Alaska, since there are no snakes, we weren't taught to fear them. I am still fascinated by all things reptile and amphibian, and indeed, my childhood dream was to be a herpetologist, until I realized this involved experiments in laboratories on the living creatures I so admired.

So Bobbie and I loved to explore the woods together, just as I used to do in Alaska with Snoopy. Bobbie, though, would not leave me to chase hares or rabbits, howling away, as mon chien did. Never did she leave my side; she'd walk as close as she could get, just touching my knee.

She was in love. It was amazing after what she had been through how she gave her heart and trust so fully and completely to me. It is something I admire about dogs. As Walt Whitman wrote in *Song of Myself:*

> *I think I could turn and live with animals,*
> *they are so placid and self-contain'd,*
> *I stand and look at them long and long.*
> *They do not sweat and whine about their condition....*

We spent so many happy hours together in those woods. Although Sacramento was violent and the bike trails were filled with signs warning women never to be alone, I felt safe, just being with my best new friend Bobbie. One time a man approached me, as dusk was falling and I was waiting for the frogs to begin their nighttime chorus, but he hesitated when he saw my dog, staring intently at him, her tail still. Her sudden tension told me this was trouble.

His glance at her gave me enough time to slip into the woods I knew so well and escape.

Fears and Comfort

Bobbie was afraid of many things, I discovered over the years. She was afraid of stairs. She was afraid of basements. She was afraid of loud voices. She was afraid of thunder.

One night there was a terrible thunder and rainstorm that lasted for hours. Bobbie was panicked, panting, desperately trying to get in. My sister forbade it. I worried about my dog, trying to go to sleep, but couldn't. When my sister finally fell asleep, I went to sneak in my dog, but Bobbie was gone.

Somehow, in her terror, she had climbed over the 6-foot wooden fence and run away. I searched the dark streets for her in the rain, calling her, desperately, so afraid for her.

I was back looking the next day, after the rain and thunder had finally stopped, and I found her, not too far away, shivering and quivering in someone's front yard, waiting for me. She leaped on me, joyously, so sorry. And I was sorry too; I was sorry I lived in a place where she couldn't come inside and stay warm and safe during a thunderstorm. I promised her I would change this; we would find a place to live where she would never be forced to stay outside again.

She never, in the next ten years together, ran away again.

One night I received a phone call from my friend Tim, whom I grew up with, telling me that my best childhood girlfriend, Allison, had been murdered.

I grabbed my leash and my dog, and we set out, walking, walking, walking, into the dark Sacramento night, through the neighborhood, finally to a crosswalk over a freeway. There, I sat down and cried. The tears wouldn't stop. I was hysterical with grief.

Into my arms shoved Bobbie, and gently she licked away each tear as it fell. We, two separate species, were so bonded, so close. There was no need for words. I needed her that night, and she gave. No words of comfort were necessary. She made sure I knew that whatever it was, she was there for me, and would always be there for me. That's how it is with a dog.

An unfortunate thing happened to me after Allison was murdered, though. I became, for the first time in my life, afraid. Mainly I was afraid to live alone, for she was alone in her bed when she was murdered. I didn't know at the time, but this fear was to leave me vulnerable to dating, marrying, or living with the absolutely wrong kind of men for the next two decades of my life.[1]

The Bite

Although my sister demanded that my new dog stay outside, when she fell asleep or when she left me in charge of her son for long evenings at home, I brought Bobbie inside. Those were happy evenings, the three of us. But one

---

[1] Allison's story, and the effect of her death of my life and relationships, is described in my book, *Poor Little Allison*.

night, something happened. Something bad.

It was November, and Bobbie had been with me for a few months. She was completely in love with me, and happy, although terrified of my sister, for if she had to go into the backyard for some reason, she came out screaming and kicking, "Get away from me!"

My sister Corrine's fear and I'd even say hatred of dogs had no reason that I could tell, and it made both me and Bobbie miserable to be around her. Otherwise, she was a fine person, a good sister, and although angrily and sadly going through a tough divorce, she was a wonderful mother to her beloved just-turned five-year-old son.

So one night my nephew and I are in my room; I am typing away on my typewriter, and Bobbie has put her front legs up on the table to be next to me, her back legs quivering.

I had warned Jeremy not to touch her back near her back legs; clearly, some permanent damage had been done there, and she yelped in pain if touched there.

But the child was only five, and unlike his mother, so happy to have a dog around. He came up behind her and grabbed her in a tight hug right there, where her sorest spot was, leaning into her. His act and hers were instantaneous; she turned and snapped and got him right on the cheek.

There was a break in the skin, some bleeding, some tears. I cleaned him up and rocked him, and Bobbie offered her paw in apology and shame. I put Bobbie back outside and awaited the wrath of my sister.

It was far worse than I could have expected. There were calls to my nephew's father, and he was over instantly, furious and concerned. There were calls to my parents, who told me I must immediately have this dangerous dog "put down."

"No," I said, stubbornly.

I had been planning to return to Alaska as soon as the semester was over, in a couple weeks. The Anchorage "cat lady," Madeleine Cibil, who I had met during my spay clinic drive in high school, had been calling me several times a week, crying about the state of the animals in Anchorage and the destruction being done to the pets at animal control, and we needed to start a spay program now; we needed to do something. I said I would come home.

Now my parents, through my mother of course, said, "You are not welcome here with that dog."

"Then I won't come," I said, absolutely, stubbornly.

The next day I began to look for an apartment that allowed pets, trying to figure out how much money I would need to move in, what kind of job I would get to pay for it. I had been working ever since I moved to Sacramento at temporary office jobs (for "Kelly Girls" and similar agencies), and I'd managed to save some money.

As far as my sister and her divorcing husband and their son and me, it was over, and it was clear I needed to move on. "That dog" as they called her "is to no longer be near Jeremy."

I wanted to tell them, "Hey, Jeremy and I played many nights, many hours with Bobbie, inside, while you were gone. We've never had an issue before. She just has a bad back, and she snapped, and she was wrong, but I know she won't do it again." (She never did bite anyone else the rest of her life, and I somehow already knew this.)

But obviously there was no use in arguing the case, especially by confirming I often broke my sister's no-dog rule.

My dog and I were to get out, as soon as possible.

In the next two weeks, as I still searched for an apartment, my parents changed their minds. They offered a compromise, which to me was an exceptional offer: I could stay in their one-bedroom rental house. I would pay rent. I could have my dog. No other dogs were allowed there.

I had a place to stay, on my own, and I got to keep Bobbie. I could go back to Alaska and help Madeleine start the Alaska Humane Society, and we would change that city for the better. We would help animals.

I would fight the use of the decompression chamber to kill dogs and cats at Alaska's animal controls, as I had done in California (and eventually helped get it banned in both states).

So, semester finished, Bobbie and I and the turtle I'd had since I was nine years old were on an airplane, back to Alaska, away from Sacramento forever.

Bobbie in Sacramento.

Alaska Rental

Living in our new little house in Anchorage was wonderful for me and Bobbie. Never again would she be an outdoor dog. We were together.

There was one place, though, that terrified her, and I could never, in all the years we were in that rental, tempt Bobbie there. That was down to the basement. I, a vegetarian, even tried to tempt her by putting a piece of meat on the stairs.

Whatever horrible things had been done to her in her life before me, at least one of them involved a basement. She trembled and cowered and whined softly, telling me, no, no, please. I cannot go there.

So I never tried to make her go downstairs again.

I got a job in downtown Anchorage. I didn't yet have a car, so along with the 8 hours of work, half hour for lunch, and almost two hours of bus rides, Bobbie was alone for 10 hours a day, Monday through Friday.

She spent that time very busy.

She would pull all my blankets from the bed, then all my pillows, then (and this must have taken work) my sheets. She would remove all my clothes from their hangers in the closet (there were no closet doors). She would pile everything, carefully, every day, in front of the door.

Every day I'd come home to a giant pile, and I'd open the door with difficulty.

"My poor lonely, nervous girl," I'd say, kneeling down and hugging her. I hated leaving her. It was clear she hated it too. She couldn't talk in my language, but she certainly expressed her dissatisfaction over my being gone.

Fortunately, by the next summer, another dog, Dane, would come to live with us, and Bobbie would never do that again, not for the remaining ten years we had together.

Humane Societies and Animal Controls

I tried to accomplish many things to help animals over the next few years in Alaska, per my life's mission made so clear to me back in high school when I watched two dogs die a slow death in a decompression chamber on the local PBS station.

I co-founded the Alaska Human Society, which at that time had an active spay/neuter program with Anchorage veterinarians) and joined the board of CARE Alaska (in which, surprisingly, veterinarians, humane societies, dog obedience clubs, and cat and dog "show" [or kennel] clubs all joined together to "fix" Anchorage animal control and get the then-contractor replaced. I say "surprisingly" because such groups are often at odds; as you can probably tell, I have strong opinions about overbreeding, for example, but I worked with breeders to improve animal control; this bothered Madeleine to no end; she felt we should spend our time on the streets, feeding and catching stray cats, not in meetings.)

I successfully ran a drive to get the decompression chamber outlawed as a method of euthanizing pets in Alaska.

A position was offered to me at animal control—public relations and education coordinator—perhaps to silence me, I suppose.

"That's like being PR director of Auschwitz," my husband told me.

I ended up only being able to handle it emotionally for two months. Three times a week I would go through the rooms filled with cages and choose one pet to take on a morning TV show, where I would give a few minutes talk about an animal issue while presenting the pet available for adoption. I was overwhelmed with guilt, as I knew the one I chose would live, while most of the others would die.

One morning I walked into a room where I wasn't supposed to go, and there, on the floor in front of me was a pile of at least 30 dogs and cats...dead. I was rushed out of the room by the person doing the "euthanizing." I gave my resignation.

I know I have strong opinions about animal issues, about pet overpopulation in particular, and some of those are reflected in these words. My hope is that my readers do not take offense but rather try to understand that I have witnessed things done to dogs that never should have happened. Overbreeding leads to killing, and I have seen the bodies of the good dogs, and cats, who had done nothing to deserve being killed.

In addition to my volunteer work, I spent the first half of my 20s working various jobs, going to college again and earning two degrees, playing and teaching flute, meeting a man, marrying him, and divorcing him. I was, as I usually am, very busy.

What Matters Most

Although I was busy, the years with Bobbie were rich with her love and companionship. All my life I've tried to make time in every day to walk with my dogs in the woods, and to snuggle and talk to and play with them at night. These are my best and proudest moments as I look back on my life with dogs.

Isn't the most important thing to do is to make someone else happy, for just a little bit, every day? That's what I always tried to do with my dogs, at least.

Fortunately, dogs are easy to please.

Some of Bobbie's and my daily walks in Alaska were actually horseback rides. While I rode my "mean ole mare" Cherokee deep into the woods bordering Anchorage, Bobbie ran alongside.

One time, Bobbie repaid me for saving her life by saving mine.

Cherokee was never a nice horse. She tried to kick your head if you reached down to grab a girth, so you learned never to use a saddle. She knocked down the guy who fed the horses hay. It took at least five men to hold her down for hoof trimming or shots, one with a twitch. Still, she managed to injure so many, including my brother, as I begged him to help hold her for one such appointment.

One day I had her tied up to groom her; I was respectful of her hooves because she'd try to kick me every chance she could. Bobbie knew this too, so she stood to the side, worriedly watching me.

Cherokee was in heat, and as I was standing in front of her, in the tight space between the barn wall and the hitching post, suddenly a young stallion broke through from his pen and into our yard, mounting her desperately. Cherokee reared and kicked in panic, and I was trapped, trying to avoid her hooves that were flying at my head and face, unable to escape the two horses crushing toward me. It was only an instant, but I knew this was bad and going to get worse.

Bobbie didn't wait. She ran straight for the stallion, biting him on the legs, herding him back into his pen, all the while getting kicked in the head and body, but never stopping. As soon as Cherokee dropped to the ground, I ducked out, and ran and closed the gate.

"Bobbie, Bobbie," I knelt down, feeling her all over to make sure she was okay. "Do you know what you've done?"

She licked my hands carefully. It's okay, she seemed to say, I owed you one.

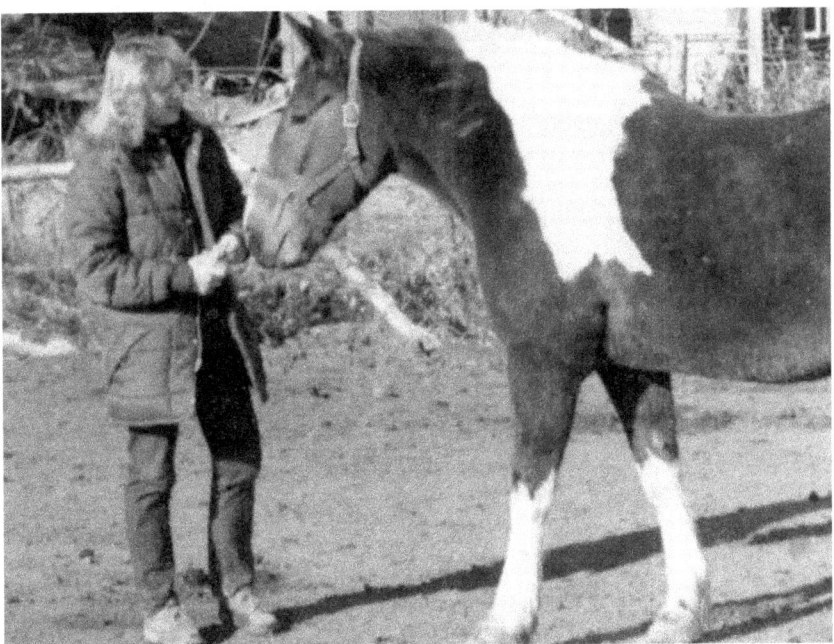

"My mean ole mare, Cherokee."

Moving to Oregon

After finishing college in Anchorage, I drove down the Alcan with my two dogs, Bobbie and Dane, along with my cat and turtle, to Oregon and graduate school. My pets and I lived in my Ford Escort for almost two weeks as I tried to find a rental that would allow pets. Finally, I found a little one-bedroom house with a fenced yard in Springfield that was perfect. It was across the street from a park where my dogs and I would spend many happy hours. (Two years later, after I moved, the landlord gave me all my "nonrefundable" pet deposits back, saying no one had ever left the house cleaner, even those without pets.)

My dogs and I explored Oregon together every weekend. Sometimes I'd get in the car and drive to Seattle, or California, or the coast, just because I could. This is a freedom those in Alaska never get to experience. One summer day, after school had ended, I packed some things and called Bobbie and Dane into the car, and we set out to go east and then up to Kennewick, Washington, to visit

Allison's grave.

I couldn't do it. Instead, we drove across country, all the way to New York. Driving across the United States with my dogs was something I'd wanted to do ever since I read John Steinbeck's *Travels with Charley* when I was 16. The problem was I had little money, one gas card, no credit cards, and—especially—no air conditioning, having bought my cheap little Ford Escort in Alaska, where such things aren't needed.

So, my dogs began to get hot, too hot. I took to renting hotel rooms during the day and driving at night, when it was cooler, for the final eastern leg of our trip. So I didn't see much of the United States, after all.

But still, we had great times. In Ohio, we stopped at my brother Aaron's for a few days, and got to explore the woods there, where a beautiful red fox jumped right out in front of us. My brother's son, a little rascal named Taylor, spent the days we were there running across the room and jumping on Dane, who took it kindly, without complaint. Bobbie, of course, avoided him, standing next to me, shaking a little while probably wondering why Dane put up with such pain and seemed to actually welcome the boy's pounces.

On the return trip, I stopped to see the "faces": Mt. Rushmore. This is the only place on my entire trip across the United States—me who had never been east of Seattle before—where I thought to take a picture...it is of Bobbie and Dane in the parking lot.

Parking Lot at Mt. Rushmore

FOR THE LOVE OF DOGS: MY LIFE IN DOG YEARS

The next summer, back in Oregon, I moved 10 miles outside a small town. It was my first home; it cost $26,900 for seven acres of creeks and woods and pasture with a little A-frame lacking insulation, electricity, or toilet, and I thought I'd found heaven.

Unfortunately, I have a way of attracting the wrong kind of man, and an abuser (Brock) came into my life, not often, but enough to cause me to "walk on eggshells" (this is the cliché abused women use, as if you make too much noise, say something wrong, think something wrong, watch the wrong TV show...you have raised his wrath) in my own home. I'm afraid Bobbie and Dane's last year or two, though happy with lots of dog walks, and living in the woods and swimming in the creeks, may have also involved some serious concern for me.

As I struggled to escape the abuser but only fell more in love with him, thinking I could help him and change him, they must have watched me and wanted to stop me somehow, but what are dogs to do in such cases? They were nearing the end of their lives, and old, I hope deaf enough not to hear his screams at me, and fortunately, perhaps, they didn't live long enough to witness much.

No, this was a tragedy for my next two dogs to experience although Bobbie, old as she was, and the puppy I later found, Woody, would crawl on my lap to block Brock from me when he began screaming at me. Later, Woody and Eb would do the same.

I did have many good friends those days, and many fun times at the cabin as well. Graduate students filled my pasture on weekends, as we'd build giant bonfires and read poetry. I also bought a horse, Dusty (a gentle mare, this time), so Bobbie and Dane, and even my cat Sylvia, would run alongside us on our rides through the woods.

One time I was riding Dusty through the woods, a typically cold winter day when the rain poured so hard it was difficult to see, and the creek my dogs and I swam in during the summer had turned to a raging river, pulling hillsides and giant cedar trees down into it, but it still all felt like a wonderful autumn day to someone raised in Alaska. Bobbie went down the hill to get a drink of water, and disappeared. I looked and looked for her, and finally saw her across the river, shaking in fear and looking like she was going to jump in. For a second I thought of riding Dusty home, getting my car, driving the five miles back toward town where the "Y" was, and going to the other side of the river to try to find her. It wasn't a choice. I knew she wouldn't be there. She would have jumped in and could be washed down by the raging, muddy, branch-filled mess. I dismounted and jumped in the water, crossing to get her. My little summer creek that came to my knees in most spots now reached my neck from the winter rainforest flooding, and it was much colder than any summer Alaska lake I'd swam in. By the time I reached my dog, I was shivering already. I picked her up and turned back, my legs now frozen, but I could think of nothing but saving my dog, so I forced myself across, carrying her in my arms. We rode back together on Dusty, Dane dry and fine running along beside us. We made it into the cabin, where I struggled to make a fire in the woodstove. I didn't know if I would make it. We were both hypothermic, or near it. My fingers struggled to light a match. Finally, the fire lit, and Bobbie and I lay next to it to get the blood flowing through our bodies again.

Was I wrong? Probably. Would I do it again? Without hesitation. I loved her as family; I loved her as one loves a child. Logic never came into it.

The gentle creek by my cabin in winter would turn to a raging river.

The Ending

When I first saw Bobbie have a seizure, in July 1989, I was standing on the roof of the "tree barn" my plumber friend had built for me, showing it to (the abuser) Brock. I'd proudly showed him the work I'd done on the roof and turned to survey the view of the mountains and trees and pasture when I saw her.

Bobbie!" I screamed, but no sound came out, and I was down the ladder, running to her...picking her up in my arms...her eyes were wild and she covered me with drool and hair. "Bobbie Bobbie Bobbie Bobbie," I said, over and over, rocking her in my arms, her slobber covering me, trying to press the sharp seizures out of her body. By the time Brock and I carried Bobbie to the car, the seizures had stopped; they probably lasted a few minutes, but we went to every vet in town trying to get someone to look at her. It was Saturday, and our search was futile. By then she seemed okay. But it was the moment I knew my dog was going to die.

FOR THE LOVE OF DOGS: MY LIFE IN DOG YEARS

Bobbie and Dane and me at the Oregon cabin.

Dogs die. They die first. That's just one of the things they do. But this would be my first experience of losing a dog to death; the first two from childhood disappeared in other ways.

Not only do dogs die, but in general people do not understand your loss the way they should. Only someone who has loved a dog and accepted that dog as family can understand what that loss means.

It means the end of the perfect relationship.

And one of the ways in which the attitude of those who cannot understand is expressed is by telling you to "Put her down; it's the humane thing to do." Put her down. Euthanasia is not taken lightly when it comes to human beings. It involves court cases and fights and moral questions and debates. It involves a pure question of right versus wrong. And yet, when a dog begins to near death, the dog "owner" is told by others, as I was, that it is "your duty" to have that dog put down.

I struggled with the conflicting messages Bobbie seemed to be giving me, still loving her treats and scratches, still full-on adoring all that was me, but her body was shutting down. I didn't want her to die, but I hoped when she did it would be without my having to make that decision for her, as excerpted in a poem I wrote during that time:

> *You fall now, and stumble often,*
> *and this past week can no longer make it up the stairs*
> *to sleep with the love of your life—me—*
> *for the first time. I don't feel*
> *your comfort at the end of my bed,*
> *so I climb downstairs and carry you up*

or sleep down with you.
Only now your sleep has become wandering.
Now your old tired body—
exhausted from its years of love and care for me,
is telling us both, it is time for you
to leave me.
It leads you into dark tiny places
you always avoided before.
It gives you seizures as signs to me
to help you rest.
But why must I make this decision?
Just because I helped you live,
why now must I help you die?

    I have always felt guiltiest over Bobbie's euthanasia in that I listened to someone else, a young man who was visiting me when he witnessed one of her seizures and became upset and left, telling me, "It is cruel to keep her alive."

    It is cruel to keep her alive. All Bobbie wanted was to be alive, to be alive for me and with me. She struggled to live long because she knew I needed her, I honestly felt. I had saved her once; I needed her now more than ever before, and now her body was failing her duty and purpose.

    Bob-dog (I sometimes called her), unlike Dane, who was "put down" the next year, struggled against the needle, even, it seemed, the fluid that delivered death as it poured into her veins, and I grabbed the needle and said, "No," but it was too late.

    She wanted to live, and I will never forget that, nor can I think of her or remember her without this guilt overtaking all the glorious perfect happy years we shared.

    But I listened to others who said, "It is time, do it, do it now, you are cruel to keep her alive." Especially that last sting. You are cruel to keep her alive. You are cruel, you are cruel. There is nothing in life I have tried to avoid more than being cruel. There is nothing in me that could ever accept that I have been cruel to anyone.

    So I had her "put down," and for the first and only time in my life, I felt cruel.

Bobbie at my cabin in Oregon.

Remembrances

Those eyes, when I first saw Bobbie there in the cage...were so sad and truly hopeless. I was the luckiest person in the world to get such a wonderful companion. I knew it the moment she was dragged out of that cage and gave life one last growl. But life gave you to me, and me to you. And I got so much more than you did. We saved each other, old friend. Dogs are that way; they give so much more than they get.

We certainly had one thing in common, and we blended perfectly because of it. We were both so lonely and needy. The way you pushed your head into my arms, demanding attention, was just what I lived for as well. The way you always stayed next to me on our walks, on my couch, in my bed, in my car...I needed someone like you in my life. Someone who needed me just as much.

And then, we experienced so much together, didn't we, Bobbie? You watched me grow up from a teenager to nearly 30 years old, as I went through various jobs, states, college, and relationships. You were the one sturdy factor in my life that entire time.

You were my dog when I was married and when I was divorced; you were my dog when we lived in my sister's house, my parents' rental, an efficiency apartment, and several other rentals, and finally in the home I'd always promised you...our own cabin in the woods. And not just a cabin in the woods, but a cabin in the woods on a creek. A creek you could swim in and fetch sticks in.

Even though by then your eyes were dimming and your hearing was going and it was getting harder for you to run around me, you were happy those last two years in the woods, weren't you? I choose to remember that I gave you the woods, just like I promised.

And you, you gave me so much more.

Those last days, weeks with you...well, what am I supposed to do with those memories? Should I push them away? As I wrote in my journal:

> *Bobbie, I miss you. Every day I miss you. I remember thinking at the time that you were ready to die, long past ready to die, and you knew you should die, but you wouldn't, because of me. You knew how desperately I needed you. You knew how alone I would be without you. Oh, I have other dogs. And other friends. But they're not you. You and I, Bob, we were something, weren't we? We were pals. I will always miss the way you slept next to me at night, sometimes putting your head on my neck—as if you knew when I was most lonely. I miss the way you used to reach your paw to me and just set it there, on my arm or leg or in my hand. Just to hold on to me. Just so I could hold on to you.*
>
> *Robinson Jeffers wrote that a little dog would grow tired living as long as people do. I guess you grew tired. But oh, Bobbie, I feel the loss of you in my life. I want to hold you again, to throw you a stick in that creek. I miss my Bob-dog.*

I finally went through my journals, and forgave myself for the needle, seeing in writing there the months of slow starvation, legs giving out, the seizures, the pills no longer working.... It was time to help her pass on. I was just not ready to lose her, as I never am when a loved one goes. The loss of someone so close makes it feel like you can't breathe, can't sleep, can't function...ever again. But you slowly realize that this is what you must do. You must go on. You have other dogs to care for, and there are others like her who need an advocate.

Dane and Bobbie.

Lessons Learned from Bobbie

When all is hopeless and even death is certain, someone can change your life. A little dog can save someone's life from a big horse. Don't follow coyotes into the woods. Having another dog around solves lonely desperation. Don't let raging rivers sweep you away. True love will never leave you. Go gently into that good night.

4 Saint Dane

Things that upset a terrier may pass virtually unnoticed by a Great Dane.
— Smiley Blanton

If there are no dogs in Heaven, then when I die I want to go where they went.
— Will Rogers

In my life, I have known three saints: my godmother, my brother Aaron, and my dog Dane.

One night at home in 1979, I heard a dog yelping. I ran up to the busiest intersection in Anchorage at the time, Lake Otis and Tudor, and found my neighbors' dog mounted on a Great Dane mix in the middle of the intersection. She was trying to get away but couldn't. Sam was very determined.

Dane did not want him, it, or the cars, and she was ever so grateful when I (carefully, I suppose) ran out and grabbed them both and dragged them home.

I put Dane in my house and then chained Sam to his chain (later the drunken neighbor came and screamed at me to never touch his goddamn dog again or else, and when I tried to explain I saved Sam's life from traffic, he cursed me more, as drunks tend to do).

FOR THE LOVE OF DOGS: MY LIFE IN DOG YEARS

Dane, Dane, what a beautiful soul.

I was living in my parents' rental house at the time. My mother said if I got another dog besides Bobbie, I was out. I believed her. (In fact, she did evict me when she drove by once and saw another rescue out front on a chain that I was trying to find a home for. She gave me three days' notice that started: "To the Tenant...." I can't really blame her; it was time for me to grow up and leave. I never could figure out my bank balance, since at least half the time she didn't deposit my rent check although if I handed it to my father, he certainly did!)

So Dane had to go to a boarding kennel while I searched for her owners.

I eventually found them. A couple 19-year-old party boys, living in a trailer park, eventually responded to my advertisement. I told them about the boarding fee ($5/day) and the cost to spay her, and they said they didn't want her anymore. They told me they could "give a shit" about her, and had only owned her for a few days, and certainly weren't going to pay the boarding fee (which had reached $50 by then).[2]

I felt so bad seeing her in a cage. I started advertising to find her a home.

I finally got a call.

"Is she female? She must be female," the effeminate-sounding man on the phone said.

"Yes," she is female, I said. "I just had her spayed a few days ago, so she is ready for a new home."

"Spayed? You had her spayed?" he was irritated and asked me questions about what that meant and why.

"Yes, about 9,500 dogs and cats are killed every year in Anchorage because there aren't enough homes. So yes, dogs need to be spayed and neutered."

"Okay," he finally answered. He wanted to see her.

Now, I didn't do much rescuing, because of my home situation, but as director of the Alaska Humane Society, I did end up with dogs and cats to find homes for once in a while. Usually we had tried to use foster homes to keep them. But one couple who volunteered as foster "parents" ended up being pet hoarders, and their house, when I went to in, was filled with starving animals and a few already dead from starvation or thirst. I never accepted foster families again, but took it all upon myself.

So Madeleine Cibil (the Anchorage "cat lady," as she was known) and I went by to check out this man's house. It wasn't far from where I lived. I had picked up Dane at the boarding kennel, so she was in my car, along with my dog Bobbie.

At this point, I was 19 years old, and innocent (actually still a virgin) about many things.

But when Madeleine and I finished our tour of the house, of meeting the two men, of seeing the padded pink room which would be Dane's, of hearing how she had to be large enough for their needs, and I finally got out of that house, I

---

[2] I think the world would be a better place for dogs if even a mutt would cost more than television sets or computers; at least then people would place some value on them and consider before getting one.

felt like I couldn't breathe.

We both looked at each other as we reached our cars, safely away from the house.

"They want her for sex," we both said, at the same time.

Madeleine, wise and 50ish or so, me, 19 and unaware that such things went on in the world—both came to the same conclusion instantly.

It wasn't a question.

I knew at that moment that Dane was mine, for the rest of her life, and she would never go to another home.

I told this to her on the drive home, to my house, not to the kennel. I was crying. "You're mine, and I'll take care of you forever, and I don't care if my mother kicks me out of her rental, I promise you I will never ever leave you with anyone else."

The policeman who pulled me over gruffly demanded why I'd been speeding (42 in a 35).

"Be-be-because!" I sputtered. "I just met two men, and they wanted to have sex with my dog!" I was wailing and hysterical. I couldn't believe it myself, and the policeman certainly couldn't, so I was given a ticket and some strange looks before I could drive away and take Dane home with me forever.

In the rental yard in Anchorage.

Of course, "forever" is a short time when we compare people years to dog years. I didn't know that 10 years from now I would be nearly comatose in mourning for my beautiful Saint Dane. For now, I was gloriously happy with my two girls: Bobbie and Dane, and I felt so lucky to have two dogs sharing my life.

Together, we would share the decade of my 20s together. "Bob-Dane!" I'd call them, as we set out for another drive, another walk, another adventure. Every morning they were happy and eager to find out what this day would bring us. Every morning, Bobbie would push needily into my arms, and Dane would be stretched out next to me on the bed.

"Dane," I'd whisper, and her whiplike tail would thump softly on the bed.

"Dane," I'd say louder, and the thumping would start to beat my bed like a drum.

"Good morning, Thumper!" I'd say, and she'd suddenly stretch those big long legs, pushing me, sometimes even off the bed! It was our morning routine, and she'd make me laugh every time.

Then I'd scratch her back and rub her belly, and she'd sigh in such grand peaceful pleasure.

Just before going to sleep, or just upon awakening...those were Dane's favorite moments with me because my focus was only on my dogs. It is the one time when I can relax and play with them and talk to them and scratch their ears without worrying about all the things I have to do and haven't done.

Bob-Dane would see me through a bad marriage, then a good relationship, then into the worst kind of all—an abuser—before old age took them away from me. They would ride in the car with me and my cat down the Alcan Highway, then on to Oregon and graduate school. They would ride with me across the United States.

They were my best friends, my loves, my family, through so much.

But I didn't know any of this the day I brought Dane home. I just knew I would take care of her, for the rest of her life, and no one would ever harm her. This was my promise to Dane.

Naming

The reason I named her "Dane" is that I never gave her a name those first weeks that she was being boarded and I was trying to find her owners, then a home for her.

I cannot have another dog, I kept telling myself. I will not name her. I will not fall in love with her.

Somehow, I thought if I didn't give her a name, I wouldn't become attached to her. She is obviously at least half Great Dane (I often thought the other half was boxer), so I'll just call her Dane, and then whoever adopts her will name her.

Of course, she became "Dane" for the next 10 years.

"You need to name her Princess," my friend Tim insisted. "Dane is not a name!" But I just laughed. She would always be my dear Dane.

Fortunately, whatever else was mixed with that Great Dane helped her outlive the full-blooded Great Danes by at least a couple of years. The larger the dog, the shorter the lifespan, the saying goes, and I suppose that's true for humans too. The heart must have to work harder, the blood flow longer, and the years go faster.

Attention Must Be Paid

Bobbie was a very insecure dog and always needy. She demanded my attention, my petting, my assurances, always. She wanted to be next to me, at least touching my feet while I typed or read, at all times. I understood this; I was the same way with the few boyfriends I'd had in high school, and I'm sure it irritated them. Why be next to your loved one without holding hands? Why hold hands without squeezing and caressing that hand?

Dane was not that way. She would sit back and wait to be petted or paid attention to. She would not drive herself into my arms and legs like Bobbie would, demanding more more more more. I understood Bobbie's insecurities. I have much the same myself.

But Dane was a wise young thing. She waited for my attention.

Maybe at first I misinterpreted that to mean she didn't have needs. It actually took my ex-husband to point this out to me. While I was wrestling with Bobbie on the floor, like she so loved to do, Dane sat on the couch, still and regal, watching us, as usual.

"She wants your attention," Bert said.

"What?"

"Look at her. She is jealous; she wants your attention."

"But she doesn't want to wrestle. She likes sitting there," I told him.

"Oh no, she's watching your every single move. Look at her."

I looked at Dane, really looked at her. Looked into her eyes.

I wouldn't call it jealously.

I would call it hope.

She sat there, waiting, hoping for me to come to her, to give to her.

But she would never interfere, never ask for it.

For the rest of my life, I remembered this. This is Dane's personality, and I must come to her, and give her lots of attention, and pet and scratch and talk to her, even though she never asks me to.

Some dogs are like that.

And my ex, whose general goal in life seemed to be to ruin (or control) mine, actually taught me something that I carried with me through all my relationships with dogs. Don't wait for them to come to you; go to them. Find out what kind of being they are, what their preferences are. Really look; really listen...listen to their souls. Communication can come in many forms.

My ex taught me that, and Dane taught me that.

Centering

She centered me and my life in the way only a spiritual leader can. She was calm and gentle and so loving. I swore sometimes I could see a slight glow around her, like a halo. I wondered sometimes if certain beings, human or animal, just had that certain thing, and why they did and I did not.

Dane had it.

There was such peace and gentleness in her; Dane was a being who understood others, who was content to calm others by her very manner. It was as if she had some special life force, or aura, perhaps, which emanated from her eyes and into your soul. When Dane looked at you, life's burdens, in that moment, went away. In her eyes, I would see a kindness and an awareness of something that I am so far away from understanding.... I believe we call this wisdom.

It was just a sense, that this was a special being, a great being, and this is why I called her "Saint Dane."

I was honored to know her.

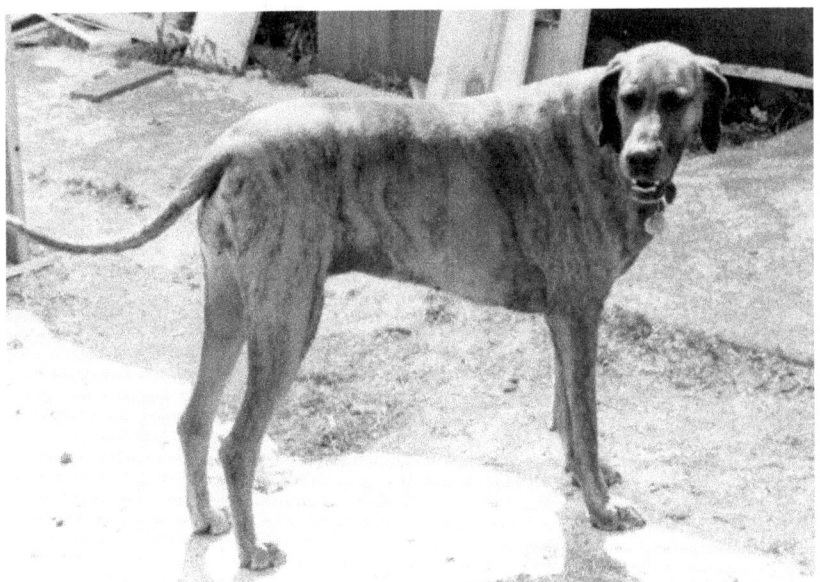

The Dane Effect on Bobbie

Dane's calming presence didn't just influence me. It also influenced Bobbie. Poor Bobbie, so crazy and desperate in her love for me, had so many struggles in her little life. I was her treasure, and her grief was when I left. Every day she had, as I explained before, piled up my bedding and clothes in front of my door, while I was gone at work. This had gone on for a year since we moved to my parents' rental house in Alaska.

Once Dane moved in, Bobbie never did it again.

And that is when I knew, a dog needs a dog.

A species needs another of its kind.

Having another dog didn't take any of Bobbie's love away from me. It didn't change our close relationship. But it calmed her. It centered her.

I would always, then, have at least two dogs, I decided. So in the moments I was gone, they would have each other. Same with cats, birds, goldfish, turtles...the animals who came to share my space would have at least one of its own kind to share time with.

Now this is not possible for everyone, and maybe there are certain dogs or cats who do better alone. It is just how I have lived my particular life, and I've been lucky to be able to.

Bob and Dane, at my parents' rental in Anchorage, getting ready to enjoy my birthday cake.

When Dog Love Seemed Not Enough

Unfortunately, I was not as deserving of her as I should have been. Oh, I was an excellent "owner" to my dogs, kind to them, fed them, walked with them, loved them, groomed them, slept with them, rode with them. I loved them fully and kindly. I'm not saying that.

What I'm saying is, their love was not enough for me. I wanted a man. I don't know if it's because I was raised by movies and television and magazines and peers and family to think that is what I needed for my life to be complete, but I assume so. Maybe it was the deep loneliness in myself as well. I couldn't seem to be satisfied with the very powerful love I had with my dogs. When I look back, I wish it had been enough. How could I really be that lonely if I just accepted that this was love, and this was enough? Certainly I should have waited for someone deserving of me.

But I didn't.

So, once I was of age, which was 19 at the time in Alaska, I started going to a bar, right next to my house, with my friend from high school, Lori.

Both virgins, both nerds, both uneducated when it came to bar men.

We had no idea what we were walking into.

What I walked into was my ex-husband, 21 years older than me, bitter toward women, recently divorced, probably more than slightly insane.

When my mother came to pick up my neighbor and her mother one Saturday morning, they informed her, "That car has been at Jory's all night; it must be a man!"

My mother told them that was not possible, and she parked in my driveway and rang the bell to show them.

At the moment, Bert was in my bed, although I was fully clothed. I had already taken Bobbie and Dane for a walk, and was now sitting on the end of my bed, my files about wolves spread out before me, arguing with Bert about the State of Alaska's shooting of wolves from airplanes and how wrong it was (Bert would argue anything, and he would take the opposite view of whatever I held [oddly, just like my mother], to irritate and rile me, I suppose).

When the doorbell rang, Bert said, "It's probably your mother," in a joking manner.

I assured him, "She would never come over unannounced; she believes that is wrong."

I opened the door and said, "Hi mom." Softly.

Bob and Dane, by the way, weren't the kind of dogs to bark hysterically or at all when a bell rang. They sat quietly on the couch, watching the whole scene unfold, probably amazed by it all.

My mother brushed passed me, turned left into the bedroom and stared at Bert.

"Forty? Hell, he's sixty!" she turned and shouted at me.

"Hello Mrs. Ames," was all Bert said, staying put.

My mother came into the tiny living room, yelling things like he's obviously an alcoholic, just look at him, and what are you doing, and I didn't raise you this way, and suddenly her anger turned to tears, and she stood there, in front of me, crying.

"Oh mom," I whispered. I had never seen her cry before. I would not see her cry again until after my dad died, fifteen years later.

She turned and went out the door.

So now I really was stuck with Bert, in a way. Because my mother wasn't speaking to me. And I was living in Mom & Pop Rental, and doing my laundry at Mom & Pop Laundry, and getting food from Mom & Pop Grocery.

Suddenly, I had to grow up.

I remember standing in line at Safeway once, counting my change, with one dog food can in my hand. My dogs liked canned dog food, and I liked to give them some, every day, with their dry. But it wasn't payday yet, and I was 12 cents short.

Bert suddenly showed up (was he following me?) and laughed and gave me the 12 cents. (That is probably the only time Bert ever chipped in for anything, for he was as cheap as I was independent).

Bobbie and Dane, why did I bring these awful men into our lives? So sorry about that. When you left me, I was with another bad one in Oregon, the worst of the worst, an abuser. You tried so hard to live long for me, but dogs must die before their people, and so we must mourn you and go on, feeling that terrible forever sorrow, trying to comfort ourselves with, "But at least I gave them a good home. At least I gave them love. And there are so many dogs who don't have that, or who don't even get a change for a life. So many, too many."

The Train Ride

Although I failed to be wise in choosing romantic paramours, one thing I have done right in life is have great friends, especially male friends. Since I was 19, one of those has been my friend Dave.

One Saturday Dave and I took the train to Whittier. I brought Bobbie and Dane, of course. Back then, the Alaska Railroad let dogs ride right with you on the seats. I believed I ruined that for everyone. Or more specifically, Dane did.

After a glorious day of hiking, Dave and I and the dogs waited at the Whittier Train Depot for the train to return and take us back to Portage.

But it was a boring wait after such an adventurous day, so Dane began wandering the rocky beach behind us. Bobbie, of course, never left my side, leaning against my leg, per usual.

Dane in Whittier on the beach; before the fish roll.

There's one thing I've never agreed with dogs about, and that is how glorious the smell of rotting fish guts are, but even though we disagreed about this matter, Dane luxuriously rolled in a tossed pile, covering her entire body with the perfume.

"Come on, Dane!" I yelled to her, as the train just-then arrived.

We boarded, and Bobbie and Dane took a seat together, as did Dave and I.

It wasn't but a minute after the train started rolling that Dave and I looked at each other. This was going to be bad.

The smell permeated the train car so suddenly and nastily that one by one, people arose, some choking, all covering their noses, and waffled into a different car. Now we were alone, and Dave and I started laughing uncontrollably.

Sadly, the next time I went to take the train to Whittier, a sign read, "No dogs allowed in passenger cars."

The fateful train ride.

Moving to "the States"

I have often felt frustrated at how difficult it is to travel or move because I have two dogs.

My dogs are my family, but they are also much more for a woman who lives alone.

Dogs are a warning and a deterrent.

"There's your biggest safety feature right there," a Springfield policewoman told me when she came out to give my rental house a safety check after I'd first moved to Oregon (in August 1987).

I looked at my two old dogs, Bobbie and Dane, and said, "But they are very friendly."

"Yes, but just the fact that you have dogs keeps strangers out of your house. They cut down tremendously on break-ins. They're too much trouble."

The only trouble I ever had travelling alone was at one hotel on the Alcan Highway that wouldn't allow my dogs in the room. The man standing behind me saw my key number, heard the clerk tell me that no dogs are allowed, and followed me to my car.

"Are you taking those dogs inside?" I heard him ask, in the dark.

I was nervous and didn't know how to answer. Maybe the hotel sent him to check up on me. "No."

Then, when I went up to my room, he was waiting, and he tried to get in.

Fortunately, that first night on the way down to the states, two kids I knew from Anchorage who were heading for college were sharing my room.

If not for their presence, I don't know what would have happened.

I think, of course, of my childhood friend Allison, and what happened to her.
My dogs, I believe, have kept me safe during the many walks in the woods, the moves, and even traveling across country. I am grateful for my "deterrents."

Bob and Dane, my traveling buddies, during one of our stops.

Wild Dog

"Bob-Dane," I'd call them, as we walked through the Alaska woods, then Oregon. "Let's go, Bob-Dane!" I'd whoop as I mounted my horse in Alaska, later another horse in Oregon, and called them to run alongside me.

Before Dane came along, Bobbie stayed right near Cherokee's feet, as close to me as she could, which was good, because one time two coyotes tried to get her to chase them into the woods in Anchorage. I didn't realize what a danger that was until years later when I read how coyotes will trick dogs to follow them and then attack.

Once Dane was with us, Bobbie was happier and more comfortable; both of them rarely left my sight on my walks and rides...certainly Bobbie didn't. Sometimes Dane would run just a little ahead, so I couldn't see her, but she was always right there. As soon as I'd yell, "Dane!" she'd appear, right from the woods, happily laughing in her way, panting and eyes gleaming.

"You wild dog!" I'd call her. She'd dog-smile at me. It was our little joke. She'd pretend to be "wild dog," free and uncontrolled, but always be just in the woods or just around the corner, watching me, waiting for me to say, "Dane!"

Her absolute favorite place to go to was the Oregon coast. I only went there once or twice a year, as life gets busy, and so you have better things to do. But every time I did I thought, "I must come here more often, for Dane."

For wild-dog would run and dance in the surf, playful and silly like a puppy. It was the only place I ever saw her act like that. She loved the waves coming at her, and would run away and run back, then run to me, dog-smiling and wagging.

I was always amazed by the complete change in her demeanor when we'd get to the ocean. It was like taking a child to a bouncy house and watching her go mad with happiness.

Bobbie, me, and Dane (shows how Dane liked to sit on couches like a human).

Dog Memory

Dogs remember people, incidents, places, and bad experiences. I believe they have very busy minds, even though some scientists and philosophers love to debate this. Animals are mere machines, Descartes insisted.

Dane was always sweet, always kind, always trusting.

Until our "regular" vet in Oregon was out of the clinic one day when I stopped in to get the dogs' nails clipped. I'd been doing this for years, in Alaska and now Oregon, without incident. Pop in, pay $5 per dog, pop out. Every month or two.

The replacement vet was old and cranky. First of all, he insisted on putting my big ole Great Dane on a table, where she trembled uncomfortably on the metal. Most vets or vet techs just asked her to lift her paws, which she did gently and kindly.

Now Dane had no way to support herself. The vet threw her down on her side, and she began to get frightened.

But the cutting is what really did it.

"Stop, she's bleeding!" I said meekly, always intimidated by vets.

"If they ain't bleeding, they ain't cut," he said firmly, continuing on and on with each nail, while she cried out in pain and fear.

I felt terrible that I didn't just grab her and kick him in the shins. It reminded me of when I took her to be "tattooed" at animal control; this was before microchips. The tattoo process was slow and painful and I was dreadfully sorry as they etched my social security number in poor Dane's shaved belly. She yelped and cried. I thought I was doing the right thing, in case she was ever lost, but I regretted it.

Well, Dane never forgot the nails.

No animal machine was she.

For the rest of her life, she was terrified of getting her nails trimmed. Never again would she gently lift her paw and offer her nails.

Patience

When I got my cabin in Oregon, I decided to rescue another animal from animal control, a kitten. I named her Bibs, as she had a white bib on her calico fur.

But Bibs, perhaps taken from her mama too soon, had an irritating habit of nursing on you—your face, your arms, your legs, whatever was available. I tried to break her of this habit some months after getting her, especially after houseguests started complaining.

After a week or two of shoving her (gently) away, she turned to the only one who'd let her nurse—the saint, Dane. From time to time, Dane would growl a little at having her jowls sucked by this cat Dracula, but put up with it.

Poor Dane, Bibs did this to her for the rest of her life. After Dane was gone, Bibs sometimes came out of the attic to look for something to suck, but found nothing—as no other being but Saint Dane would tolerate it—and retreated.

Bobbie and Dane, watching me.

Aging

As Dane made it past eight years, then nine, I felt blessed, but frightened. She meant so much to me. I was scared of what I'd read about Great Danes living such short lives. She was already an adult, so at least a year old, when I found her.

Bobbie went first, and I depended on Dane more than ever. By then I lived in my Oregon cabin. A little irritating puppy had joined us that last year, Woody. I called him "my transition dog," as I desperately watched Bobbie and Dane stumble into old age. Then, Bobbie died, a little Labrador-mix pup named Eb joined our household, and Dane took more to her couch. Our walks slowed. Her life would not be much longer.

One day we went down to the ponds, and Dane seemed unsteady. She tried to sniff the water but tumbled in and couldn't seem to right herself. "You silly girl!" I said, trudging in and helping her out. I made light of it and scratched her ears, but I was frightened.

Perhaps I had made a mistake when I let my vet surgically remove the fatty tumors that had sprung out from Dane's belly and sides. He was only supposed to remove one, but he happily confirmed "I got 'em all" when I picked her up. She never got her strength back after that surgery (and so I have always ignored my dogs' fatty tumors ever since).

Our Last Walk

My last walk with Dane was probably in May 1990, a fiercely blooming spring for someone from Alaska and used to melting mud instead of the sparks of color and earthy smells in Oregon. I think the sun had come out that day, and I decided to head up to a dead-end road where a favorite dog of Dane's, a Great Pyrenees lived.

Per usual, when we got to his house, he came and greeted Dane, nose to nose, gently, quietly. I watched the two giant old souls touch each other, communicate with each other, knew they were having a discussion just through the way they held their bodies and noses. No sound came from either.

The walk was enough for Dane. She looked at me quietly, those deep soulful eyes telling me our walks were over.

We turned and slowly headed back to the cabin, Woody and Eb bounding wildly around us, all youth and energy.

I was probably 29 or 30 now, but I felt as old as the gravel road I lived on, long ago an abandoned train track. The walk back, which might usually take 10 or 15 minutes, lasted almost an hour, as I went at the pace Dane set for us. She sniffed every so often the grasses and trees along the way home, took special care with her now graying eyes to notice everything, as if she knew this was it.

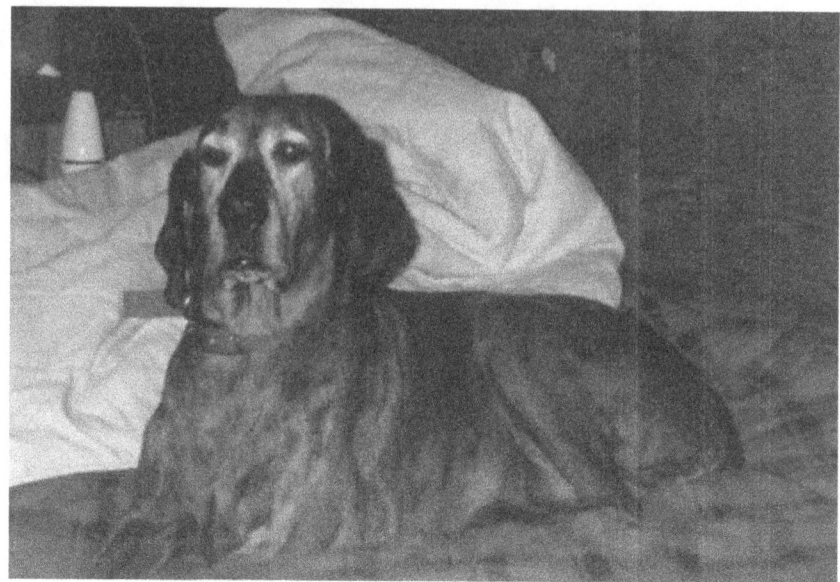

Dane in her old age, on my bed at my cabin in Oregon.

The next day I had to leave for work and school. I hurried home after just a few hours.

As I stepped out of the car, Dane came up and told me she was dying. She was having trouble breathing. I lifted her into my car and drove to the vet, who told me one of her lungs collapsed, and it was time.

Maybe it was her time, but it definitely wasn't my time. I took her home.

The next few days, Dane and I had our first disagreement in the decade we'd shared together.

Her opinion was she wanted to drag herself into the blackberries lining the pasture, deep in the woods where I couldn't reach her, and die.

My opinion was no, you will stay with me, you will hang on for me, I need you, my god, don't leave me.

I would drag her back out, get her into the cabin, put her on her beloved couch.

"Please don't leave me Dane," I'd say. "I know you have to, and you want to, but please don't leave me. I am nothing without you. I can't bear it."

I had the abuser Brock stalking me, and a current boyfriend, younger than me, using me for my money, conning me out of my credit cards, using my kindness to try to save him, like I saved animals. I didn't know the depths of his evilness yet, but I was suspecting it.

I still had to teach, and I remember trying to lead a poetry class at the university that day, after leaving Dane, so clearly ready to go, but needing help passing this life.

"My friend Mike told me, 'No one can write a poem about a dog or a child that's not sentimental,'" I told my class.

"I disagree with him," I said. "I believe we can write great literature about pets and children without delving into sentiment," and then I followed this by reading them an example of a very sentimental poem about a child's dying.

"My old dog, Dane, is dying now," I said. "I don't know if I can write a poem about her that's not sentimental."

"Your dog is dying?" one student asked.

"Yes," I said to the young man.

"Do you want a puppy?" he asked gleefully.

I thought to myself, give that bastard an F, but I said, "No, thank you."

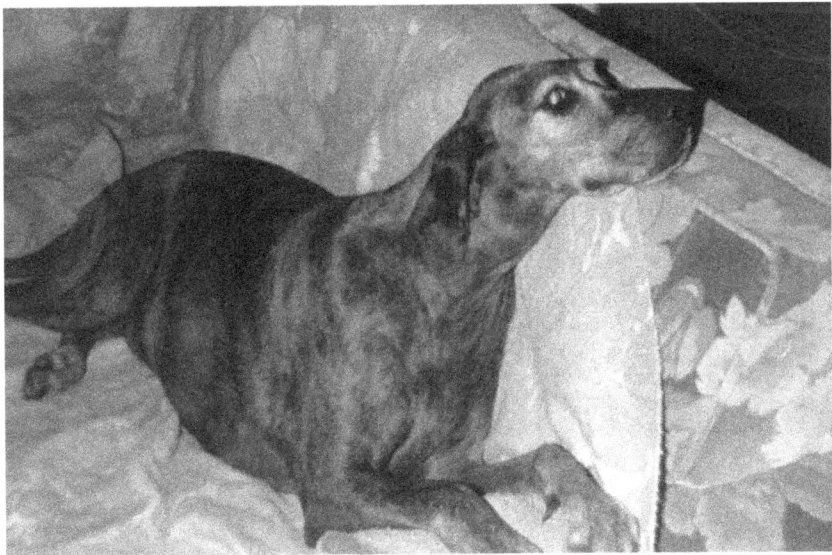

But he wasn't the only one who seemed so callous. I finally asked someone, "If your child died, how would you like it if someone kept telling you to get another child?" Those who don't understand how close people can be to their pets would find such a comparison offensive. But for others, a dog seems to function in many roles: child, best friend, parent, partner. Dogs are uncomplaining, loyal, forgiving, understanding. And yet, they are also all unique. The loss is tremendous.

After I recovered from my student's comment, I challenged my class to write a poem about a child or dog that wasn't sentimental, and the next class they came up with such wonderful poems that I typed them and made a little book out of them for the entire class.

My poem, I'm afraid, was sentimental.

Dane's Dying
There on the strangely soft carpeted floor
I could not do it
Though a moment before I'd told him, "Okay."
What passed in those seconds between
when he told me you had no chance

*but only more suffering
and when he came back, bottle in hand,
reaching for your leg, rubbing alcohol-soaked cotton
on that paw.
That paw. "Shake, Dane," I used to say,
and you'd dog smile and gently reach that paw to me.
He filled the syringe with yellow fluid
and bound the rubber cord around your leg,
"Stop," I said.
They looked at me. The vet. My friend.
But you did not look.
You just struggled to breathe.
I suppose it was that struggle,
though there are other reasons.*

*You struggle still to live, though you can no longer swallow
and with one lung, can barely breathe.
Yesterday, I tried yesterday to help you die,
but I couldn't.
I took you home.
"Go ahead, you can die, Dane," I tried to say, "I'll be all right."
But will I ever be all right?
I try to let you go, but you know, still, that I cannot.
"Dogs die. It's cruel to keep her alive," they tell me.
But can't you die like we lived? Just let me hold that paw,
and scratch that now-white head, and rub your ears,
and you can put your head in my lap, and sigh,
and let go.*

*I'll stay. I have to. But you, now,
you have to go. You can't wait for me to grow old.
This, then, is the thing that separates us.
It's not that I go to school and work, and
play flute and talk on the telephone. It's not that I have other
loves than you, and you, you have always just had me. No,
it's that you grew older so much faster.
this is what separates man and dog.
It's not your fault.
It's just the punishment
for one species falling in love with another.*

The Wild Dog in Oregon, near where we took our last walk.

Like I did with Bobbie, I took Dane into the vet one or two or ten times before I could say yes. But unlike with Bobbie, when I finally called my neighbor, the nurse, and said, "It's time," I knew it was time.

Dane couldn't get off the couch that morning. She couldn't move at all. I tried to drag her outside, so she could go "potty"; she was much too polite to relieve herself inside. But she was too heavy to lift. It felt cruel; it felt wrong, seeing her on the floor where I'd dragged her.

She looked at me with those still, deep eyes, and asked, Will you help me, please? You have to let me go. Will you help me go?

So, sobbing, knowing yes, I will do this for you, I called my vet.

He wasn't in that day, and the one who was, I didn't like. I was mad at her over a deer incident. I thought she was cold and uncaring.

But unlike Bobbie, I had no doubt anymore. My beautiful dog needed help passing on. She was suffering too much.

Paula, my neighbor, came over and helped me carry Dane to the car and into the vet's.

There, we laid Dane on a table, and I held her beautiful now-gray head, and I bravely told her, "It's okay, Dane. You can go. I'll be all right."

I'll never be all right! I wanted to scream. I wanted to sob and cry and demand more of life, that dogs live longer, that dogs outlive us! It's not fair!

But to Dane, I stayed calm and comforting and thanked her for so much love for so many years, for being so much to me, for being my "saint."

The cold, cruel vet I didn't like, watching us, actually started crying as she injected Dane with the end of her life. The cold, cruel vet I didn't like actually made a donation, later, in memory of Dane, which none of the other vets I've taken my dogs to over the years ever did.

Life without Dane would get a lot worse. I was home, lying on Dane's couch, a $3.00 monstrosity I had bought at Goodwill just for her, that she liked to "sit" on just like a human being, her butt to the back, her back legs under her, her front legs on the floor.

Tom, the con artist, and my neighbors would try to get me to go out with them and have fun at the bar. They literally dragged me like I dragged Dane.

Tom decided he had got all my money and so it was time to dump me and go onto someone else. He left me with a forever lack of trust in men when it comes to money, a $5,000 debt on my credit cards, and the necessity to drop out of school for a year while I got those credit cards paid off.

I became bitter and hateful. Mostly I hated how heartless and cold he was after I lost my Great Dane. I didn't realize he was just using me until she died. I was no longer fun, and broke, so he quickly escaped to his next woman to con. I remember thinking, at least the abuser, Brock, truly loved me, and was a million times better person than Tom (as if these were the only two choices for men in the world).

I felt so alone in my mourning for Dane. It was another dog who pulled me out of my slump. As discussed in the next chapter, Woody was to undergo a rather miraculous change after Dane died.

Dane on her precious $3.00 couch, near the end of her life.

Forget-Me-Not

A year before Dane died, when I had to bury Bobbie, I chose a spot near my cabin, so I could see it from my window, keeping her close to me. Now the day had come where I had to place Dane beside her in the dark Oregon soil.

My twenties had ended, and my decade with the "girls" was over. I was devastated; I felt as if I had buried my two children. But dogs aren't children, are they? They are companions, friends, quiet listeners, comforters, faithful at love, and so much fun to be with.

An Alaskan friend sent me a packet of forget-me-not seeds, and I desperately planted them over their graves, side by side as they were in death, just as in life.

But nothing happened, and I assumed it was because I knew nothing about growing flowers, and there, under the shadows of the giant cedar trees, no flower could grow.

The next spring, suddenly, Bobbie and Dane's graves were covered with the happy blue forget-me-nots, Alaska's state flower, and I felt peaceful and happy for the first time when visiting their graves. I will forget you not, Bob-Dane.

Bobbie and Dane's graves

Forget-me-nots

I met a wonderful fellow teacher, years later, whose golden retriever had passed away, and he said he could never bear the pain of losing another dog, so he would never get another dog.

"But you are the kind of person who should own a dog," I said. "There are so many who need homes, and you are so loving and kind."

"I couldn't bear it," he said sadly.

I understood.

When Bobbie and Dane left me, I felt like I too could never bear it. After Dane died, I didn't want to get up from her couch. I didn't want to move. I was in so much pain.

The thing about another dog is, it's never too soon. They need you and love you instantly, and that love carries you through.

Now as I began my thirties, I had my boys, Woody and Eb; before, in my twenties, I shared my life with my girls, Bobbie and Dane.

No love for Bobbie and Dane, and no memory of them, was diminished. But I was able to go on, to have reason to live, to get the cuddling and love I so needed but only seemed to really get from my dogs, not any of the men who stomped through my life and just took took took.

My dogs gave.
And no dog gave more and demanded less than Dane.

Years bring solace, and so I can look back at the gift in my life that was Great Dane. All good and love and unselfishness and giving. That was Saint Dane.

Glorious, happy, and wise Saint Dane, in my pasture in Oregon.

> *I've changed my ways a little, I cannot now*
> *Run with you in the evenings along the shore,*
> *Except in a kind of dream, and you, if you dream a moment,*
> *You see me there.*
> —*Robinson Jeffers, "The House Dog's Grave"*

Pencil drawing of Dane by Selena Rose.

Lessons Learned from Dane

Your family needs your presence, even if they seem to pay more attention to each other than to you. Stretching your legs in the morning feels good. Have your nails cut regularly, but gently. Avoid rolling in dead fish and getting on trains. If you have a bad home life, keeping trying. You'll find the one who will love you completely and fully till the end. Tell her when it's time to let you go.

5 Bear, Who Waited by the Road

The greatest fear dogs know is the fear that you will not come back when you go out the door without them.
—Stanley Coren

Photo of a dog similar to Bear (although cleaner and not matted and without brown tones). Photo courtesy of wallpapers.com.

Ten miles of out of town, next to a former one-room schoolhouse near my cabin in Oregon where locals liked to abandon pets. This is the spot where Woody and the rest of his litter were found.

A neighbor, Paula, and her family lived on the other side of the school. Paula is the nurse who went with me to Bobbie's and Dane's final vet visits. I didn't know her well, but I knew she was strong enough to get me there and get me home after the impossible tasks of taking my beloved dogs in to have the vet help them die peacefully.

It was summertime 1990. Dane's death was imminent, Brock the abuser was stalking me, and the new con-artist boyfriend was running up all my credit cards so I was in debt. I was at risk of losing my home and dropping out of graduate school.

But despite my troubles, and my desire to add any more stress to my life, I couldn't help, on my daily drives to work and on the way home, seeing two dogs sitting next to the road waiting for their owners to come back.

Day after day they waited. One was large and as ugly and long-haired as a dog could be...he was probably mostly Newfoundland, but with mixtures of brown in his black-matted fur; he looked like he'd never been brushed or cleaned. The other was a half-grown pup. One day, the pup was gone. Paula said she thought she saw him in the back of someone's truck, so someone had taken him.

Day after day I came home to take care of my dying beloved Saint Dane, and I'd see that poor, homely, giant dog, looking something like a black bear, waiting patiently for his owners to return. Of course they never did.

I checked with Paula from time to time; she said she'd go out and leave food for him, but Paula didn't want another dog either, and anyway, he would never leave the exact spot where he'd been dumped. Fortunately, there was a tiny creek behind where he waited, so he had water.

Once in a while I would stop and pet the poor soul. It broke my heart to see him waiting so confidently and sure that his owners would come back.

The first few weeks, every time I drove by, he sat, watching each car, seeing if it was his "owners' (how I despised them) returned at last. The fourth week, during which my beloved dog Dane died, the big Newfoundland-mix was lying down, the exact same spot, but no longer sitting in anticipation. Something was changing in him. Another week passed when I saw it.

I was driving home from another long day of teaching, and "Bear," as I'd come to call him, had finally gotten up and was headed toward town. Town was ten miles away. He had about seven miles to go. I suppose he figured they'd forgotten where he was, and he was going to go find them.

I pulled my little Ford Escort over and said, "Come on in."

Bear jumped gratefully in the car and came home with me, just as if this is what was meant to be. It really was, but I couldn't see it then.

All I could see was my grief, and darkness, and missing Dane, and I told Bear, "I can't keep you. I am not strong enough. But I will find you a home."

But for about ten days, Bear lived with me, ate with me, and slept with me.

One day Woody, Eb, Bear, and I even went for a swim in the creek, and it was a brief happy moment in my time of grief. (I probably thought it might be a way to get this poor dog clean.) For the first and only time during my seven years at my Oregon cabin, I saw a raccoon. Since we don't have raccoons in Alaska, I was overjoyed, but I quickly saw he was running right toward us, jumped in the creek, and swam full speed, teeth bared. Bear leapt between us, and he and the raccoon tangled into a fight, until the raccoon just as quickly disappeared back into the woods.

The creek by my cabin where I swam with my dogs.

I finally had the mental capacity to sit down at my computer again, the first time since Dane died, and I wrote a flyer, describing Bear's story. I said he was so trusting that his owners would come back for him, but they never did, and he needed a loving, forever home. I printed 20 copies and put them up all over town, including the post office. By the time I got back to my cabin, I got a call.

"We saw your flyer, and we'll take him!" the man said.

"Come on, Bear," I said, and we drove back to the small town. Bear jumped out of the car and headed straight for the little, dirty house right in downtown. The man and wife and their filthy children (who never spoke a word) showed me briefly around, particularly a shed in the back where "the dog can stay." They seemed pleased with their offer.

I left Bear there, and I regretted it immediately.

As soon as I got home, I got a call from a woman. "We have a 20-acre farm, and I was so moved by your story of Bear," she said. "I promise I will provide him with a wonderful home, bless him."

I had absolutely no doubt she was telling the truth, and that this is the home Bear should have gone to.

I admitted I had already left him with the first callers, and I didn't feel good about it. I went back and said I found a lady with 20 acres, and they said absolutely not. Any attempt they had made previously of acting nice was now gone, replaced with the threatening stance I had come to know from the locals in this town, and I backed up and left.

Bear was lost to me forever.

Sometimes I've wondered if those people were Bear's original owners, by the eager way he jumped out of the car and went right to their door. Maybe they saw my flyer and felt ashamed.

Or maybe he just jumped out of the car to follow me for the same reason he'd jumped in my car that day I found him finally walking toward town. He completely trusted me, as dogs do so trust humans, even after they've been dumped and left for weeks ten miles from anywhere.

One more time, weeks later, I drove downtown to check on Bear. The house was empty.

If I could go back in time, I would keep Bear. It was not worth the worrying and forever regrets. The place and the people just felt wrong, and I should have trusted my instincts.

Honestly, I have never stopped thinking about him, just a little, just enough to feel ashamed.

I hope I am wrong about those people, and it was a good and happy home for him. That is what those of us who rescue animals always pray for when he leave a dog or cat with someone.

If ever a dog deserved a loving, forever home, it was Bear, whose trust and loyalty in the people who abandoned him, and then in me, and then in the home I left him at, were so inspiring.

I guess I was so lost in my grief over losing Dane that I couldn't see at the time that the universe, or perhaps God, had sent me another saint.

Maybe his outside appearance was so homely because his inner beauty was too rich and deep. I didn't give him enough time with me to find out. I didn't want to find out. But I was beginning to suspect it.

Our time together was so brief, but I was honored to know ugly but oh so beautiful Bear.

My hope in telling this little story about Bear, even though he was never really "mine," is that others will learn from my mistake. Take the dog in, and keep him, even if you think you're not ready, or you have two dogs already. Even if it is bad timing, and he's the ugliest dog you've ever seen. At least, I'm quite sure, you won't regret it.

Photo of a dog similar to Bear (courtesy of DanDee Shots).

Lessons Learned from Bear

Sometimes the ones who left you aren't coming back. Eventually, you have to stop waiting for them to return, and get on with your journey. Swimming is good. Raccoons don't belong in the swimming pool.

MY THIRTIES IN OREGON, ALASKA, & WASHINGTON (1988-1999): WOODY, EB, & BOOTS

6 Woody: My Transition Dog

Dogs are not our whole life, but they make our lives whole.
—Roger A. Caras

Not the least hard thing to bear when they go from us, these quiet friends, is that they carry away with them so many years of our own lives.
—John Galsworthy

My beloved companion, Woody (Photo by David Jensen).

I was a woman in love—so deeply, utterly in love that I couldn't look at him without feeling that quick spasm in the chest that people call "butterflies."

And oh how he loved me. He never said, "I love you." But I'd be typing away at my dissertation or articles that seemed to have so much importance, or I'd be sitting in bed grading freshman composition papers, with a diet coke, cigarettes, and coffee to sustain me through this torturous duty, and I'd feel it.

I'd look up, and there he'd be—on the floor or on the bed—looking at me. It was possible he was even more in love with me than I was with him, because his love could travel across the room and hit me in the heart with its powerful beauty.

"Woody, I love you," I'd say, and sometimes—usually in the morning when his head was next to mine, he'd sigh-moan back to me, attempting to explain it to me in my species' limited language—"Harrrrooooow"—and then he'd kiss me on the cheek.

I'd hug him and pet him and sweet talk him, and then Eb, my feisty black lab, would come over from his place near the end of the bed, and grab Woody's neck or back and chew on it just like Woody loved him to. Eb was in love with Woody too. Woody—Woodson—Woodhead—he was our leader; our joy; our inspiration.

If I had to choose my favorite dog, which seems unfair somehow since they were all so special to me, it would be Woody. But this didn't happen instantly. It took more than two years for the greatest bonding of my life to occur.

Transition Dog

Woody on my bed (just a mattress on the floor) in Oregon.

In March 1988, I was driving home from school and work to my cabin in the Oregon woods. A half-mile from my cabin was a little park (actually the remains of an old one-room schoolhouse) where the locals liked to dump their animals, and this day I saw a litter of black puppies playing in the field. No cars or people were around. I kept driving, thinking of them, wondering what I was going to do, hoping it was all some kind of mistake, knowing it wasn't.

Standing on the cabin porch roof waiting to greet me were Bobbie and Dane. When they heard my car coming down the gravel road, they'd run upstairs and out the giant hole where a window should be onto the porch roof, which would shake with every wag of their tails.

"Bob-Dane!" I'd greet them. They'd leap in the window and run downstairs, where I would let them out. We'd hug and play and run down to feed the horses, Dusty and Jeffers, who always came running from the pasture, neighing happily—"Hay! Hay! Hay!"—when I came home. It seemed such a perfect life, except that I had to leave them so much for graduate school and part-time teaching at three colleges 70 miles apart.

I'd light the wood stove to heat up the cabin but had to take my bath in an old claw-foot tub on the porch. The tub was filled with a hose from the creek, into an aging, leaking water heater on the porch. (They were the most comfortable baths I've ever had.) After feeding the dogs and cats, I would begin my grading and studying. My life was simple, relaxed, and happy. I had my dream home in the woods; dogs, cats, and horses; and my dear graduate school friends.

Then, that night, the phone call came.

It must have been a Friday, because I had graduate school buddies over, spending the night. We were watching a movie on my new VCR, since I'd just gotten electricity in the weekend before. Partial plumbing was soon to come. Septic approval would take the county four more years, so the outhouse would stay.

"Hi Jory," said my neighbor, Wade, a boy who lived next to the park where the puppies had been playing when I drove by that day. I'd met Wade and his family months before when I rode my horse to their house one day and asked if Dusty could meet Riley, their horse, since she was lonely. That was before I bought Jeffers as a friend for Dusty.

"Hi Wade!"

"Do you want to see some puppies?"

"Oh, I saw them...." I knew what would happen if I went and looked. I just didn't want to do that to Bobbie and Dane, not in their old age. Two dogs were perfect. They had each other, and I had two hands to pet them both. A third...someone would be left out. And a puppy. How could they stand it? How could I?

But I knew before I hung up that in a minute I'd be in my car, going over, to take a look. No matter how much I didn't want to admit it openly, Bob and Dane were going to be leaving me soon. There were the signs—the soreness after our walks or rides, the white hairs, the fatty tumors covering Dane's body, the cloudiness in the eyes. Just starting. I maybe had a few years left, I hoped. Bobbie was 13 by now, and Dane was probably 10. Getting old for a Great Dane—even if there probably was some boxer in there too. So yes, I drove right over there.

I came home a few minutes later with this little boy puppy, maybe six weeks old, who couldn't stop chewing on my fingers and kissing my face and wriggling his little black body like an eel. He had golden circles around his eyes and looked at lot like Bobbie. That's why I picked him. How was I to know he'd change colors later and look nothing like her, except maybe deep in those rich brown eyes? I thought I'd brought home a black lab, but as the months passed by he slowly changed colors, and black turned to gold and brown and yellow, and by the time he was eight months old it was obvious one of his parents was a

German shepherd. The other was probably some out-of-town visitor, often the source of offspring in rural Oregon.

But after that first night, I took him back to the neighbors' house the next morning on my way back to Eugene. "I just can't keep him," I said, as I dropped him into the pile of his siblings.

Young Woody, tormenting Dane (on her beloved couch) while licking her paws.

I'd told Wade I'd only keep him for a night, and one night with a puppy was even worse than I expected. Especially for Bob-Dane, who couldn't stand the little beast. He was chewing on them and jumping on their sore backs and it just took everything they had not to pinch his little head off.

And me! I had found homes for a lot of puppies over the years, but I hadn't had to raise one. There was the whining, the messes, the destruction, the needing out all night long...I was too busy for the full-time job that a puppy was obviously going to be.

All day I thought about him, the way he chewed on and kissed me. The way he was bursting with happiness and curiosity, even though he had clearly not had an easy start of things in life. Who ever thought of the dog's point of view in these matters? No, we tend to think of the trouble they are instead of the trouble they've been through. He'd been taken from his mother, thrown out of a car far into the woods, left without food or water. Then I'd come along and taken him from his brothers and sisters to this cabin with two grouchy old female dogs who growled at him and refused to play. And still he was just all bubbling with joy and gratitude. I certainly could learn something from his attitude.

He'll be my transition dog, I decided. I won't give him too much attention or affection in front of them because I don't want to upset Bob-Dane. But he'll be the one to pull me through when they...the thing I can't admit.

"I hope I'm not too late" I chanted to myself on the hour-long drive back home that afternoon. I wasn't. I took him home again, and I never thought of returning him. Okay, maybe I thought of it from time to time—as my shoes, books, furniture, carpet, Dusty's reins—the few things I owned—became Woody toys. Now on my daily returns to the cabin, there would be a slightly different feel, as Bob and Dane sat on the roof and stared disapprovingly at me, their wags not so fierce that they shook the porch, telling me of the misery of their day alone with this puppy. As I picked up the remains of his destruction each night, Bob-Dane followed me, seeming to be saying, "What are you going to do about this Thing you brought home?"

I built a little fence outside after he ate my precious 1956 $5 encyclopedia set, which seemed like the end of the world to me at the time. I decided to leave him outside while I was at work, for Bob-Dane's sanity as well as to protect what few things I had left.

I started to drive away, and little Woody raised such a ruckus and then scurried right over the fence. I wasn't even to the end of the driveway when I saw him running after me.

"No, Woody, you *stay* in that fence," I reprimanded.

I walked back up the driveway, holding that wriggly kissing little beast, with Bob and Dane glaring at me from the porch roof, and I stuck him back in the fence and watched him climb right back over all 4 feet of it.

Woody, have grown.

So I put him back in the house where he could eat my phone cords and computer wires and *Shakespeare's Collected Plays* and other tasty things, and drove to work thinking how lucky I was that Bob and Dane were adults when I found them. But then, of course, I assured myself, Bob and Dane must have *always* been good dogs, they were born good, they would never do the things Woody is doing.

And what about this thing called housebreaking? Sure he was breaking my house, and he was also making messes all over it—it was unbelievable how many piles one little puppy could manage to create in a day. My least-favorite thing to do was clean up his messes. "I have a master's degree in English," I'd tell him as he followed me with my paper towels and spray bottle in hand through the cabin, "and I'm an incredibly talented flute player. And here I am, every day, all day, cleaning up your puppy poo! This is not what I'm trained for!"

He liked to hear me talk to him, and he'd wiggle his ears so cutely, and smile, his tail wagging proudly every time I found a mess he'd left for me.

"I will never never *never* get another puppy, you Woody you," I'd say, and he'd laugh at my joke by panting, mouth open wide. "I'm not kidding," I'd continue, just because he liked to hear me talk: "I will only rescue *old* dogs from pounds. That is my vow!"

I never follow through on my vows—just ask my ex. And it's a darn good thing, too. A year and a half later, a ridiculously happy Labrador puppy, Eb, joined my little family. Woody thought I'd brought him the best toy ever, and never stopped playing with it to the minute he died.

But Eb and Woody were a study in contrasts when it came to learning anything. Eb might have begun to nibble on my shoe or a book once; I said, "No, Eb" and he looked at me with eyes that said, "Okay. I understand. No problem. It will never happen again." And it didn't. He might have started to "do his duty" one time on the floor, and I said, "No, Eb. Outside for that." And as I carried him outside, he looked at me and informed me quite clearly that he got it, a rule was a rule. One-time Eb. Hundreds-of-times Woody.

I think back when my former student and later friend in Oregon, Alan, who was in his 70s, met Woody, smiled knowingly, and said, "I have a policy not to eat any animals that have intelligence in their eyes, which is why I don't eat pigs. But you'd better keep an eye on Woody around me."

Dogs are individuals just as people are. One baby will cry hysterically for the first year or two; another will be happily quiet. Eb learned everything the first time—tricks, housebreaking, leashes, what not to chew, leaving the cats alone, respecting his elders (which was now only Dane). But Woody. My dear, slow, special Woodson. There was the couch, for example.

It had been several months now; he should have known better (really, I suppose, looking back—I should have known better). I had no problem with dogs being on furniture—I wanted them there. I liked to cuddle with them in bed or on the couch. I loved it when they were comfortable.

But besides Dane's couch, the $3.00 eyesore from Goodwill, there was another couch, the one nice piece of furniture in my cabin, which my mother bought me on her first visit to my cabin from Alaska. She saw I had no bed and just this "awful couch," so she went and spent what seemed like a fortune to someone with a $3.00 couch—$495—on a hide-a-bed. The upholstery was velvety bright green with yellow flowers. It was a beauty and about as hard as training Woody.

My mother commanded that my animals were not allowed on it, which was of course a silly thing to say. My animals are allowed on everything. But I knew I'd better keep it blanketed because if she ever came back, first thing she'd do is check it, and if anything was wrong with it, it would just be more evidence to her that I would never amount to a plug nickel, whatever that means.

But sometimes blankets need washing, and I'd finally got indoor plumbing (although not yet septic approval or a toilet) and a used washer and dryer, so I picked up the blanket from the hide-a-bed, explaining briefly to Woody to not do any damage in the three minutes it would take me to throw it in the washer.

It actually only took him two minutes to take off one of the two green and yellow cushions and throw pieces of foam and upholstery all around the living room. Such joy, such abandon! What a wonderful toy I had given him! I stood there looking in horror at the results of his playtime, not thinking of what fun he'd had but of what my mother would say.

When my mother returned to Oregon, the first thing she did was inspect the couch, pulling off the blanket I'd so neatly tucked in over Woody's onslaught, knowing full well before she even touched it that the couch was ruined. I never could fool my mama.

Woody starting to change colors, from black to gold. My mother's couch, which he later destroyed, is behind him.

The Miracle

When I first got Woody, I kept my promise to my old girls, Bobbie and Dane, and I did not show him too much affection or attention. Plus, Bobbie being as needy and as she was, probably made sure Woody didn't get too close to me. He was a happy, silly pup; he didn't seem to notice that I paid more attention to the old dogs.

After Bobbie was gone, I adopted Eb, so now Woody had a best friend to play and sleep with at the foot of the bed, and my focus was on Dane. At night she'd stretch out next to me, and side by side, me hugging her.

During the day, while Woody and Eb would wrestle happily, with all their energy of youthful puppyhood, on the floor, Dane would sit on her couch, watching them, watching me work, wise and quiet. But Dane was slipping away. Her body began to shut down. Nearly a year after Bobbie died, she was gone too.

Now I had lost both the dogs I was closest to, the two who loved me the most and who had shared every adventure with me the last decade. I was instantly plummeted into depression.

But something very amazing happened right after Dane died. Woody, my rambunctious, destructive, troublesome puppy, grew up. Immediately.

First, he smelled me over thoroughly when I got home from the vet. He looked at me and sighed. He read with his nose exactly what happened, and he knew that Dane was gone.

He did something then that he had never done before. He stood up, walked over to Dane's couch, and climbed on it, lay there, and looked at me. His look said, *I understand, she is gone now. I will take her place. I will do what she did. I will take care of you.*

Woody on the porch, where we were both attacked.

That was the miracle, and that's when I completely fell in love with Woody. It had been two years and three months since he came into my life and my home. No longer was he a wild silly destructive puppyish fool. He took on her wisdom, her quiet love, and he simply, somehow, encompassed me with his love. It was like he suddenly went from having the role of my child to the role of my parent, or caregiver.

From that moment, Woody the most giving dog I've ever known. He had no insecurities or abuse in his background to make him needy, like Bobbie was. His entire purpose became to just give all his love right to me. And, of course, he loved Eb too. Dane was a giver too—but she would never come up to me. She would wait until I was ready to receive, and then she was there to give.

But Woody, although the slowest dog I'd ever had when it came to training, knew what I needed most. He did something else. When I went to bed now, for the first time, instead of sleeping at the foot of the bed with Eb, he would lie next to me, kissing my face, and every night, he would touch his forehead firmly to mine, as I held him, using that action to tell me he would take care of me. For the rest of his life he did this. Later, when the abuser Brock came back in my life, Woody would sleep behind me, on my pillows, but still put his head next to mine, separating me from Brock, perhaps to keep me safe, but certainly to ensure I felt loved.

Woody grown up, in Oregon, after he took over Dane's role.

The Abuser

My dogs and I were to experience something that I could have no idea of predicting. We all wish we could go back and do things over, do them right, but we cannot. But perhaps my mistakes will help save others; I hope so.

The man I loved in Oregon, Brock, turned out to be a violent man. One of the reasons I loved him was how wonderful he was with my dogs, especially Woody. But when he turned violent against me, Bobbie and Woody, and later Eb and Woody, would come between, jump on my lap, blocking me from his rage and violent hands.

Abusers tend to go for a woman's pets, but I was fortunate in that he had not yet done so. This changed one night. Bobbie and Dane were still alive then, and Woody was two years old.

I had told Brock I didn't want to see him anymore. I had realized his temper could not be "cured." My nature is to rescue, to help, to save. No matter how good I was at rescuing dogs, I was starting to realize, there was no rescuing this man. I could not, despite all my efforts, save him from his darkness. I am the one who needed to be saved...from him.

He called from a bar after midnight, "I'm going to come out there and fucking kill you!" he screamed. I rushed to get the dogs in the car, but I only got Dane and Woody outside before Brock drove in. Bobbie couldn't make it down the stairs. I told Brock to leave, and so the beating and choking started. Then he lay on the floor crying, which, I had learned, was his pattern. In the old days I would have comforted him. But this time I told him to leave again. So his anger and punishment flared once more. Then he was begging me to take him back again.

When Brock reached the crying "please take me back, I won't ever hurt you again" stage the second time, I opened the door, walked out on the porch, and told him firmly to leave. Woody, who had been outside, came up and stood between us, gently wagging his tail, staring Brock in the face. It was a purely gentle move but a protecting one. The man took it for what it was—a preference for me over him. Rejection he could never handle. He grabbed Woody by the neck and began slowly wrenching it back.

"No, not Woody! Not Woody!" I screamed, leaping in between them, and then I got thrown onto the porch for the worst beating yet.

I later studied domestic violence as I tried to understand how I could have dated someone like this, and to try to "get over" Brock. One thing I learned shocked me—pets are often the victim of the abuser's rage. In his attempt to get the woman's attention—or perhaps, in my experience, in his jealousy for her love and affection—he takes it out on the animal she loves as well as her. I shudder to think of those nights, those screams, those women, those dogs.... And I cringe in shame to think of poor Woody.

I should have put him and Eb and my cats in the car that night and driven away and never gone back. Quit school and jobs, given up friendships, called around to find someone to take my horses until I could send for them. The thought of doing such things never crossed my mind then. I loved my cabin; it was my perfect little Eden and the home I'd always dreamed of having, outhouse and all, and I had put all my money into improving it. I was a year into my Ph.D., and I was happy with my teaching and editing jobs, my many wonderful friends, and the gorgeous woods I walked my dogs and rode my horse in. Everything was perfect except for two things: the abuser, and my conflicted love-pity-hate for him.

My "Woodhead," as I liked to call him.

Now I know better. Watching my father die, losing my mother so abruptly—those things tend to teach one the precariousness of living.

Especially, I remember two phrases my father later said that didn't register at the time. First: "It's just a place. You can get another place." No, I'd argue, my cabin is my dream! But he was right. Yes, it was a very special place, which I will treasure in my memories forever, but it truly is better to be alive someplace else than dead there.

Second: "Let it go." One time, my dad was lying on his death bed, and I was complaining to him about a phone call I just received, something about a former boss firing people unfairly, and he looked up at me and said so softly, "Let it go."

Let it go. I messed up; I could never make right the wrong that had come into my life in Oregon. I had to let it go. Yes, if I could go back, I would call my parents, digest my pride, and admit I needed their help in getting away from Oregon, back to family and safety in Alaska. I would confess that I had made a nearly fatal mistake by dating someone violent and ask them to get me and my pets home. And they would have helped me. But I was both stubbornly independent and frightened of their disapproval.

I did do two things that were probably "right," after the terrible night of abuse. First, I filed charges and got a restraining order. You would think that would be a good thing, an empowering thing, but somehow this made me feel in even more danger. I didn't know that Brock's friends and family would begin an onslaught of threatening me, or that Brock would not be arrested for at least three weeks and then be bailed out immediately. Perhaps that's why the police and District Attorney discouraged me from filing charges, but I think it is really because they knew that too many abused women reverse their decisions, change their stories, try to undo the filing.

What I *know* I did right was put my old girls, Bobbie and Dane, and my young scamp, Woody, in my car, and drive down to San Francisco. My sister Corrine, the dog hater, was up visiting my parents in Alaska, but when I called her to explain that if I was killed, it would be Brock who did it: "Don't tell mom and dad; I don't want to upset them, but I want someone in the family to know." (I'm sure the murder of my best childhood girlfriend, Allison, and the years of not knowing who the murderer was, affected my decision to call Corrine. I wouldn't want my family and friends to go through years of questioning.

Corrine said I could stay at her house. "My dogs come with me," I reminded her.

Brief silence. "That's okay," she said. It had to be quite a struggle. I knew my sister loved me beyond sibling requirements, because she sacrificed much that day. Her house was perfect, white, clean, urban…the opposite of my cabin.

I stayed for a week, feeling some sense of peace at last. One day a friend of Corrine's walked in to check on me and saw Dane stretched happily on my sister's white couch, and Bobbie and Woody comfortably in her white chairs, and she shook her head.

"Your sister would have a heart attack and die," she said, and I just smiled.

I now had a funny story for my sister. And I was ever-grateful to the "dog hater" for giving up her house, and her furniture, to me when I needed to escape Oregon.

Woody rolling happily in my Oregon pasture.

I'm ashamed to say that after a year of a restraining order, a year in which Bobbie died; another pup, Eb, came into my life; and, then Dane passed away too; a year in which I dated a different man but was conned out of all my money and my credit cards were maxed out; a year in which Brock was in a near-fatal accident and wrote letters of apology, I took Brock back, believed his tears and promises, and thought I loved him still. Months went by; tensions mounted, he lost his temper; he was screaming at me, his face swollen red, his eyes bulging, his rage expanding, exploding...just like old times.

Woody and Eb jumped on my lap to cover me; he jabbed them both hard with his fingers right in their foreheads; they yelped in pain, I ran with them for the door, so ashamed for letting him back into our lives to hurt my dogs, let alone myself. Brock chased us down the driveway with a chunk of wood he had grabbed from the wood pile.

I drove for hours, past the Oregon border, far into Washington, before I felt safe enough to get a hotel room and sleep the deepest sleep of my life, with my dogs at my side. But the next morning, I had to go back—to feed the horses and make sure my cats were okay. To make sure my cabin still stood.

My life became a jumbled mixture of good and bad—I lived trapped by both terror of him and love of him, as abused women so often do. I thought my only escape might be death, but how could I leave Woody and Eb, as well as my cats, and horses, and parents? Those who needed me and depended on me? Those who loved me?

Sometimes I tried to find a rental, but someone with three cats, three dogs, and two horses can't. Later, I found a place for my horses, but still my dogs and cats and I were rejected by scores of rental owners I called.

"How many pets?"

"Five, but they're all spayed and neutered and trained and I have perfect references...."

"Sorry." Click.

Yes, I wanted to leave, but I loved my cabin, had nowhere else to go, and was also, ashamedly, trapped by my own love for Brock.

Woody and me in the Oregon pasture, communicating our love.

FOR THE LOVE OF DOGS: MY LIFE IN DOG YEARS

Woody, Eb, and me in my beloved Oregon pasture.

Woody and Eb and me at the Oregon cabin. This is blurry, but still my favorite picture of the three of us.

Going Home to Alaska

It took my father's cancer for me to finally get in that car one day, with Woody and Eb, and leave my cabin to head up the Alcan to Alaska. The cats were supposed to come too, but at the last minute my sister-in-law told me I couldn't stay with them if I brought them. I was upset, but I had planned my escape for eight months—the last time the man I loved kicked me in the stomach. I finished my dissertation, bought a car good enough for the Alcan, found someone to watch my cats, and drove away when Brock was at work, letting him know I was going to visit my father while I still could.

I really waited too long to return. My father was very ill. He had about seven months left to live, but they weren't comfortable months. He died in my arms as I tried to help him sit up. I was devastated, guilty, and so sorry I had not come home sooner.

My first reaction was to jump on an airplane and go visit my cabin, my cats…and Brock, in Oregon, just for a few days, then fly back to Alaska.

Now my mom and I lived together in the big house I'd grown up in, both quieted by our sorrow. She never asked me why I flew back to Oregon; maybe, perhaps, she knew. I loved her so much, but I couldn't tell her how flawed I was. I wish I had had the courage to tell her everything; she was always a much stronger woman than I am, and she could have helped me. But I thought I'd have time to silently mourn my father's passing, and then someday, when I was ready, my mom and I would talk about everything. I was wrong.

Losing Mom

Less than three months after my father died, I lost my mother too. I instantly plummeted into the darkness I'd fallen into after Dane died. My older brother Aaron told me the siblings wondered whether I was suicidal. (Three of them had spouses, and all of them had children, while I had neither to help me through this time.)

Aaron told them to stop being ridiculous, that I would never kill myself because I had my dogs.

I admired him for being so right, so understanding.

Here's how I found out about my mother.

Every weekend, for a couple months now, she's talked about driving down to the Kenai house, the house my father built for retirement but didn't live long enough to retire there. Colon cancer ravaged him too young.

But every weekend my mother finds an excuse not to go.

Woody, Eb, and I are living with my mother and my dad's dog Boots now, in the large house I grew up in. Both my mother and I are in a sort of shock over losing my father, but I bury myself in work, as always, writing report after report for an agency, teaching, editing. When I'm not working, I walk the dogs.

We talk very little.

I do encourage her to go to the Kenai, though, thinking it will be good for her.

"It snowed last night," she says. "I might not be able to get in the driveway."

"Just call the plower," I say. "I'm off to teach, so long!" I tell her. I'm supposed to babysit my niece that afternoon, but my last words to her are, "If you wait till tomorrow, I'll go with you."

Later, I'm home from teaching, and I am reading a note from my sister-in-law that she doesn't need me to babysit after all.

Then the doorbell rings. There's a policeman standing outside the door. I feel that clutch-heart-spasm-stomach fear that even good little citizens feel when a policeman appears in the rearview mirror or walks up their driveway.

All I can think is that it's my dogs. Someone has reported that we have three dogs here, my two and my parents' dog, and that violates some strict city code that says "two only" and I am in trouble.

I must make him understand that my dogs are family to me, that no one will touch them or take them from me. I don't care what gray-permed-teased-bouffant-haired neighbor lady with six TVs and polyester clothes said in her call to the police; these dogs are staying. My dogs, who snore in my ear and cuddle me at night, and my parents' dog, Boots, who has lost much too much already this year, who struggles confused through each day, looking for the man she worshipped. As we all—my mother, my brothers, my sisters—do.

I open the door, my stance forced by such thoughts during the last 10 seconds—it is one of fear, surprise, feigned strength and real conviction. He will not take one dog away today.

"Hello," I say, my voice much weaker than what I think my body language projects.

He looks at his notes. "Is your father here?"

I'm shocked. Why would he ask for my father, who has been frozen now for almost three months somewhere—wherever the deceased in Alaska are stored until the short summer allows the ground to be cut open and swallow them? Didn't the neighbor at least have the decency to tell the police that my father is gone? It's not like she wouldn't know. Everyone knows how he fought a battle with colon cancer for seven years. Everyone saw the ambulance drive up when it was too late, and he was dying in my arms, and I couldn't do anything but scream at him not to go.

I've been frozen too, since that day. Frozen and mannequinned and frightened and lonely. Only today have I been able to reach out again...visiting both my brothers at work for the first time since pop died, joking with my mother this morning before I left to teach and she left for the Kenai—her first trip since he died.

"No," my voice falters worse now, "My father—he's—he's no longer living." I still can't say that word.

The policeman looks at me. My dogs, Woody and Eb, look at him from where they sit at the top of the stairs, grinning and wagging their tails. Boots is gone with my mother; probably a good thing since she would bark and be protective; my dogs are everybody's pals.

"Well, is your husband home?"

"I don't have a husband," I say, very confused now, thinking I must be in much more serious trouble than I thought, and at the same time, slightly irritated at the not-so-implied sexism of both his questions. Then I open the door a little wider for him to see the loves of my life. "I have *dogs*." I emphasize *dogs*, so he knows how important they are to me when I have to tell him there's no way he's taking them away from me.

He looks up the stairs at them vaguely, then back at me, and asks an even more curious question. "Does anyone else live here?"

"Yes. My mother. But—" something warns me I shouldn't say anymore, but he is a policeman, "she's not home right now."

"Can I come in?"

Yes, the warning was there, and I should have listened. He's a serial killer in a policeman's uniform. My deepest terror is about to come true—the terror I've had ever since my best childhood girlfriend Allison was stabbed to death in 1978. I feel helpless. I have to let him in, but I don't move back far; he is crowded against the still half-open door when he speaks again, and this time it isn't a question, and suddenly I find out there are worst things that can happen to you than serial killers. Much worse.

"I'm afraid I have some very bad news for you—" and I don't see his face again at all; I don't see anything; I have floated up above myself, up above the stairs where my dogs are; things have gotten very dim and very foggy and very terrifying, and I am watching a very bad very clichéd movie, where the following scene unfolds:

ME: "Not my mother. Not my mother."

COP: "Yes, it's your mother."

ME: Backing away, to the edge of the landing, toward the basement stairs. "No no not my mother. It's not possible." This has to be just a badly written stupid movie.

COP: "There was an accident—"

ME: "No no no not my mother—"

COP: "She was taken to Providence."

ME: Hope in voice. Why couldn't he have been clearer? She's okay! Just injured a little—she'll be okay! "Is she all right?"

COP: "I'm sorry. We need you to identify the body."

ME: I am running down the stairs, flailing my arms back at him to stay away, telling him to stay away from me, telling him to not say anything I have to call my brothers I cannot hear this alone I cannot hear this at all.

ME: I am now downstairs, in the rec room, which I have turned into a makeshift office since I moved back here to my parents' house, to Alaska, nine months ago. I can't recall what I'm supposed to do or how to call my brothers; all I can do is push redial on the phone and my sister-in-law says, "Hello," and I have to tell her my mother is dead and I need my brothers and then I pace and mumble and don't breathe and stumble through the fog until they get here.

The fog takes a long time to lift.

Woody and Eb were there with me in the darkness. They stayed in bed with me all day, long days, months of days. Twice a day I'd have to get up, get dressed in some way, to take them for their walks. That was my only reason to move, except for a semester of teaching to finish. My dogs just gave me that gift of dog love, and waited out my depression.

FOR THE LOVE OF DOGS: MY LIFE IN DOG YEARS

One day, I got out of bed, packed a bag, found my one credit card, called the airlines, took Woody and Eb to my brother's house, and flew to Hawaii. It wasn't to vacation, but a desperate attempt to find happiness again, and to get out of the house I grew up in, now hollow without my parents and no longer feeling like "home." The sun, the sand, the ocean, the noise, the people—Hawaii and Alaska are complete contrasts and yet somehow an Alaskan can feel quite at home on the islands, perhaps because both states are so isolated from the "lower 48."

I didn't want to leave Woody and Eb that day in 1995 in Alaska, but I couldn't take them with me to Hawaii because of a strict quarantine law in 1995. [3]I stayed in Waikiki for two weeks and found the will to live again in the warmth, the sun's vitamin D, the music, a man I met the first day there, and especially the ocean waves...I didn't want to come back quite yet...just one more week...but my parents were to be buried at last, since summer had arrived and the ground could finally be dug into.

Woody

So I came home and plummeted into darkness again, fighting with siblings, not knowing where to live or what to do—but having one consistency in my life—my "boys," my Woody and my Eb.

Two months later, I called Woody and Eb into the car and headed south, back to my cabin in Oregon (Brock had moved out of it at last). In the fifteen months since I left for Alaska, life—through the deaths of my parents—had changed me. I no longer feared I would return to Brock, and I was determined to get my cats and sell my cabin, to "let it go," as my father would say.

I was, for the first time since childhood, okay with the thought that I might

---

[3] I guess my dogs do get disappointed in me in one area—when I leave them. Oh, that is a tragedy. I try not to do it very often—mostly because I can't stand leaving them myself, and because I can't call them from Hawaii and say, "I'm coming back in a week, so don't worry! I love you!" When I pulled out the suitcases to pack, my dogs knew. All of them, all my life. They pouted, grieved, nervously watched me, and waited for the tragedy of my disappearance to happen.

never be in another relationship again. Finally, I realized that my truest loves were my dogs, my friends, and my parents. I had few friends and no parents left, but always, through everything, I had my dogs.

The six days of driving out of Alaska to the states was healing, in some way. I normally detest road trips, especially the tedious boredom of the Alcan Highway, but dogs take such pleasure in long drives that it is contagious. Their enthusiasm was catching, especially when we pulled over to explore the woods or a lake.

Two months later, late one night, I touched the rugged wood walls of my cabin for the last time, and cried. Despite what my father told me about "it's just a place," I have never felt the connection to a home like I did my little cabin in Oregon, with its cedar trees, two creeks, and seven acres. I destroyed my own dream by dating something violent, but there were other reasons it was ruined for me: the cockfighting neighbors who staked 56 endlessly crowing roosters next door, the neighbor beyond them who threatened to shoot Woody and Eb because he said they killed a chicken, the pot grower who pointed a gun at me when I was walking my dogs in the federal lands, and especially, the way the locals and state madly wiped out the beautiful forests that surrounded me, even stealing my own precious trees (where I saw a beautiful forest, they saw "board feet'). No, my Oregon days were over. Woody, Eb, my three cats, and I headed back to Alaska.

Woody and Eb and me before heading down the Alcan to get our cats.

Language

Woody's roles in my life were many; he filled those I didn't have: my son, my best friend, my parent, my husband, my confidante, my protector, my shielder from loneliness, my buddy—my dog.

"Woody, do you want to go for a ride in the car?" I'd say it softly, with no inflection, no rise in the word "car," just to show off to friends who didn't understand dogs that he understood certain words. For example, I'd just be talking to my friends, and say something like this: "And we were reading Shakespeare in the car." Woody, who would seem to be asleep, would hear "car" and would be off the couch, to the door, barking happily.

Dogs recognize many words, but just because animals and humans don't speak the same language does not mean we do not share the deepest, richest forms of communication.

Words seem useless, in fact, when it comes to describing the powerful love that Woody had for me. He woke in total joy every morning just because I was next to him and we were to have a new day together.

Sometimes, I learned, dogs can communicate their love through a special odor they emit. This has happened rarely, or I've noticed it rarely because, after all, we humans don't have anything near the olfactory skills of a canine. But I certainly noticed it most with Woody, of all my dogs.

It would happen like this: I would be scratching him and baby-talking him and cuddling him, usually at night, when I'm most relaxed. All my focus would be on him—not on television or books or another human. Woody would play with me joyfully, and then, finally, when we were done, sit back or lie down, stare at me, and emit a sweet little odor that is different from anything I've ever smelled in the world. I don't know the scientific source or reasons for it; I just know that it means, "I love you so much!"[4]

His message of love for me was so clear when Woody did this that my heart would flutter like when you're falling in love.

Woody Love

Woody love. How many nights—months—years of my life I spent seeking the love of a man when the fullest, richest love of my life was waiting at home for me, eagerly greeting me at the door? Friends, parents, and dogs have never let me down—but one man beat me, one stole from me, one lied about his marital status. It's not that men are bad—I adore men. It's just that they can't live up to dog perfection. They always disappoint; dogs never do.

"Woody, would you be my husband?" I would baby talk him. "Howrrrooooh!" he'd sigh, and kiss me.

Where could I find a man who's like you? I'd wonder.

"The more I know men, the more I like my dog" reads some post-it note my mother gave me. It's funny, but seems a little mean. I have known wonderful, glorious, sweet men (but that's not the type I usually dated!). But my dogs—what makes my relationship with them so perfect? They're so nonjudgmental.

---

[4] I never heard of the various odors dogs emit to communicate until I read *The Hidden Life of Dogs* by Elizabeth Marshall Thomas. She describes what happened after she brought home the collar of her dog who had been euthanized. Her other two dogs smelled her carefully. "When they had finished, they both stepped back and looked at me.... Then...they suddenly began to emit an odor. It was the odor of dog, of wet dog, musky and penetrating...seeping through their skins.... I...had no idea what was happening. I have no idea now.... The odor was a dog thing."

They never try to change me, they never tell me I'm too fat, they don't care if I want to sit in bed all day reading and watching old movies, or go for a walk or ride, or scratch their silly ears, or type on the computer. Their love is truly nonconditional.

Sometimes, living at my big childhood home in Alaska without my parents there, alone but for my pets, I'd catch him staring at me with so much love, and I would think: I don't think I could bear losing Woody; I think I'd die. I'm not yet strong enough.

I would add up his age, figure it out that I had until I would be 42, maybe even older, before he'd die. Maybe by the time I'm in my 40s I'll be stronger somehow. I'll be able to live without him, to take joy in what we had. I'll start working on it when I'm 41 or so, I figured. I thought I had about seven years left to learn to be strong. It would be seven glorious years of his pure love for me, I was certain of that, and I would appreciate every minute of every year with him.

Woody, in Alaska just before we moved to Washington (Photo by David Jensen).

Washington

In the fall of 1996, I drove the Alcan once again, moving from Alaska to take a job in Auburn, Washington. I had finally been offered a full-time job at a community college...which is what I thought I wanted to do with my life and had worked and studied for some nine years. The faculty were instant friends, the kindest colleagues I'd ever had. But I had left my healthiest relationship ever—Greg—when I left Alaska, and now I was, like in Oregon, in a house in the woods alone with my dogs and cats. Greg put a ring on my finger the night before I left for the Alcan, which only confused me more. Why is he asking me to marry him now, now that I'm leaving, and I've bought a house, and signed a contract in another state? Why is he claiming ownership yet staying in Alaska, especially after I've done all the hard work and flew down and bought a house, and packed my parents house up and rented it, and asked Greg ten times if I should take the job?

"Yes, it's your dream," he'd say, every time. What I really wanted him to say was, "I would miss you. I am in love with you. Move or stay, but I would like to be with you." Years later, Greg says he saw it differently; he planned to move to Washington, but I never saw him take a step in that direction although he visited me frequently.

I was frightened in Washington with its freeways and the way people drive—like they have to get somewhere *now* and they don't care who they kill to get there. (I sometimes wondered how anyone raised in freeway-less Alaska ever could be comfortable in big city traffic.) But I was even more afraid of the violence that seemed to surround me, always a concern ever since my childhood friend Allison was murdered when I was eighteen years old. And here I was, living in Green River Killer land, alone. Once again…alone.

Except for my dogs, of course.

Woody and me in Washington

Sometimes I wanted to go back to Alaska, mainly because of Greg, my brothers, my nieces and nephews, and my godmother, but I panicked at the thought of living in my parents' house without them again, the house of memories of childhood, and of losing them.... And I did love the weather, my home, and my colleagues in Washington. I guess I just didn't know what I wanted.

But Woody, he had no such confusion. He was so happy wherever we were, as long as I was with him. Often, I caught myself admiring him—his joy in running, living, eating, chewing rawhides, playing with Eb, and his most favorite activity—riding in the car.

"How much I learn from you, Woody!" I would think, as I would watch him live, really live. He never disappointed me, never became angry, never criticized, never snapped. He just loved.

Isn't it ironic that the thing he loved most—besides me and Eb—the car, was what killed him?

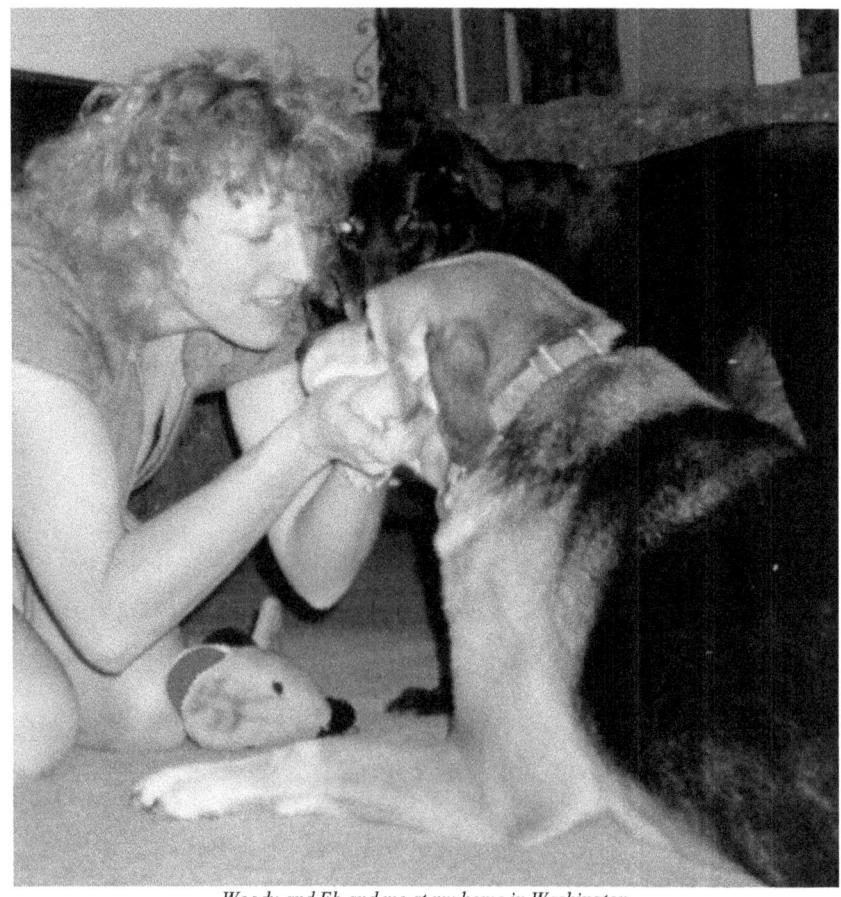

Woody and Eb and me at my home in Washington.

My Mistake

For most of the last decade, my "boy" had slept on the pile of pillows next to mine or behind me, kissing me softly on the cheek before sighing his contented sigh and shifting to a gentle snoring that lasted all night long. I didn't know when I woke up that day in May 1997, nine months after I'd moved to Washington, that I had just spent my last night with Woody.

I made a mistake. I left the gate open.

The day he died, as in every day I knew him, I caught myself admiring him. Oh how he bounded and bounced and played with Eb and jumped up and kissed me and ran some more during our walk. I found myself letting go of my worries, and found myself ready for another day of teaching, all because of him.

That morning, Woody and Eb met a new dog, a sweet pit bull, who was living with his camping owners across the road, and Woody played with him as we passed. Later, before I left for teaching, the pit kept running across the road to saw hello to mine, so perhaps Woody thought he could too.

It was one of my long teaching days, where I didn't get home until almost 9. Winter nights in Washington in the rural areas are dead black, not like Alaska with snow to reflect the moon and stars. Afraid to get out of the car and close the gate, I left it open, as I usually did after night classes. The driveway was long, and the dogs never went out that far without me, so I wasn't worried. I did do one thing differently that night; usually, when I got home, I'd walk with the dogs; if it was a late night such as this one, just around the yard. But I had to hurry and drink that awful medicine for a colonoscopy I didn't end up making the next morning.

It was 9:00 and the controversial finale episode of *Ellen* was starting, but Woody and Eb needed out. I waited till the first commercial to let them back in. But when it came and I called, "Woody! Eb!" only Eb came running back.

Eb had never come back without Woody; they always stay together; in nine years they have never been apart.

But I pretended that Woody was just taking his time even though I knew it wasn't true.

Because I could not possibly face losing him. I could not survive it.

I went back upstairs and pretended to watch *Ellen*. Instead, I smoked and was in some fog, staring at the TV but seeing nothing. Then it came, a pounding on my door, and the terror spasmed my heart because I was too far out from civilization and too far from the road to have ever had someone pound on my door and something in me knew but didn't accept and then I was out there on the side of the road by my driveway, holding him—the guy said he was trying to crawl home when he drove up—and blood was coming out of his mouth and I don't know if he was still alive but I was shaking so bad I tried to drive and couldn't and the guy drove my car the 30 miles to Pet Emergency, me in the back holding Woody, and I told the vet, "You have to save him I'll do anything he's all I have," and she said, "I'm sorry it's too late" and I held his body in shock all the way home.

Not Woody. Not Woody, I kept saying. Not my truest love. Not Woody.

No no no…you were supposed to be with me until I was at least 42; I calculated it; I mapped it out; I said I'd be ready by then somehow.

Whoever hit you didn't stop, and I've seen them drive around those corners on that rural dark road, leaving the bodies of deer, dogs, cats, squirrels, rabbits, raccoons, and opossums behind them, and I hate them, I hate who killed you.

And sometimes I think, Woody, you knew better, you knew the limits of the yard, but then I think how you were always kind of dumb about learning things, not like Eb.

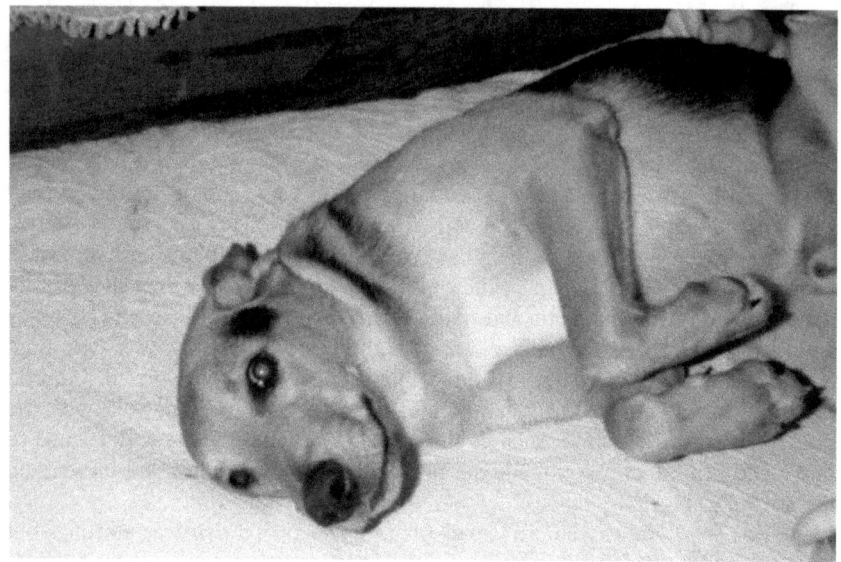

"Woodson"

And then it was just your body left to me, with its silly gold and yellow and brown and black hairs—your body that stiffened in my arms and your blood that covered my shirt. So that when I came home and collapsed on the stairs in disbelief, Eb came up and smelled me slowly and carefully, and then sat down sadly, not touching me. Our lives were to be different now, he seemed to know, not so nice in some important way, without you.

I didn't make it to work the next two days; when I returned, people tried to understand but mainly I felt like I was in trouble for missing work "just" for losing a dog.

I remember sitting staring at my computer, having to ask the department secretary for help because I couldn't type my password: "Woody." I couldn't drink coffee out of my mug at work because it was a special one I'd had made with Woody's picture on it.

The worst part was how I was expected to somehow still be funny in meetings and entertaining in the classroom when really all I wanted to do was die.

After every loss, there is that period of shocked disbelief—of reaching, dreaming, even calling your pet's name, wanting to forget you'll never see him or her again. I read once that people who love their animal companions can find their loss the hardest to take because that dog or cat is so key in their lives. They represent friends, playmates, children.

Woody was with me for six years at the cabin in Oregon, then the two years in Alaska, and finally the first year in Washington. He carried me through much of my thirties, through losing Bobbie and Dane, and during the years I was living with or hiding from the abuser. He was with me through the worst time of all—after my parents died.

And he wasn't just *with* me. Woody gave all the love and warmth he had in him, all to me, and, of course, to Eb. My department chair told me she thought his death overwhelmed me because I was finally mourning the death of my parents as well. That may be partly true, but it is not all true. It slightly belittles the role he had in my life. Even if my parents had been alive still, I have no doubt I would have plummeted into the same depression. I was in love completely with my dear friend Woody, the closest being of any to me on earth.

Woody on one of our adventures, to the Kenai Peninsula in Alaska.

I messed up. Bad. And Woody was killed. One can't help hating oneself when that happens. Piles of hate cramming itself into your mind, into your pillows where he used to rest his head. That's when I miss him most—at night. I miss his hugs, kisses, and soft snores. I miss the way he touched his forehead to mine just to let me know he was there for me.

I've little doubt I would not have made it through losing Woody except that Eb was trying to die first. Both Eb and I had no idea how to go forward. Woody was our centerpiece. He was the one who gave nothing but love and admiration and happiness to us. How were we to give to each other when we had nothing coming in?

It took counseling and antidepressants for me to be able to grade those last papers and get through those last weeks, to teach one foot to go forward and the next to follow. Plus I jeopardized my job some more when I didn't return from a conference in Toronto after three days; instead, I stayed the whole week, skipping one day to go see Niagara Falls, hoping the grandeur of it would pull me back to life, like seeing the ocean in Hawaii did after my parents died.

As my dean was berating me upon my return, I sat very still trying to listen to him, hurt and wanting to cry, "But don't you understand? I lost Woody! I will never be the same. I don't even want to live!" He didn't know that when I got out of the airport in Toronto a week earlier, I had just sat on the curb, unable to move, to think, to find a bus or a taxi. He didn't know how some stranger, hours later, pulled me up and put me in a cab to my hotel, because I couldn't do it myself. He didn't know how hard it was for me to get my feet to move to find a way to come back home. And I didn't try to explain it to him, just listened, but didn't really hear anything he said. My teaching days in Washington should have ended then, but I gave it another year, even though I now hated where I was living, having to drive by the spot where my "Woodson" died.

Eb didn't have a counselor or antidepressants. He had seizures. I'd try to explain it to him. Sometimes I'd pull out Woody's collar, and look at the hairs and cry, and Eb would sniff it and go across the room, into a corner farthest from me but still in my vision, and lie down, staring at nothing.

I was sure the loss of him would never end for me, nor for Eb. I took to sleeplessness and job failure; Eb to seizures and isolation. Both of us called out for him at night, during the day, in our separate ways.

Some people don't know dog love. They would tell me, "He's just a dog. Get another one." In a way, I hated them; in a way, I grieved for them, because they have lost out on the most wonderful relationship there can ever be.

Ultimately, it wasn't the medications or nodding counselor at $95 per hour or even each other that got Eb and me through our mourning, but a puppy named Buddy, who could never replace Woody but tried to by being obnoxious and destructive. So those people who told me to "get another one" were in some way absolutely right. But it was harder to get over losing Woody than any other dog, partly because it was my mistake that caused his death, and partly because, perhaps, I loved him the most of all.

Woody and Eb (Photo by David Jensen).

Just a Dog

You—you were just a dog, and oh how I wish I could be "just" like you, how I wish we all were—so kind and gentle and loving and playful and joyful and understanding.

I miss you my boy, my Woodson, my Woodhead, my dearest love—Woody. Perhaps you were the closest to pure true love I will ever experience. I can take pleasure in that now instead of sorrow. At least I got to have a few so perfect years with you. I was very lucky that day I saw you in the woods.

Thank you for being my "transition dog."

Photo of Woody in my Washington back yard by David Jensen.

Lessons Learned from Woody

You can protect someone you love just by being in the way. Sometimes you have to take on a whole new role in someone's life, and that's good. Just because a gate is open, you don't have to go through it. Most of all: just love.

My friend Dave came to visit me in Washington a couple months before Woody died. After Woody's death, Dave sent me some photos he had taken of my dogs. I was surprised that the pictures showed Woody's face whiter than he was, almost ghostly, and in this photo my "Woodhead" is lying exactly where I buried him (Photo by David Jensen).

7 Eb: Woody's Best Friend

It's just the most amazing thing to love a dog, isn't it? It makes our relationships with people seem as boring as a bowl of oatmeal.
—John Grogan

One of the greatest gifts we receive from dogs is the tenderness they evoke in us.... By their delight in being with us, the reliable sunniness of their disposition, the joy they bring to playtime, the curiosity with which they embrace each new experience, dogs can melt cynicism, and sweeten the bitter heart.
—Dean Koontz, A Big Little Life: A Memoir of a Joyful Dog

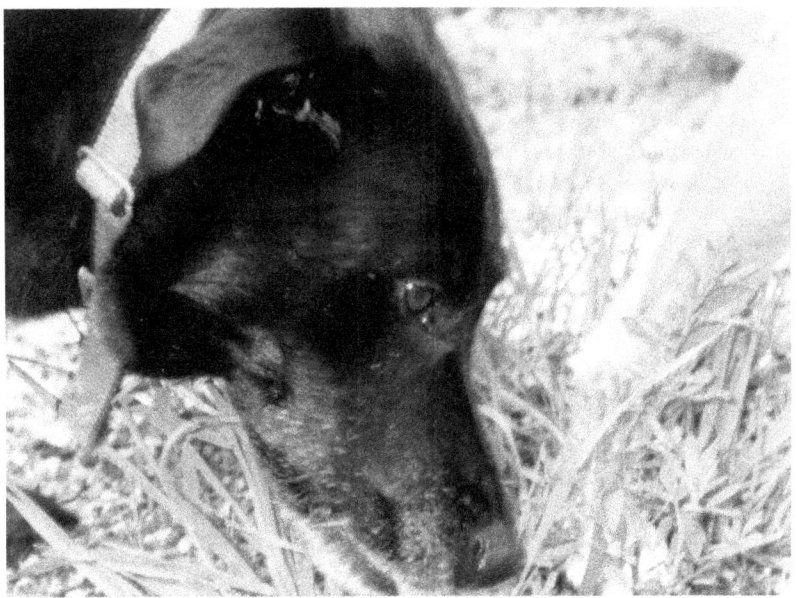

The Meeting

I met him in a veterinary reception area in August 1989 in Oregon, and I said goodbye to him in a veterinary waiting room exactly 10 years later, in Alaska.

I called him my "boy."

I had always paid my vet bills the day I went, even if I had to put it on a credit card, but when Bobbie died, back in 1989 in Oregon, I had left the vet's office in such emotional trauma that I didn't pay.

A week or so later I finally went back in to settle my account. I thought maybe I could get in and out quickly without crying.

While I was standing at the counter, a silly black Labrador-mix puppy came up to me, his tail as long as his body, wagging, wriggling, and smiling, acting silly and ridiculous as puppies tend to do.

"Who are you?" I asked, picking him up and cuddling him, accepting his little puppy-breath kisses.

"Oh, he was found by the police and dropped off," the receptionist said. "A stray. We call him Mac."

She looked at me steadily. "He needs a home."

I paid my bill, played with the little puppy again, and left. Too soon. Too soon. It's much too soon. I can't. I won't.

I knew there was no way I was going to get another dog. Two was a perfect number, and I couldn't go through the pain of losing one again. No way. I left the office and ran some errands. On my way home I drove passed the vet office, and stopped in just to say hi to that happy puppy.

Oh, the kisses he greeted me with! It's like we had been best friends for years. It's like he knew I was going to take him home and love him for the next decade. He just knew. But I didn't.

Not yet. I left again. Later, I met my former student, octogenarian Allen, for a late lunch in town.

During lunch, I kept talking about this silly black lab I saw at the vet's, and Alan agreed to go there with me to meet the little guy. The puppy jumped back in my arms and kissed me, and I hugged him tightly. That was the third time I was there that day, and the last.

"Too soon," I told Alan, and then I adopted him.

He rode home with me just as he knew he was supposed to, happy and content.

Woody was ecstatic! A puppy! Someone to play with! They instantly began wrestling and tumbling and turned my tears to a soft giggle. They were instant best friends.

FOR THE LOVE OF DOGS: MY LIFE IN DOG YEARS

Woody and Eb and play in my Oregon cabin, while old Dane complains.

Unlike Woody—the little puppy gave old Dane the respect and distance she wanted. Woody liked to chew on her paws and make her just a little bit miserable, soft growls coming out of her throat similar to what she did when Bibs nursed her face, but Dane never moved from her spot on the couch during these injustices.

I liked the name "Mac" that the vet office had given him; I liked it a lot. I didn't know why, but that night in the cabin a new name came to me: Eb. Maybe it's because he was the color of shiny ebony. But I think the real reason was he reminded me of Mr. Haney's goofy young neighbor in *Green Acres*. Whatever it was, I began calling him Eb.

Later that night, Alan called and said, "I thought of a name for your new pup."

"Oh, I already got one," I told him, slightly irritated. Why would he think he has the right to name my dog?

"Well, mine is better," he retorted, reminding me of what he was like in my Creative Writing class.

"What is it?" I asked, in spite of myself.

Alan replied, "Eb."

So my "Ebbers" or "Ebony" or even "Ebenezer" as I sometimes called him, came to live with me, my dogs (Woody and Dane), my three cats (Sylvia, Clover, and Bibs), and my two horses (Dusty and Jeffers) in my cabin in Oregon, back in 1989. I didn't know at the time that he would live with me throughout my 30s, in three states, and see me through the playing out of the violent relationship with Brock, the death of my parents, and a new relationship with a kind man named Greg. I didn't know that at the time Ebony passed away, I would be pregnant with my son, 39 years old, living back in Alaska. I just knew he was mine, till the end of his days, and I was his, and it was all decided the moment I walked into the vet's to pay Bobbie's euthanasia bill.

Ebony (Eb) and me in Oregon.

Best Friends

Woody and Eb were pals. There was no question that Eb loved Woody. They played and played. They also enjoyed "humping" each other, although Woody was not entirely faithful in this area. He liked all dogs, always. He never had a fight or argument in his life, even when someone's pet wolf didn't take too well to his hump-style greeting. I only mention the humping because it bothered some people—particularly men. They think it's sexual, and since they're two male dogs, it must mean they're homosexual, as if that even matters. "My God! You have homo dogs!" I'd hear.

I'd explain that there was nothing sexual about these two—they'd both been neutered as soon as they were old enough to be.

Teenagers and best friends, Woody and Eb, in Oregon.

In fact, here's how the humping came about. Next door to my cabin I had neighbors. These neighbors had a little different philosophy about dogs than I did. If you asked them, they'd say they "love" their dogs. But their dogs—purebred Dalmatians—were not allowed inside their precious manufactured home. They lived in kennels and were bred for show and money. Their stud dog—Jay—was unfortunate enough to earn enough points to be called a champion of some sort, so that meant more money for the pups. That also meant that not only was he stud dog to others' dogs, but to his own pups!

The one pup they kept from the latest litter—Baby—was the same age as Woody. This was before the kennels were built, so she was free to come over and play with Woody all the time as they were growing up. She must not have been seven months old yet when the neighbors began trying to have her bred—by her father, Jay. How is this breeding accomplished? They told me that they would put a female in heat in a cage, and then Jay in there, and then hold the female so she couldn't get away as Jay mounted her. Very romantic.

One day they said Baby's mother had snapped at someone so they had her "put down." There was something wrong with her. Yeah, there's something wrong with her, I thought. She had you for owners. And she was past her breeding prime.

In the meantime, Baby was learning from her mating sessions with her dad a new game to teach Woody. So when she came over she'd mount him and hump him. He soon caught on to this fun new game and did the same to her. And when Eb came into our lives, he taught Eb this game too. That's all it was to them.

But what ridiculous responses people have when they see dogs "hump" for play. They assume it is only a sexual move, and since sex is "bad," then the dogs are bad, and the dogs' owners are bad, and it's all dirty and disgusting and everyone involved should be punished! How I pity dogs of such owners.

I remember walking on a trail in Alaska once and encountering a woman who obviously knew nothing about dogs. Woody and her dog began playing, and then Woody mounted her dog, and I told her, "It's just play. He's neutered," but she yanked her dog away and screamed, "My dog doesn't play THAT way!"

A close family member actually kicked Eb in the side when he saw Eb mount Woody. I was furious. That's when I came up with my "let dogs be dogs" philosophy. Too many dogs are punished—physically or by law—for merely being dogs. The "one bite and your dog is dead" laws in many cities or the "one livestock chase and your dog is dead" laws in several states are perfect examples. My horses like to chase my dogs around the pasture, and then wheel around and let my dogs chase them. It was play—just play. Nothing more. When I sit on the floor and wrestle with my dogs and we tumble around happily, I am using my hands on them and they are using their teeth on me. It is play. They don't hurt me and I don't hurt them. But because their teeth touch my skin they could be killed, by law, in some places. Let dogs be dogs.

Woody and Eb with their typical game.

Nights in Oregon

It is almost midnight, and I'm driving again. It is one of those black Oregon summer nights, and I am going deeper into the wilderness, driving desperately, fleeing my life, or rather, the man in my life. And his temper. I drive and drive until I think he can't find me, and then I pull over. My dogs, Woody and Eb, whine in the back of the car. I let them out.

We stand there, in the woods, together, always together. When I flee I always take them. I have studied enough about abusive men to know they go after what a woman loves, particularly her dogs, and anyway, I would never leave my dogs. They are my best friends, my loves, my only family in Oregon.

The stars show themselves as the clouds pass away, and in my fear I still am overwhelmed with the sharp beauty of a summer night. Growing up in Alaska, I never saw a night like this. Up north, midnight is as bright as midday in the summer, and when stars can be seen it is too cold to stand outside admiring them.

We stay there until I stop shaking, and then I call the dogs back in the car, and we head for home.

Why am I going home, back to my cabin, back to him? My cats, my horses, my books are there. My life is there. I have nowhere else to go.

And plus...he is there. And I love him. I can change him. I can make him better. He'll be sorry by now, maybe. Sorry he hit me.

I am lonely, and he is all I have.

Of course, even as I think this, I know it's not true.

The abuser back home at my cabin does not really love me, not the way Woody and Eb, sitting in the back seat, do.

Why is their love not enough for me?

"Why don't you have any pictures of me on your walls?" the abuser once demanded. "All you have are pictures of your dogs."

Because, I thought but did not say, my dogs truly love me, not like you. They don't make demands on me I cannot meet, they don't ever yell at me, they don't hit walls in anger because of something I said or didn't say, they don't hit me.

The love of my dogs should have been enough, I think, looking back, wishing I had never brought him into our lives to nearly destroy us.

True love, I know now, is the dogs in my life, the dogs who have lived every memorable moment with me, and who have served as my teachers and friends.

One time, my dear friend Mike, who'd never had a dog, made a joke, something like, "Sure, they'll stick around, as long as you feed them." I really thought about this comment, and I haven't been able to think of one dog yet who wouldn't stick around anyway, starving right with you, to the very end. However, I have a feeling my cats would leave me flat if I stopped putting out food, but I could be wrong. They'd certainly complain about it a lot more than a dog would, I'm sure of that.

Eb playing in the Oregon creek near my cabin.

Alaska

It took me seven years to finally escape Oregon, escape the abuser. I hurried to finish my dissertation after his last kick in the stomach, planning my escape. My father was dying of colon cancer, and I needed to get back to Alaska to see him, I told the abuser, but I'd be back soon.

Of course, my escape plan included my dogs, Woody and Eb. I would never leave them. But sadly, I did leave other animals behind, temporarily, I was sure. My sister-in-law called just a few days before I was to leave, telling me I couldn't bring my cats to her house (where I was going to stay until I found a place). She said her father would be visiting later in the summer, and he was allergic. (Of course, my sister-in-law didn't know about the abuser living at my house; I just couldn't bring myself to tell my family he was still in my life, all these years.)

I was devastated. This was the end of my plans. How could I leave them behind? Doing so was against everything I believed in.

A woman desperate to leave an abuser will find a way, at least I did. I found a fellow teacher, a strong woman, unlike me, to watch my cats in exchange for living at my cabin, even though Brock still kept his things there and would be back between jobs. She knew him and had no problem with him: "I can handle Brock," she said. And she could. She was either crazy enough to not understand his sickness, or strong enough to handle it; either way, she did fine over the 15 months I was gone, and he eventually got the message and moved out.

I also had to leave my horses behind, but I found a home where—I was told—they would never be used for breeding, were in a large herd on 80 acres, and would never be sold. I could visit all I wanted, and if the couple ever had to sell for any reasons—they assured me they would not—I would get to buy them.

About 14 months later, Woody, Eb, and I drove back down the Alcan to

Oregon, after my parents died. I was going to sell my cabin, get my cats, and check on my horses, and leave my beloved cabin and the abuser forever.

Woody and Eb and me, on the Alaska-Canadian Highway (Alcan) once again.

When I went to see my horses; they were gone. The man said his wife sold them all and moved back to Florida, and no, he had no idea where they were. I was especially worried about Dusty, because she was a registered quarter horse who had been used for breeding so much she was worn out at the age of eight when I first got her. She constantly tried to escape and go back to the place where her last colt was, but they no longer wanted her and had sold him. I promised her it would never happen to her again.

For now, I had other things to deal with, and I vowed to find Dusty and bring her home, as soon as I figured out where home would be.

Eb and Woody and Dusty in my Oregon pasture.

The Moose Kick

During our daily walks in the woods, Eb liked to stay next to my knee, like Bobbie did, once he was over his first year of puppydom.

"How are you doing, Eb?" I'd ask him while we strolled and Woody ran ahead. It was courtesy and habit, and in the last few years of his life, worry.

I was walking Woody and Eb and my parents' dog Boots at University Lake in 1995 in Anchorage when a moose came charging out of the woods. Eb and I didn't see him until it was too late, until his right front foot was kicking forward, hitting Eb in the stomach, and barely missed me. I didn't know if the moose was aiming for Eb or me, but Eb got it, and so his life became a battle ever after.

My father had died in my arms two months before. Now my mother and me, and Woody, Eb, and Boots shared the large, mainly empty home I had grown up in.

Eb began vomiting that night after the moose kick, and I drove him to Pet Emergency. I came back with bad news.

"Mom," I said, eyes wet, "they don't know if they can save him. He is bleeding internally, his pancreas is torn, everything is messed up." By now my tears were falling, and I said the stupidest thing to the woman who was suffering so much too...after losing her husband of over 40 years. "I don't know if I can live without my Eb."

"I know, I know," she said, comforting me. (I didn't know that less than a month later, my mother would die in a car accident, and I would have to suffer the unbearable shock of living without her.)

Hundreds of vet visits, many nights in Pet Emergency, many days on I.V.s in vet clinics. I became his nurse in that March of 1995 till his passing in August 1999, and despite the stress, strain, expense, and tears, it was the most rewarding job I ever had. Many nights I stayed up with him. It was very little compared to what he gave me.

Eb and his toy box.

When a loved one is gone, you look back of the moments that seemed drudgery and think, "Why couldn't I enjoy that?" But I had already learned my lesson from two dogs grown old, from my father dying in my arms. When Eb needed me, I did everything I could to spend every minute I could to make his life wonderful.

I remember a job interview I had, about four years after the moose kick. It was exactly the job I wanted and loved—technical editing. But I told the committee that although I was a thorough, dedicated editor, I had to work some of my hours at home because my old dog was ill. I didn't get the job.

I don't regret it now, because it was more time with Eb. I knew his time was coming, even though I kept telling myself, "He's too young. He has to have many years left. He's only ten."

Losing Woody

Eb, me and Woody, back in Alaska, 1996.

From the moment I brought little puppy Eb home from the vet in Oregon , Eb and Woody were best friends. They loved each other so powerfully that I can't think of anything else like it, except, perhaps, Woody's love for me.

Both Eb and I worshipped Woody; he was our hero, our leader, our everything. The bond between Eb and me was really the bond of being in love with Woody.

So the night in Washington after Woody was killed by a car, I was not the only one in mourning.

Eb was waiting for me, confused. I had never gone anywhere with just Woody and left Eb behind before. He hadn't known Woody was hit since he was running ahead and came inside first.

When I came into the house and collapsed on the stairs just by the door, Eb carefully smelled me up and down, and the blood and hair and smell of Woody's death on my clothes and hands told him the whole story.

We had both lost our best friend. He looked away from me, into the sheet rocked wall, and didn't look back for a long time. He didn't push into my arms, like Woody would have, if Eb had died.

Dogs don't have tear ducts like humans do, but I have no doubt that I wasn't the only one crying.

Eb no longer wanted to sleep on the bed, for he always slept next to Woody there. He stayed in the far corner of the bedroom, his expression a vacant, sad stare. He didn't seem to sleep, and he hardly if ever ate. Our walks were different now; we didn't know what to do. We kept looking at each other. Where's our fearless leader?

The next Monday I had to return to work, and when I came home and let Eb out, he stepped over the threshold onto the porch, looked up at me, and then collapsed in the first of what would be many seizures over the next few weeks. The vets could never find a reason for the seizures, but I already knew. They were caused by a broken heart.

Woody and Eb hangs in Washington, shortly before Woody's death (Photo by David Jensen).

The seizures continued for a couple months, until one day when I brought home a pest of a puppy—a lab-shepherd just like Woody—and named him Buddy.

Eb pretended to ignore him and growled at him from time to time, but he began eating again, our walks perked up, and the seizures stopped that very day, and never returned.

One day, over a year after Buddy came into our lives, Eb mounted him and humped him. Just for a moment. But that was the only time he'd ever done such a thing with any dog but Woody.

Buddy looked quite confused. He didn't know this game. But he turned around and wrestled happily with Eb anyway. And I sat at my computer, watching them play, smiling at my dear old Eb, back to living again.

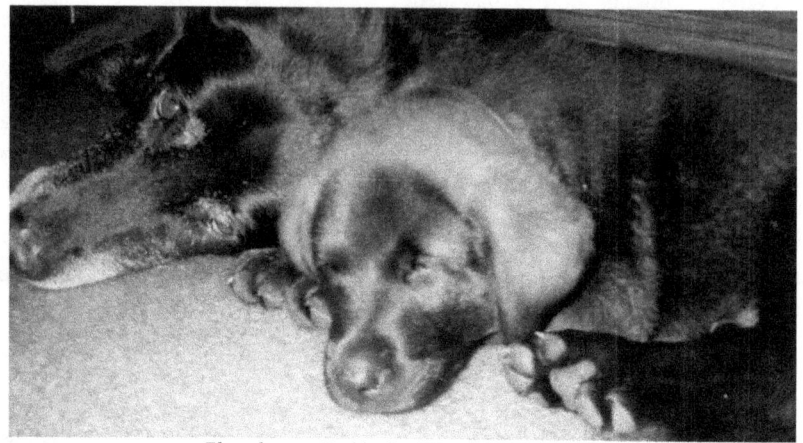

Eb and puppy Buddy, the "Woody replacement."

Eb probably would have preferred it if I hadn't found Schatzy, a yellow lab mix someone abandoned at a Fred Meyer parking lot, not long after, as she took instantly to Buddy and claimed him as her own, but somehow Eb and I became much closer than we ever had been.

Buddy and Schatzy walked and played together; Eb and I walked and played together.

Eb's job became "staying between 'mama' and that obnoxious yeller dog," and as he aged so quickly, mine became "making Eb's days as happy and pain free as possible."

Dogs Grow Old...

Dogs grow old so much faster than their humans. We love our old dogs fiercely. We know better, but still we hope that we can extend that time we have left together, even while we watch a dog who is losing his grip on this life more and more each day, a dog we value so much that we bring him at least once a day on a little walk. Maybe sometimes we have to carry him a little.

Eb had the old Labrador soul: faithful, grateful, and full of love for me. You tell yourself you gave him a good life, a beautiful life, and a glorious dignified old age. You try to remind yourself that he has to leave your soon, and don't feel too bad about his passing. In my humane society work I have seen too many old dogs left to die in animal controls or taken to a vet for a quick shot long before their time, just because the dog could no longer run with a bicycle or needed a few hundred dollars of vet care. I knew that an old dog—no matter how expensive, no matter how much "trouble"—is the most glorious of creatures.

As we watch our old dogs age away, it breaks our hearts, but it strengthens us too. We learned from their love and faith and devotion. We learn from the courageous way they face the end.

FOR THE LOVE OF DOGS: MY LIFE IN DOG YEARS

Eb, in 1997, two years before he died from the moose kick complications (Photo by David Jensen).

It was fall 1998 in Alaska, after I'd moved back from Washington, and Eb did something he's only done once before in his life, and it broke my heart. Because I knew what it represented.

What he did was, he struggled his arthritic body off the bed, got down on the floor, went into the closet, and urinated on the floor.

Eb only did that once, when he was a silly little black puppy who first came home to live with me 10 years ago. He "tinkled" on the floor, I said no, picked him up, carried him outside, and explained that this is where he was going to go from now on. Now, most puppies require further convincing—Woody took about 4 months to agree with me on this outside thing—but Eb understood right away that this was the best place to go.

I decided Eb was a genius dog, while Woody—although pure love—was a little slow. Take the command "shake" for example. Or "sit," "stay," or "come." Woody kept forgetting even though he desperately wanted to remember because he loved the treats involved in this ridiculously difficult game. But Eb—he was a dog trainer's miracle. One time for everything: shake, sit, lie, come. Just like housebreaking.

So, that night, I was shocked and he was shocked.

We looked at each other stunned after it happened, both speechless and embarrassed.

It seems unfair, I thought, looking at him, that he grows old so much quicker than I. At nine years old (so young because of the moose kick four years before), Eb's body—and perhaps a little bit of his mind—is breaking down while mine is still relatively young, at 38 years old.

I pulled myself together, "No, Eb, you go outside for that."

I started to lead him to the door, but he panicked and ran back to the bedroom.

I thought about it as I cleaned up, and how my initial feeling was how could he be so bad and how he should be *told* he was bad, and then I thought, of course he knows he wasn't supposed to do that, and he's as confused and scared as I am over this.

So I hugged him and talked to him about it and assured him it's okay and that I love him and will do everything I can for him through this tough old age. Slowly he relaxed and trusted me and managed to jump on the bed (which got harder for him every day), and snored himself to sleep.

I vowed to try to be more careful about taking him outside more frequently—like many dogs, the only time he enjoys going out is when I go along—on a walk together. He wanted to be with me as much as possible, especially as he grew older and weaker.

Eb in 1996, a year after the moose kick, aging rapidly (Photo by David Jensen).

Hip dysplasia, arthritis, seizures, moose kick repercussions such as liver and pancreas problems, and eventually diabetes. Eb seemed to have all the health problems a dog could have. But still he always knew how to live. He took such joy in the simplest of things—an ear rub, a brushing, chunks of ice to chew on, rawhide and squeaky toys, and walks in the woods. But most of all, he loved to soak in a lake. Just ease his tired sore body into the cold Alaskan waters and groan in pleasure.

All that winter I had worked hard to keep him alive, hoping he'd have his lake soaks again, and he did. Every night we'd walk to the park, and I'd break the ridiculously strict Anchorage leash law as usual, letting the three of them run and splash into the water. While Schatzy would chase sticks and Buddy would chase Schatzy, Eb would just soak with pleasure.

Eb and me in Washington, both of us cheered up after Buddy, and then Schatzy, joined our pack.

Maybe it was the lake where he caught pneumonia. Maybe it's just that an old dog with so many health problems couldn't fight it, no matter how many antibiotics we put him on that last week. But I think it was just his time; I think he was finally ready to go. He died very bravely, with great dignity. He seemed to wait for me to return to the vet office that last day. I wasn't going to put him down there; I was going to take him home to die, if it wasn't too painful.

"Do you want to go home Eb?" I asked him, trying not to let him hear the pain and fear in my voice.

He got up from the hot dark cage where we'd tried to give him oxygen as a last resort, and followed me out the back door, urinated outside politely, followed me to the car, but then circled around and wanted back into the front door of the vet office. I opened the door for him, as he wanted me to, and we went inside. That was where he decided to die. He looked up at me, his front legs collapsed, and he bravely and quietly let go.

It was a tremendous circle, his life, our life. Our saying hello and goodbye in vet reception areas took place ten years apart. When he left, a whole past went with him...a whole history of people and animals and places I have known.

For the first time in several years I didn't have constant nursing duties, and I didn't have to worry and watch him every minute, and ask, "How are you Eb?" just to make sure he is still alive. I missed that so much.

My walks with Buddy and Schatzy could be much longer now, much more vigorous, but somehow they seem emptier.

I moved to a new home in the woods, one I was trying to rush the contractor into finishing because I wanted Eb to live here, but he didn't make it.

But...someone else did.

A few days after I moved to my new home near Palmer, Alaska, I could look outside my window and see an old horse, a horse who needed me, who was not treated well the last few years of her life, who was now 21 years old and had seizures and Cushing's disease, and who would need to have medications and special care the rest of her life.

But because I didn't stop searching for her, she was to live an easy old age, and have her son with her, and she would never be mistreated again.

Her name was Dusty, and 14 years ago in Oregon, when I brought home a little black puppy named Eb, he and Woody would run alongside her during our many rides through the forests. I had promised her I would find her again, and though it took much longer than I thought it would, I did.

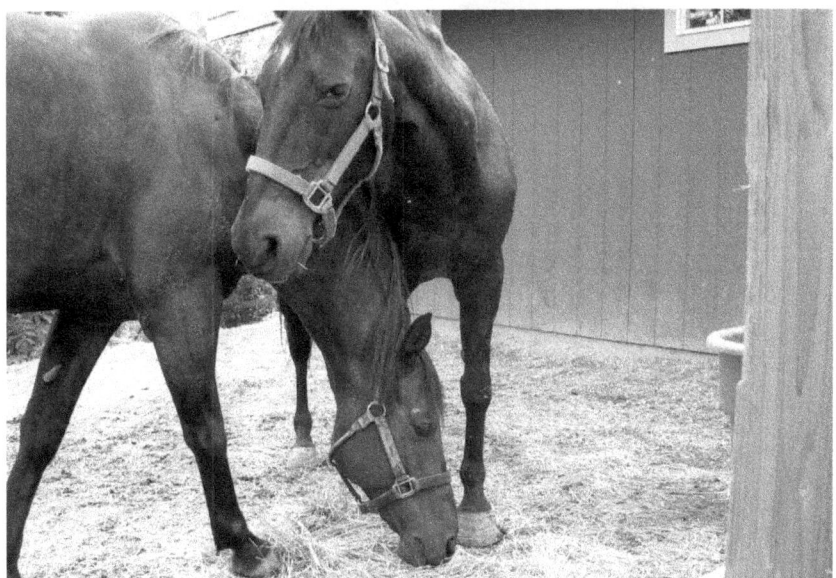

Old Dusty (right) with her son, Stargone, at their new home (with a heated barn I had built for them) in Alaska.

And I think how in some mysterious ways, things do work out sometimes, just as they should. And once in a while, you can find true love in life, and even the pain of loss cannot destroy the strength and beauty of that love. I have been so blessed to know so much love from friends, from family, from animals. And sometimes we have the grandest of opportunities to find pure love in the simplest of ways, like rescuing a silly black puppy or recovering someone we lost a long time ago, like an old black mare.

To you Eb. Thanks for giving me ten years of your precious life.

Eb and me, 1999, his last year (Photo by David Jensen).

Lessons Learned from Ebony

Sometimes it is good to be silly. Pay attention and you can learn things the first time. Obey the rules. When your true love dies, it feels like you can't go on. But you can. Sometimes, all you need is a warm puppy to get you out of your depression. If a moose runs at you, get out of the way.

8 Boots: My Father's Dog

The dog's agenda is simple, fathomable, overt: I want. "I want to go out, come in, eat something, lie here, play with that, kiss you. There are no ulterior motives with a dog, no mind games, no second-guessing, no complicated negotiations or bargains, and no guilt trips or grudges if a request is denied.
—Caroline Knapp

My parents' dog, Boots (Photo by David Jensen).

After nine years in Oregon, I left my cabin with my dogs Woody and Eb, and headed back to Alaska. I needed to escape Brock and I had finished my doctorate, but there was another reason, the main reason.

For seven years my father, not yet old enough to retire, had been battling colon cancer. Now he was dying. Tumors had blocked off his intestines and filled his stomach; he could no longer eat or even drink water. Some infection forced him into the hospital, which was the only thing he'd ever complained about, and even then, not really. I just sensed that he wasn't happy with the way he was ignored or basically told—by his doctors—to give up and die already. One night he had no luck summoning a nurse, and tried to reach the bathroom on his own, but fell and gashed his head on the nightstand.

Seeing his deep scar the next day only added to my frustration and helpless anger. Why isn't there anything I can do, I thought, as I waited for the elevator.

As if in answer to my prayers, when the elevator opened, two dogs greeted me.

Dogs? In a hospital? Personally, I couldn't think of a better place for dogs, but I was shocked the city laws, hospital codes, and heavy-handed orderlies let them in.

"How did you get to bring dogs here?" I asked the owner, as I stepped in.

"They are therapy dogs. I take them up to the sixth floor once a week, to meet with the patients in rehab."

An idea grew stronger and stronger as I walked out of the hospital and to my car, and then drove home to get my Woody, Eb, and my parents' dog, a springer spaniel named Boots, to take them for their walk.

My dad had bought Boots for my mom for a Christmas present a few years before. My mother insisted that she wanted a dog, and it had to be a spaniel, my dad had explained as he asked me to go for a ride with him up to Wasilla to pick out a puppy.

I realized the genius of my mother's plan immediately as I saw the tension ease from my father's face when he picked out that wriggly kissy puppy. The dog was not for her; it was for him; it had to be a spaniel so he could have the hunting dog he'd never had since he was a boy.

Boots as a puppy in Anchorage, Alaska.

Growing up in Alaska, all children want to do is leave for the "lower 48" or the "Outside," and many of them never move back. I was one of those children.

FOR THE LOVE OF DOGS: MY LIFE IN DOG YEARS

My brothers and sisters had moved away, also, although one brother (Robbie) moved back to Alaska—but was at this time living in Fairbanks, over 400 miles away—and the other brother (Aaron) was soon to return to Alaska as well. But Boots became the perfect child my father never had. She was an eager, loving, obedient pal and hunting partner for him.

In fact, she seemed too obedient to me. Unlike my spoiled dogs who didn't know the word "No," Boots was not allowed on the bed or any other furniture, and she never broke this rule. Sometimes I wanted to tell my dad when he was lying on his sick bed, "Call Boots up here! She'll give you love and kisses and hold you like I'm too restrained to do...and you need it." But I didn't. And he didn't. And Boots didn't. Instead, she sat near his bed, watching him protectively and lovingly, as the months rolled on and he could no longer walk or even sit up without help. Once in a while he would get very sick, and go to the hospital, and she would await his return hopefully. But I never knew until this day how much they meant to each other.

That day during my walk, I decided that if I could give my dad nothing else, I was going to give him a few minutes with his beloved dog. So I went back to the hospital, and asked a nurse about it. She told me that if I was to bring his dog in, she would not "see anything." I took that as a yes.

Later that day, I came back for another visit, but this time with Boots. All I told my dad was that I had a surprise for him, but it was in my car. I went to get her, and the strangest thing happened.

Boots, who had never been anywhere near that hospital, and who was perfectly leash trained, yanked me across that snowy parking lot to the front door, then dragged me down the hall to just the right elevators (I could never find the right ones myself), and then, when we reached the fourth floor and the elevator doors opened, pulled me harder than ever down the hall, around two corners, down another hall, into his room, and jumped on his bed! Ever so gently, she crawled into his arms, not touching his pain-filled sides or stomach.

For the first time, Boots was on a bed, just as she knew she should be. And for the first time in a long time, I saw my father smile.

Boots, my father's dog.

My father and Boots (Photo by David Jensen).

Lesson Learned from Boots

Sometimes it is the best thing for everyone to break a rule.

MY LATE THIRTIES TO FORTIES IN WASHINGTON AND ALASKA (1997-2012): BUDDY & SCHATZY

9 Buddy: Woody's Replacement

Dogs lives are short, too short, but you know that going in. You know the pain is coming, you're going to lose a dog, and there's going to be great anguish, so you live fully in the moment with her, never fail to share her joy or delight in her innocence, because you can't support the illusion that a dog can be your lifelong companion. There's such beauty in the hard honesty of that, in accepting and giving love while always aware it comes with an unbearable price.

—Dean Koontz, *The Darkest Evening of the Year*

"Free Puppies"

After losing a pet, some people never get another one; others do. There's no right or wrong way, but for me, another pet heals.

It was near the end of May 1997, and I'd been living in Washington for nine months when Woody was hit by a car and died. After he died, I was irritated when people suggested I get a another dog. Woody was irreplaceable. But they were right, of course. I knew I had to, at least for Eb, I told myself, who was still seizuring and not eating.

I forced myself to go to an animal control or two, but I couldn't make a decision there. The dogs were all so worthy, and it was so unfair that they were there, and they were all beautiful souls. I can't choose one when so many will die. I kept thinking of the movie *Sophie's Choice*, and I left feeling worse than ever.

One day I took a long road back from college, and this was when I saw a sign that said, "Free Puppies." Now, I hate these signs, and I detest the people who don't spay and neuter because of what happens in this country to millions of dogs and cats every year just because there are too many.

But I told myself I'd just turn in and take a look.

Of course, I should have known better.

The mama is a black lab, and her large litter...at least 10...look to be lab-shepherds, just like Woody was, only they are almost all black, except for one.

He has an odd orange stripe across his head, from ear to ear. (As he grew up, the beautiful orange colors on Buddy's ears and head faded and slowly disappeared, and his head turned black, just like his brothers and sisters. Browns and reds glowed through other parts of him, from time to time, but I lost that cute stripe. Just like Woody went from black to gold as he aged, so Buddy's colors changed too, but to dark and rich, almost black.)

Anyone would say bringing home a puppy that looked almost exactly like Woody did would be a bad idea.

"You can't replace Woody; you can't force another dog to become Woodhead; dogs are unique, just like people are," I told myself, but clearly, something happened.

I even named him the closest name I could think of to Woody without being Woody: Buddy.

Eb's undiagnosable seizures stopped, never to return, the minute the pesky puppy came through the door, and he growled peacefully at little Buddy when the puppy would wear himself out with mischief and curl up next to the old lab. And maybe I slept a little again, with a little black pup snoring on my chest.

Buddy was instantly more effective than the medications and counseling sessions I had turned to after Woody died. He couldn't be Woody, although he seemed a little dense like Woody was, a slow learner when it came to housetraining and destruction of property. (Poor old smart Eb just watched him, patiently, and I think of how Eb learned everything the first time.)

My little "Buddapest," as I called him while he ate another shoe or book or rug, was our savior. He couldn't be Woody, but he was, indeed, a silly, joyous, playful, and pestering rascal that brought happiness to our home.

Maybe I saved him from a trip to the pound, but he saved me in some indefinable, beautiful way that only dogs can.

Buddy as a puppy in Washington, with his cute orange ears.

Buddy was so loving and unselfish and gentle with us. Although Eb showed no outright interest in the little puppy, Buddy would tire himself out, and then plop down right next to Eb, sleeping with his head touching Eb's head, while I typed.

It was so sweet and kind and served to bring Eb back.

My overwhelming guilt of not closing the gate, which led to Woody's death, was slowly being replaced by overwhelming love for this new joyous life.

As he grew, I thought Buddy would learn to hug and kiss me and snore in my ear at night, like Woody did. But he usually had no interest in giving me hugs or kisses, unless I happened to have food in my hand or lotion on my face. He didn't even care to sleep on the bed unless he felt like pestering Eb.

Sometimes, late at night, when I couldn't bear the loneliness of having to sleep without a dog to hold or who is holding me, I would find Buddy somewhere on the floor in the darkness, and I would curl myself behind him and hold him. In the dark, he felt just like Woody. He was the same size, had the same texture of fur, had the same soft floppy ears and giant rough paws and broad sloping head. He bore the pretense without turning to look at me, just slept on. I felt a sense of comfort but also sadness, and I knew I'd given this boy a tough assignment.

But I reminded myself...Woody didn't become a giver and our love did not fully bond until after Dane died, when he was over three years old. Of course, Eb got my fullest attention and empathy after Woody died, because he needed it most. Sometimes I think that he too wanted to imagine in the darkness that Buddy was Woody.

I remember the first time I laughed in three months. I was lying in the sun in my yard, in my swimsuit, soaking up sun. My dogs were next to me.

The little puppy Buddy grabbed my large plastic coke cup and ran around the yard, spilling the coke everywhere, then stopped and stuck his black and orange head into the cup.

Suddenly, he was stuck, and his running was more desperate this time, frantically crashing into bushes as I was chasing him, laughing, to get the cup off his face.

When I pulled it off, he looked at me, jumped in my arms, and kissed me. I was his hero! I had saved him from the dastardly vengeful cup, and he was overjoyed.

Eb and Buddy in my home office in Washington.

Living in Washington

So now I'd lived in Washington for a year, in a home in the woods again, alone, except for my dogs. I was not sure I'd done the right thing leaving Greg in Alaska, but then, we hadn't dated but six months when I was offered this job, and he didn't ask me to stay. I tend to fall in love quickly, and with the wrong kind of man.

Greg seemed honest and good and kind, but I could never quite trust myself and what kind of man I would attract after Brock.

And I was afraid in Washington, the state where Allison was murdered back in 1978, when we were 18.

Now I had a special kind of fear, living and working near the great Green River. I'd heard of the "Green River Killer" for many years, but the local police told me he'd died long before, they were sure (they were wrong). Also, he tended to like to murder prostitutes, and I was certainly not one to charge for sex.

But the Green River, too, made me think often of Allison, supposedly murdered by a serial killer.

One day I was out in my yard playing in a wading pool with my three dogs, and I stood there laughing as little Buddy played in the pool, before I noticed the two men who had pulled over, just outside my gate, staring at me, no longer hidden behind my bushes where I'd been sunning before.

All my fears of Washington and the Green River Killer came rushing back, and I called Eb and carried Buddy into the house and locked the doors, trembling.

The Gun

One night I wanted something from the store...probably chocolate...and put the dogs in the car and headed the five-mile drive in the dark to Safeway. At the last minute, I grabbed my handgun and put it under my seat. I was afraid of being followed, of breaking down, of someone trying to get in the car with me when I got out of the store.

I was pretty much afraid all the time.

Having nice lab mixes like Woody and Eb, and then Buddy and Eb, was great for not getting a pet owner in trouble because of how they treated people and pets on the trails, but they weren't the kind of dogs to make you feel safer either. Sometimes I wished for a pack of Dobermans or rottweilers, because I was sure I would have nothing to fear then.

However, the law approves gentle dogs, and those are what I had.

So I took my gun. Fully loaded. I really had no idea how to use it, although I believe my father showed me once. I had bought it in Oregon, after Brock tried to kill me, and slept with it each night for a year, just in case he returned to finish the job. I didn't know if I would ever be able to actually shoot someone, especially Brock, if he broke in, but my brother had told me what to buy, so I bought it.

We arrived at Safeway, I told the dogs I'd be right back, then I shoved the gun as far under my seat as I could reach as I left them.

When I came back, 10 minutes later, little Buddy had the gun between his paws in the back seat, and was chewing away on the barrel, the muzzle aiming this way and that, his silly paws touching the trigger. I was mortified. I never took the gun anywhere with me again, and a few years later, when I was living with Greg in Alaska, I felt safe again, and got rid of it forever.

Me finding happiness again after Woody's death, as little Buddy chews on my fingers (in Washington).

Schatzy: And the Pack Is Born...

I had avoided adopting a dog after Woody died because, as I told people, dogs find me. One day, one will appear, like Dane did, or Woody did.

My new dog did appear, but about three weeks after I brought Buddy home. She was to become Buddy's best dog friend.

Unlike Eb, Schatzy was young and vigorous, and played madly with our little black Buddy puppy on my lawn.

Eb and I would sit on the porch, my arm around him as he leaned into me slightly, and watch the two tumble and wrestle about the yard. They were peaceful times. Both Eb and I missed Woody, still, but we enjoyed watching the two youngsters play so energetically, and we bonded closer to each other.

Buddy and Schatzy at play in Washington.

Leaving Washington

I began walking again, my pack of three now, long walks through the Washington woods. Schatzy was a little more protective and less trusting of people than the other two, and so I felt somewhat safer with her in our lives. One time I was deep in the woods across the street from my house when I ran into two hunters, and the look on their faces and the way they leaned in and whispered to each other while staring at me gave me chills. Schatzy stayed protectively next to me while we moved on quickly, disappearing into the trees. Something about their look made me feel like the potential prey.

One day, at 4:00 in the afternoon, a woman walking with her golden retriever was murdered in the woods not far from where I lived. Her dog was found, still leashed, tied up near her body (perhaps one of the reasons I don't like leashes). The police said, a few days later, that someone they chased down and who died in a car wreck in eastern Washington was the killer, even after the DNA evidence came back (over a month later) saying he wasn't a match.

I went to the police station. "Look," I said to the officer, "I walk in those woods every day. Am I safe?"

"Yes, we got him," he insisted.

"But are you sure?"

"Of course."

I was frustrated. I knew this game...closing unsolved murder cases was priority in police departments. My friend Allison's murder was pinned on a serial killer for some 20 years, before DNA was finally used to prove it wasn't him. In the meantime, since her case had been closed by the police department, her real killer was free to kill again.

"Listen," I said, staring in his eyes, "are you so sure you'd let your wife or daughter walk in those woods?"

"Yes," he said, and by the look on his face, I didn't believe him.

FOR THE LOVE OF DOGS: MY LIFE IN DOG YEARS

I was missing Greg, missing my godmother, missing my family, sick of Washington, sick of the dangers, and even sick of teaching, for the first time in 12 years of teaching English and another five years of teaching music.

The truth was, I knew I had to leave the moment Woody was killed. It had been a year since his death, but Washington, and particularly my home, had never been the same for me. While my first year there I had been happy, made lots of friends, and was an enthusiastic teacher and fun department member, the second year, after losing Woody, even with the addition of Buddy and Schatzy in my life, I was stiff, unhappy, frightened, and lonely. Although everyone I met in the English Department I truly cared for and loved, I just couldn't make life work for me there anymore. I could never get the happy part of me back. It died with Woody. What teachers and students had come to expect from me the first year was no longer me anymore.

Nothing, really, was fun or funny to me anymore. I suppose the death of Woody had aged me, seriously, as it had Eb, whose sudden splashes of gray hairs confirmed this.

Buddy was all love, and he pulled us through, but this did not change the fact that every day I had to drive next to the spot in front of my house where I found Woody, on the side of the road (not in the middle, so sometimes I wondered if someone swerved to hit him on purpose). He'd been trying to crawl home, leaving a blood trail behind him.

I quit my job, put my house up for sale, loaded the dogs in the car, and headed up the Alcan. But this time, unlike when I left Oregon, it felt like I was leaving *for* something instead of escaping. I was going home, instead of leaving home. I was going back to see if Greg and I could make it work. I knew and loved Greg much more than before I had taken this job, when we'd only been dating a few months. For two years we'd lived apart, yet visited each other. I told him everything, including about my dates, and he showed no signs of violence or "ownership" I'd suffered with my ex and Brock. He was kind and understanding.

Plus, after Woody died, Greg gave me my first smile. He had flown down to be with me after Woody died, and I asked if he could build me a cross for Woody's grave.

"I don't know if Woody was a Christian," he said, deadpan.

I stared at him briefly, then the smile broke through. "Don't make me laugh," I said, squelching it, but there it was. Life again. Living again.

Going on.

"I'm going back to Alaska to have a baby," I'd joked to a teacher who was shocked I was leaving.

I didn't know at the time that this was to be true. In two years, Greg and I were going to have a son together. Life, even when it seems too painful to go on, can always throw a wonderful surprise party.

Buddy and Schatzy and me in Washington.

The Last Hurrah

Although the Ford Explorer was the perfect dog car, or so I had thought when I first saw one pack-full of dogs at a gas station, there was something I didn't think or know about when I bought mine back in 1994. That was automatic windows.

As soon as I got it home, I called the dogs to take them for a drive, pushed the buttons to roll down the windows (I'd never had such buttons before, just the old-fashioned roll-up windows), and glanced back to see Woody put his head happily out the window and then screamed when the window started to roll quickly up and trap and nearly murder him in just a few seconds.

The button was right on the door armrest just under the window, so when Woody stood on it to look out, the window rolled up to close. Fortunately, in his panic, he had lifted his foot off the button. I don't know how many dogs are killed in such freak window accidents, but statistics are kept on children, and there are many. I hate automatic windows.

So when I moved back to Alaska in 1998, I found a Ford Explorer that had the old-fashioned manual roll-up windows. I drove all the way down to Kenai to get it, a southern twisty drive south of Anchorage that I had avoided since my mother had been killed on that road. I figured it was worth the time, risk, and expense to avoid the constant fear of my dogs cutting their heads off.

(People would say, "Just push the lock button," and I'd say, "I don't trust it; what if something goes wrong?" Also, when I was out of the car, often one of my dogs would bump the lock button and I didn't know it was now unlocked. There had been too many close calls to ever trust the windows, yet my dogs so loved putting their heads out into the fresh air, so I vowed to get a new car as soon as I could. Another time I had a rental car, which came with the windows down; as I started putting the back window up, Eb had stuck his head in the window; in that car he was able to do so from a lying down position, as it was open partially at the top and all along the side; I almost didn't notice it in time.[5])

Now I found one, with manual windows, so I picked it up and brought it home. Buddy was almost a year old now, so out of the chewing destructive stage, I assumed.

I was wrong.

He had one more chew left in him.

He ate the cruise control switches in my new car the first day.

Then he was finally grown up and done with his chewing stage.

Pack of Four: Eb, Buddy, Schatzy, and me in Washington.

---

[5] According to www.www.kidsandcars.org, At least 50 children have died and over 2,000 children a year are maimed by power windows, and one potential solution, automatic reversals on car windows, at a cost of $6 per window, was supposed to be required in all new cars, but this requirement was dropped in 2011 by the U.S. National Highway Traffic Safety Administration. Statistics on how many pets are killed by power windows have not been kept.

The Baby

There was a special bond between my son and Buddy, from the moment I brought baby Winston home from the hospital. Buddy, as I knew he would be, was very gentle and loving with the new baby. He carefully stood over him, and licked the top of the little baby's head, and that was it. The two were in love with each other, just as Poochie and I had bonded more than 35 years before.

When I was pregnant, by now living with my son-to-be's father Greg and our combined household of four dogs and four cats in Alaska, I predicted this bond. People who share their lives with dogs understand their unique personalities and interests.

Even though he'd never been around a baby before, I absolutely knew that one dog would be the happiest to welcome my son into our lives. And that was Buddy.

Schatzy loved the baby because Buddy and I did.

Greg's dogs, Bailey and Newt, were fine with him.

One of my cats, Clover, was a bit grumpy about this new addition, especially because he was placed in her spot next to me on the bed while I recuperated from knee surgery (thanks to Buddy crashing into my knee one night while I was pregnant). She took to lying on his other side and reaching over once in a while and patting him on the head, claws kept in. But I knew it wasn't intended as a loving pat, but a pat of protest over losing her place.

But Buddy was in love, and his fullest love was now expressed to the baby, no longer to me. As a new mother, this didn't trouble me at all but gave me great joy. My son had a dog, his own dog. My son was born into the world with a best friend at his beck and call.

Buddy with baby Winston.

Buddy stayed near the baby at all times. Once Winston learned to crawl,

Buddy followed him around the house, fascinated in everything his "boy" was interested in, such as pulling all the books he could reach out of the shelves. Winston's first words were "dada," "baba" (bottle), and "buba" (Buddy). "Mama" came fourth. Soon after, my son began talking in full paragraphs, telling stories about each of his toys to Buddy. I would sit at my computer and work, and the two of them would be on the floor behind me, examining each car. Buddy would listen attentively to the fascinating tales about the cars and superheroes, occasionally licking the top of my son's head in absolute adoration. I had a full-time free babysitter.

Those were good days.

The Sickness

Buddy died in my son's room when Buddy was eight and Winston was five. I remember I had to work in Anchorage that cold January day. It was a Friday, so I had brought my wonderfully rambunctious niece Rachel home with me. The two children were playing in Winston's room. Buddy had waited for me to get home, I'm sure, and for my scratches and sweet talk, and then he pulled himself up with difficulty, dragged himself into Winston's room, and died.

Buddy was much too young to die.

But it was not because I didn't try to save him.

Suddenly, that July, he couldn't do our daily trail walks. Oh, he'd start out fine, but then he'd slow, and fizzle, and finally stand, panting, unable to move. He'd look at me, his expression apologetic.

I'd spend the next hour walking slowly with him the ½ mile back to home, where he'd lie down for the rest of the day.

Buddy and Schatzy on one of our daily Alaskan wood walks.

He'd try to eat dirt and rocks and even lick the sheetrock in the hall outside my office as he lay there, waiting for me to finish my work. His body was starving for iron, starving for nutrients.

His gums and tongue were white. He was bleeding somewhere, inside.

The summer was ruined for me, desperately trying to save him. I went to nearly every veterinary clinic in the Valley, Anchorage, and in between trying to find out what was wrong with him. Every vet had an opinion (but never expressed as an opinion, but as a fact) of what was wrong with him.

Every one, even though I brought previous x-rays, demanded their own tedious, slightly cruel tests, to my poor, weak, dying dog.

Every one prescribed different medications.

Nothing helped.

My Buddy was slowly dying, and there was nothing I could do.

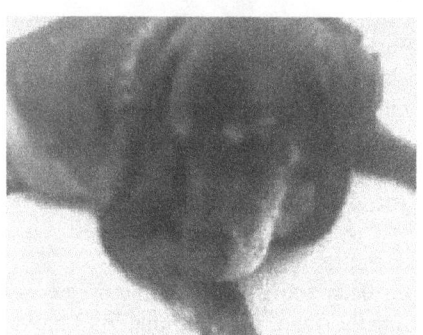 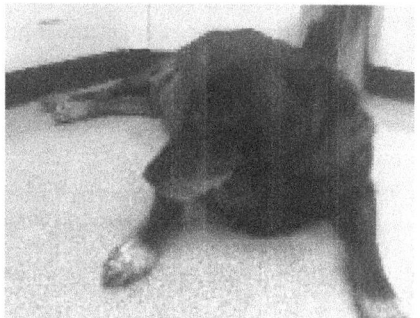

Buddy, sick, on another veterinary clinic floor.

Finally, I went back to the first vet. He was the one who insisted Buddy had ulcers.

"I want you to do an exploratory surgery," I said. I was desperate, clearly.

Understand, it was as if my child was suffering, and so I spent thousands of dollars and dozens of hours in vet appointments, trying to find the answer that would save him. Anyone who loved a dog like I loved Buddy would do the same. I was not happy about the loss of money or time, but what else was I to do?

I had been terrified that Buddy wouldn't make it through the exploratory surgery, but when I came back, he was jumping and excited to see me!

I was so joyous! It was my old Buddy! And right after surgery! What miracle had the vet found?

The vet explained it was the post-surgery steroids that were making my dog feel so much better. He said he sent tissue samples to Washington State's vet laboratory, and we'd have to wait.

The call came a week later, and a week is a long time for a dog who is dying, and for the "mom" who has raised that dog and loved him for his whole eight years.

It was actually the vet calling and not some receptionist or assistant, so I knew this was important.

"I have the results back on Buddy," he said. "They had a hard time finding it."

"But they found it?" I felt such hope.

"Yes," he said, and he explained something about the white blood cells or eosinophils were attacking Buddy's organs, and the lab guys at Washington State had never seen this before, and had to do a lot of investigating. But they were sure, he assured me.

"That's great news!" I said, so happy to at last, after 4 months of vet visits and medicines and x-rays and ultrasounds and watching my Buddy-boy slowly dying, that we had an answer at least. Something we could treat.

"What do we do?"

Clearly, my voice was happy and excited, as he sobered me up quickly. "Let me, er, explain that this—this—isn't treatable."

"What?"

"There's nothing that can be done. It's terminal."

Terminal.

I said nothing.

He filled the silence. "What we can do is give him steroids. That will make him feel better."

Yes, I remembered how Buddy was when I picked him after the exploratory surgery, hyped up on steroids and wagging his tail and even jumping a little.

So we put him on steroids.

And he clearly felt better.

There was one negative side effect, I suppose. That is that Buddy, always hungry and a healthy eater (and overweight) to begin with, was now hungry beyond anything I'd ever seen.

My big dumb black lab did things I never thought him capable of before. He actually moved the child's stepstool to the end of the kitchen, next to the refrigerator, stepped on it, and somehow managed to open the cupboard door to get food.

All he wanted was food. He was so desperately hungry.

One morning I woke up and he was standing next to my bed, licking my arm.

"Really, Buddy?" I asked, petting him. "Are you going to eat your mama?"

I was just joking, of course, but his desperate hunger did scare me a little, as the Buddy I had always known had disappeared into drugville. He wasn't "himself" anymore. He wasn't the gentle giant I knew so well. The drugs were making him voraciously hungry and desperately intensely focused on food. He would have eaten all day long if he could.

Perhaps, I just should have let him happily eat himself to death.

For I didn't know that "terminal" meant that only two months were left.

And so, late on a cold Alaska Friday night, just after Christmas, Buddy left me, left Winston, left us.

He did not want to leave; I am sure of that.

But he was gone.

It was too soon; he was too young, but his suffering was over, and the slightly crazed steroid monster that had been pacing the house looking for food the last two months was gone too.

Buddy, the summer before he got sick, in Palmer, Alaska.

Recently, I found something my son, then nine years old (four years after Buddy passed), had written for school:

> *My favorite object or animal is my dog Buddy. A funny thing he did was chew my mother's car lock in the back left. I have known him since I was born. He was my dog.*
>
> *Buddy had a sickness where you were always hungry. He ate some ducks that we had just because of that. He also ate chocolate because of that. That is about when he died. I was seven years old when he died. He came to my room to die. It was very very sad. Buddy died when he was eight years old in human years.*
>
> *Buddy loved to go outside. That was his favorite place to go. He would never get bored of the outdoors. He loved to walk in miles of trails to walk through. That was my outdoors dog Buddy.*

Lessons Learned from Buddy

You can change someone's life and give them hope again just by being in it. Babies are special. Enjoy any food that comes your way.

Buddy, baby Winston, and Schatzy (Photo by David Jensen).

Buddy, his last year.

10 Schatzy: My Treasure

We give them the love we can spare, the time we can spare. In return dogs have given us their absolute all. It is without a doubt the best deal man has made.
—*Roger Caras*

I have found that when you are deeply troubled, there are things you get from the silent devoted companionship of a dog that you can get from no other source.
—*Doris Day*

Schatzy young and old (Photos by David Jensen).

Schatzy. At the point I am writing this, she is the longest live-in relationship I've had in my life—over 15 years. We grew old together, "mein schatz" and me.

It is July 1997 in Washington. Just three weeks before I had brought Buddy home. So now I had enough dogs...the perfect number of two: Eb and Buddy. Two to entertain each other while I worked; two to fit in my car and walk with me in the woods every day. A Perfect Even Number. No one to be left out, as I was, in a family of odd-numbered (five) children.

I'm pulling into Fred Meyer on the way home, and there she is. A yellow lab mix, probably thrown out of some car by an owner who never deserved a dog. This becomes clear when I see her still at the door, watching, hoping, expecting, even after I have gone shopping. I get in the car. No More Dogs, I remind myself. I Have Two. She Is Not My Problem.

I notice she has no collar, no tags, her ribs stick out with thinness. She's probably thirsty.

I go back inside and ask them to page, again and again, the person who owns her. No one comes. I take her to my car and give her water. I take her back and wait with her.

I will not love you. I will not take you home. Someone else will. I have the Perfect Pack of Two, and anyway, you don't look like Woody, or any other dog I've known.

An hour later, I pull up to my house and introduce Eb and Buddy to their new roommate. Just a temporary thing, I explain, as I call up the newspapers and animal controls and report a found dog. The owners will call.

I call my new yellow dog "Schatzy," which means sweetheart or treasure in German, but not for a few days. The first night, she didn't seem very sweet at all, and for the first and only time, I was afraid sleeping with a dog.

That night, I called her up on my king-sized bed, and fell asleep surrounded by three mutts. I woke up to Schatzy in a terrible nightmare, growling and snapping and biting...right next to my throat. I carefully moved out from under her and talked to her till she woke up.

Something is wrong with this dog! I realized. I was, for the first time in my life, afraid of a dog. It brought back the terrible nightmares Brock would have back in Oregon (and the reason Woody slept with his head between us). He would suddenly jump up, grab me, shake me, scream insanely at me—all the while still asleep.

Was it something in this dog's past, something she would never be able to talk to me about, being communicated that night in her dream? Did something terrible happen to her?

Schatzy, soon after I found her at a Fred Meyer parking lot in Washington.

After she came out of her dream, she looked at me, confused, as I stroked her head and talked to her. She slowly calmed and curled up next to me, sighed, and fell asleep. I admit that sleep did not come so quickly for me that night.

Many people would have said to get rid of her, she was too dangerous, but it never occurred to me not to show her that things were different for her now. Although I'd failed at such a lesson with the abusive man, Brock, years before, I knew dogs were far more capable of change and far more responsive to love than people. Dogs forgive and move on.

Dogs, I used to say, are the "codependent" animal. They will stay faithfully, no matter what. I was determined to be her best "no matter what." Life would be filled with walks, and scratching, and sweet talk, and chew toys, and hugs. Life would be better from now on.

I'm holding Schatzy, and she's reaching to play with her best friend Buddy, in my Washington home.

So the years blend...I move back to Alaska, filling my car with my three dogs and two cats and a computer, leaving Washington behind. We move into my parents' house, which I have inherited through their untimely deaths, and eventually I begin to build my own home in Palmer, backed up to the most delicious dog-walking trails I have ever known (although the Borough in its wisdom has deemed this park to be the future landfill). I rush my builder, pleading with him to finish, as Eb's life is fading away; he lets go of us a few days before I can move in.

So now it's Schatzy and Buddy and me...but just as I've moved to my new home in Palmer, I'm about to learn there is something growing inside me, something I never thought would come into my life. A baby.

"You never know what love is till you have a child," one of my friends says to me. "You think you love your dogs, but you don't. Not compared to what you will feel for your child." Maybe it's the hormones, but I want to slap her.

How can you say I don't know what love is? I want to tell her. I have been overwhelmed with love from these dogs who have shared my life. "Can there be a human-animal bond?" some scientists attempt to ask and prove. I have lived this bond; that is my proof.

Schatzy and me on the couch in Washington; Buddy is to the right leaning in.

In some ways, she was right, of course. There is a different kind of love, that between a mother and a child. It is protective and determined to do what is right. But there are also similarities. My love for my son did not come at the expense of my love for my pets. I did not have to choose between them. It made me sad to see so many signs at Anchorage Animal Control where the people wrote, as reasons for giving up their pets, "Having a baby." Why should it be either/or? The gifts of love my pets would bring my child were precious. And just like him, they are family. They will never be tossed, nor should they be.

Three things would definitely change from the moment I had a child. One is my level of worrying increased dramatically. I had someone tiny and precious and completely dependent on me that needed my constant attention and supervision. Another difference was my work habits had to change. I couldn't sit and write and edit all day with the baby sitting under my desk, like my dogs, content there until I was ready to go for a walk or play.

But, the final change was wonderful, unexpected, instant. My loneliness ended instantly and permanently. Never again would the death of a dog be so devastating to me that I thought I couldn't go on myself. I had a little human being dependent on me, and it was my purpose to raise him well and loved and make sure he outlived me.

Just like people, some dogs love children, and some are unenthused. When baby Winston came home from the hospital, Buddy was ecstatic, and loved him as his own, going everywhere Winston did, sleeping next to him, swallowed up in love. At first, Schatzy loved him because she loved me, and I loved my baby. He was an extension of me, so the baby was an acceptable addition to the household. But although her love was perhaps not instant, it grew, strong and stronger with every year, especially after Buddy passed and no longer had full ownership of my son.

The years blend by. Winston grows. Buddy passes on, crawling to Winston's room to take his last breath. Schatzy has learned to love Winston as much as Buddy did; she's seemingly as fascinated with every stage of his development as I am. I tell Winston—heartbroken over losing his beloved Buddy—we will foster puppies for the Alaska Dog & Puppy Rescue since we have room in our home and lives for them. But we will not get another dog, not yet. I pick two to take home for the week. One looks like shepherd-lab-husky Woody; one reminds me of my childhood beagle in her eyes and the chocolaty circles around them, even though they are sisters. I can't choose between them, so I take both. "It's just for a week," I tell myself, knowing better.

Two days later, I adopt them. And this is how I am back to three dogs...sisters Blue and Chewie, and, of course, Schatzy.

Schatzy is the always-good dog. Well, there was that first night at my throat, and a couple days of ripping the sleeves off my shirts as she bit at me with overzealous joy. But those are forgiven, of course, and were easily fixed. One took comfort and love; the second just took a few "No's" at the moment of snapping. Forever after, she is what we would call a "good dog." She never ventures from me on our walks, never starts a fight with another dog, never chases a car, never chews one thing, never even barks at a neighbor. While Blue and Chewie struggle to learn that bikes and cars are not toys to chase, furniture is not to be eaten, joy must be subdued when running toward other dogs, and spring lake ice is not to be pounced on, I never have to teach Schatzy anything again. No, she just teaches me.

My son with his beloved Schatzy.

Lessons learned from Schatzy: be calm. Enjoy the walks. Sleep soundly without fear of snoring. Tolerate the changes in the household without complaint. Don't bite. Don't fight or argue. If food comes to you, savor it, and don't ask for more. Make friends with people. Show gratitude. Most of all, of course, that eternal dog lesson: Love. Love completely and without question.

Winston's schooling moved me back to Anchorage, now saddled with a leash law, but fortunately the city also had a few dog parks. The dogs accepted this situation much better than I did. Blue-Chew were fascinated with the dog park. Instead of walking for an hour without seeing anyone, now we might meet 10 to 30 dogs and their people. I missed the quiet walks, but I enjoyed watching their sometimes-too enthusiastic greetings of every dog they saw. The people they never noticed. But Schatzy did. Now in her early teens, she would slowly walk over to and greet every person, interested in them more than the dogs. Sometimes she would get confused since her eyesight was failing, and follow someone she thought was me. "What a sweet old dog," they would say, and I would feel so grateful for those words, for they understood. We understood what was coming.

(Then I'd scratch Schatzy's ears, reprimanding her: "Schatzy, why do you always confuse me for fat ladies?" Of course, I knew why.)

The future awaits me. It will be not long. It's been six months now since she could go to the dog park. She made the decision herself one day. No longer was she up to the car rides. Her hearing is gone, and her sight is poor. Her back legs don't want to carry her on walks anymore; she struggles to arise and go out of the house a few times each day. At night, she barks at ghosts. My quiet girl has found her voice late in her precious life. Several times a night Winston or I go down and comfort her and scratch her back and belly since she cannot make it up the stairs anymore. She always greets us with a wag and a grin.

Old Schatzy, cooling off in the lake at the dog park.

FOR THE LOVE OF DOGS: MY LIFE IN DOG YEARS

There is something so beautiful about an old dog. There is a peace and wisdom and gentleness that reaches from her, teaching me. She would lie next to me as I worked, happy when I took a break and petted her. I thought it was to soothe her, but really it soothed me. I still had her. It was the first thing I checked for every morning. But she would go there soon, that place we all wonder about.

I tried to tell Winston that one day the vet would come and help her pass to the other side. He insisted that I must let her pass in her own time. Others told me to end her suffering. I debated this in my mind, but mostly I listened to her. She was going to tell me when it was time. I hoped that she could let go without my help, but if I had to help her, I would.

Fifteen years before, she had been tossed out of a car and into my life. There was nothing special about her, nothing at all. I have no grand stories to tell about her. She was just a dog. She was also the longest relationship of my life. My son's baby photos are with her. Her clouded eyes speak of places we'd lived and traveled together, forests we'd explored together, injuries and sorrows she'd comforted me through, people and pets who had come into our lives, and most of all, those quiet moments when we just shared love and friendship. No grand stories at all; she didn't save my life from a moose or a car or an abuser, but still, she saved my life, in the quiet way that dogs do. Mein schatz.

Schatzy and Winston (Photo by David Jensen).

Schatzy struggled for another year, before the final vet call had to be made. Fortunately, back then, I had a wonderful vet who came to the house. Winston was there as well; I made sure he was, so he could see we were giving her a gift at the end, not a punishment.

Schatzy lived the longest of any of my dogs. By the time she passed, I had shared 15 years with her, and she was at least a year old when I found her. That is old for a lab. But the last three years she was really slowly dying. Blindness, deafness, legs weakening, steroid shots so she could keep walking, unable to get up the stairs, night barking.... It was like caring for an elderly sick patient. I was her nurse, and I found it both rewarding and exhausting. Many would have given up long before I did, but I also had a son who had known her since he was born. When she finally left us, she had shared all 11 years of his life, so that was why he fought so long and hard to prevent me from the Final Decision.

When the vet finally said there was nothing more to do, I was relieved, in a way, which I never felt at the end of any other dog's life. I felt that she had long exceeded a quality life. I suppose what kept me hanging on to her was that in spite of everything, when I came to reach for her during her night terrors or early in the morning to help her out of the house, even blind and deaf, she knew it was me, and her tail gently wagged. Almost everything that made a life was gone, but still she loved me in that old-dog way, and showed me that love with a wag and a gentle, but tired, lick to my hands.

I had her cremated, and went to pick up her ashes, to bury them in the yard. The man handed me a small can, and I thought, how can a Labrador fit in this tiny thing? How can a whole life of 15 years shared together be here now?

I took it quickly and left, and went out to the car, sat for a while, holding it, then opened up the card from the crematorium. It said, "Dear Sally, sorry for your loss of Schatzi." I took it back and got the right dog, this one in a larger, heavier can that made sense.

At her funeral, I read a poem by Robinson Jeffers, "The House Dog's Grave," and over Schatzy's grave I planted a tree, which would grow roots into her ashes and feed off her and become one with her. With this ending, I felt satisfied.

To "Mein Schatz": I'm so lucky I found you and knew you. I will remember you as a kind, old soul.

> *You were never masters, but friends. I was your friend.*
> *I loved you well, and was loved. Deep love endures*
> *To the end and far past the end. If this is my end,*
> *I am not lonely. I am not afraid. I am still yours.*
> —From "The House Dog's Grave" by Robinson Jeffers, 1941

Lessons Learned from Schatzy

Nightmares don't last forever. Sometimes, it just takes finding the right person to live with that ends them. Take pleasure in long walks in the woods. When you live your life at peace, others calm down around you. Don't envy that she has others in her life; you know she loves you fully no matter how large the pack grows. Even when your sight and hearing go, life can be filled with happiness.

FOR THE LOVE OF DOGS: MY LIFE IN DOG YEARS

Schatzy and me in 1998, after I moved back to Alaska (Photo by David Jensen).

*Ain't but three things in this world that's worth a solitary dime
But old dogs and children and watermelon wine*

—*Tom T. Hall, Old Dogs, Children & Watermelon Wine*

Schatzy and I (in my early 50s) grew old together (Photo by David Jensen).

MY FORTIES IN ALASKA (1999-2010): NEWT, BAILEY, BLUE, CHEWIE, & STRAYS

11 Bailey and Newt: Not My Dogs

> *"When you have dogs, you witness their uncomplaining acceptance of suffering, their bright desire to make the most of life in spite of the limitations of age and disease, their calm awareness of the approaching end when their final hours come. They accept death with a grace that I hope I will one day be brave enough to muster."*
> —Dean Koontz, *A Big Little Life: A Memoir of a Joyful Dog*

Bailey

Newt (Photo by David Jensen)

Greg moved in with me while I was pregnant, along with his two dogs, Newt and Bailey, in fall 1999.

Both dogs insisted immediately that they were mine.

I explained, no, I already have two dogs; you are Greg's dogs.

But of course, they came on my walks (I couldn't leave them behind) with me and my dogs, and they slept in my room with me and my dogs, and they went on the car rides with me and my dogs.

I do not have four dogs, I think, as they follow me throughout the house.

Obviously, I did. Here's how it happened.

Bailey: Chained Dog

Bailey (with toy) and Schatzy.

Of the two new dogs in my household, Bailey irritated me the most, but what most upset me was how she had been raised before Greg inherited her from a family member. From puppyhood, she'd been left on a chain for the entire first two years of her life. What could this create but insanity?

She certainly, by the time she came to live with me, now three years old, had never learned housetraining. The first thing she did was mark my precious treadmill, the most expensive thing I owned, and the only thing that kept me slim the previous few years. I was never able to use it again without smelling that horrible urine smell, no matter how much I cleaned it. I even left it outside an entire winter. Nothing helped. As I lost my treadmill, I lost my body. (I blamed Bailey for this, of course, not my increasing dependence on chocolate.)

I've never had to teach an adult dog that houses are not to be urinated in, but fortunately, old dogs learn fast, despite the adage which says otherwise. Within a week, training was done, and she never had that issue again.

So Bailey moved in with no manners, no training whatsoever, having spent her first two years on a chain. But, like most dogs, she aimed to please, and the one she wanted to please the most was me. Despite my protests that she and Newt were not my dogs, they both followed me everywhere, begging for the love I doted on Schatzy and Buddy to be shared with them.

It didn't take too many years—perhaps just months—for Bailey to become kind and gentle, although it took some work, work I didn't really want to do but had to. For example, when I encountered people on the trail, she at first tended to "tree" them, which means run at them barking hysterically so they huddled together and quivered against a tree.

How embarrassing! How humiliating! I have never had a dog do this. She's not my dog, I'd say, grabbing her collar and dragging her away. She's not my dog not my dog not my dog.

So I had to teach "not my dog" to stop doing that. It wasn't hard. As I said, she wanted to please me.

I really wanted nothing to do with her or Newt. I had just lost Eb, and now here I was, almost 40, pregnant, stuck in the tiny two-room upstairs apartment I had built for myself and my dogs (the downstairs was rented to pay for the upstairs, a technique I learned from Greg, the builder) with four large dogs and a man and a baby on the way.

So I was just irritated pretty much all the time with her.

Bailey with baby Winston.

Bailey and Buddy began getting fatter and fatter after we moved to Palmer. Greg, always thin, blamed this entirely on me. Of course, I was also the one tasked with feeding, watering, walking, and giving treats to the dogs...a task I happily assigned to myself.

Why are Newt and Schatzy thin? I would ask Greg. They all go on the same walks, eat the same meals. It took a few years to find out the answer, but it was my horse vet who clarified it for me. Buddy and Bailey liked to chow down on horse manure, every day as we passed by the barn on the way to our hikes on the trails, on the trails when we walked where horses had been, and again when we returned home. The other two dogs did not. "Horse manure is very fattening," my vet informed me, as if he'd actually tried that diet. "Lots of grain in there."

So unfortunately, Bailey gained weight, lots of weight. She was the only long-haired dog I'd ever had, and the two factors led to her early death, when she was about nine. It was on my beloved trails.

It's always either very cold or cool in Alaska, but this summer we had one hot day. Well, not what anyone in the lower 48 states would classify as hot, but it hit the 70s, and that's hot to an Alaskan.

I had had Bailey's hair shaved the day before, something I did each summer, to help her with the heat. Unfortunately, the groomer (who was the only local one at the time), tended not to give her any water all day, and she was in a hot salon. I mentioned it to them that morning: "Be *sure* she gets plenty of water. She comes out thirsty every time." "Oh, we do!" she insisted, but once again, Bailey came home hot and drank nearly half a bucket of water.

Water, water. Such a simple, precious little thing. A thing that saves a life, it turns out.

I was angry at the groomer, once again, but Bailey seemed okay once she drank up. And anyway, she's not my dog, I reminded myself. If it was my dog, I wouldn't use the damn place, and I'd scream my bloody head off at them for making her suffer so.

I didn't know the next day I was going to kill her myself from thirst. Maybe it was the groomer day plus the long, hot walk day, but Bailey was going to die of thirst. More specifically, of something I'd never heard of in Alaska, of heat exhaustion, or heat stroke.

My then 6-year-old son's drawing of him ("Me" in the picture) and our dogs Newt, Schatzy, Buddy, and Bailey walking the Crevasse Moraine Trails in Palmer, Alaska. (Note that "My mom" is not in the drawing, but notated with an arrow to the left. I love my son so much! He always makes me laugh, and I am so happy that he is filled with "dog love.")

The dogs and I set out on our typical walk on the Crevasse Moraine Trails this day, a surprisingly beautiful hot day. None of us is used to temperatures higher than the 60s, typically more the high 50s. So I decide to vary my walk a bit and head for the pond, so the dogs can swim. I found it once before, and I'm sure I know how to find it again.

An hour later, I'm still looking, and Bailey is starting to pant heavily. "It's just over the next hill," I promise her, but I'm only leading us farther and farther out.

By the time I give up and turn around, it is too late for her. I have yelled for help unsuccessfully; I am alone on the trails this day. I have tried to get Bailey to stay while I run back for water, but faithful dog as she is, committed to me completely although I remind her she is not my dog, she struggles to stay with us, her breathing getting harder and heavier. I try to stop and let her rest, but this is not helping. She needs water now! In the eight years I've walked these trails, I have never brought water with me and most of the time, such as today, I don't have a phone. We've always done fine. I would do anything for water. I am desperate. I keep walking toward home, telling her to stay. At 140 pounds of fat (at this point I'm only about 20 pounds heavier than that), she is far too heavy for me to lift, and I must keep going, with her dragging herself along.

Finally, she falls over, and I hug and pet her and then run for home as fast as I can, grab Greg and as much water as I can, and we race back.

I forget exactly what trail she is on when we come to a Y; I send Greg up the right one while I go on the left. I hear a happy yelp, and then nothing.

Greg found her; she waited for him, yelped happily to see him, and then, as I arrive, despite water being poured on her head to cool her down and attempts to get water into her body, she dies.

Bailey, at the end of one of our previous walks on the Crevasse Moraine Trails.

This is my fault.

I will have to live with this for the rest of my life. I will have to think that just taking a few minutes to pack water would have saved that dog's life. That a dog died too young, too soon, because of me.

I try to tell myself she was overheated already from the groomer; it was their fault, but I know, in my heart, it was mine. I made a mistake; I took the wrong trail; I got lost...for the first and only time on those trails, and it happened to be the hottest day of that summer in Alaska.

And Bailey paid for it with her life.

Baby Winston leaning on so-patient Bailey.

Being a dog, as kind and loving as such creatures are, she would have forgiven me of course. She would have expressed gratitude for all the years of petting and brushing her, talking to her, the kindness I gave her, the glorious trail walks, the never-ending supply of toys, and, of course, for her favorite snack: horse manure. She would have taken on the guilt herself, saying she should have listened and stayed when I told her, and she should have had a good drink before we left instead of worrying about how much manure she could fit in her tummy while passing the barn.

If anything, I think she would have "tsk-tsked" me about the groomer, for she never did care for it there, and she didn't like her own smell and lack of hair after. (The other dogs always treated her like a stranger for the first minutes after she came home from the groomer, not recognizing her look or perfumed smell, circling her curiously, and this always made Bailey furious. "It's still me!" she'd bark and growl at them.)

Bailey and I would argue about the annual grooming appointments, for I would try to tell her I was only trying to help her, and she'd remind me, "You know I hated it. Every year. You know they didn't treat me right."

"Yes, of course," I'd say. "You're right. I should have known better."

But what I'd really want to say to Bailey is, "I'm so sorry. I made a mistake, and it cost you your life, and I am so terribly sorry."

Greg got the wheelbarrow and went back and got his now-lifeless dog, and buried her down in the pasture, which she would have liked, with so much horse manure around her. I never visit her grave.

Bailey before her annual hair cut, on the porch in Palmer, Alaska.

Lessons Learned from Bailey

Even if your youth is scarred and miserable, life can get much better. It's not necessary to bark at people on trails. Old dogs can learn new tricks. Certain foods might be terribly delicious, but they are fattening. Always bring water.

Newt: The Accused and Sometimes Guilty

Newt, typically sweet and happy, but for the occasional odd snap.

Newt, a large, laughing malamute, whom Greg had saved from a now-defunct animal shelter near Big Lake, was also used to outdoor, doghouse living when I met him. Newt had a fenced area and a doghouse when I met him, and that's all he ever saw before I came into Greg's and Newt's life (Greg didn't have Bailey yet). The first time I went to my then new-boyfriend's house, I immediately brought Newt inside (despite Greg's light arguments against it) and said "outside only" was no way to treat a dog. And so forever more, Newt was an indoor dog.

So Newt was pleased with his new life with me. But there was something wrong with him. It reminded me of Bobbie, actually, the way he snapped if you touched his lower back, near his hind legs. Bobbie never bit anyone again after the terrible incident where she bit my nephew; if touched there, she would just yelp in pain. But Newt never stopped the snapping.

Newt's back pain and snapping issue did not become apparent until three years after I first met him. By this time, Greg and I moved in together, I was pregnant, and I was worried about the level of pain his dog seemed to be in. I ordered Greg to take his dog to the vet and find out what was the matter. I suppose I should have gone with them, as I would have discussed medication options and such. But what Greg came back with was that the vet diagnosed Newt with something terrible (I forget the name) causing his spine to deteriorate rapidly, and if we didn't keep him still (no stairs, confined to a room the size of a bathroom, no walks) the rest of his life, his spine could break in two at any time.

Newt was, at this point, about four years old, strong and big and healthy, and I'm sure the happiest he had ever been in his life, now living inside, in love with me, and going on daily car rides and long, intense walks with me and the rest of my pack.

"Ridiculous!" I told Greg. "He will not live in a bathroom. He will go on walks. He will have quality of life rather than quantity, if that's what life has given him."

And so Newt continued on walks and rides for the next nine years. I eventually had to switch out my SUV for a van so he could still get in the car (as I by this time had a serious neck injury and two torn rotator cuffs and could no longer lift him), but we adjusted.

My favorite trails, the Crevasse Moraine, in Palmer, Alaska; Newt is facing the camera. Even though Bailey died on these trails, it still upsets me that the Matanuska-Susitna Borough is turning all these gorgeous trails into landfill.

What I couldn't adjust to was his snapping. It maybe happened once every two or three years, but every time the consequences were serious and frightening. I took to moving my child into my room as he became a toddler so he wouldn't stumble across Newt in the middle of the night. Fortunately, Newt never bit Winston, but it was a concern. Of course, we raised our son to never touch the dog on the back, only pet him on the head or shoulders.

One bite occurred when a dear friend with multiple sclerosis came to visit me. Tom had brought his teen daughter and her friend, as well as his youngest daughter, perhaps about six years old. I put all the dogs out back in the fenced yard.

The girls eventually bored of listening to Tom and me visit about old high school days, and they went out front to play. The older girls began throwing a baseball to each other, ignoring the younger girl, I soon learned.

What we heard was a commotion of tears and cries as they brought the little girl in, a bite mark on her hand. She had been pulling Newt's leg under the fence, wanting to play with the "puppy." It sounds like he patiently accepted it for a while before giving her one bite to let go.

So off to the doctor, who of course, by law had to report it to animal control, who sentenced Newt to home confinement for two weeks, which seems like a fair punishment; however, I did remind the officer that Newt was in a fenced yard, at his own home, and was being pulled under the fence by a child not supervised by the older girls. But this is the way dog laws are written. The officer said she was being very kind to me, that usually this kind of dog would have to be taken in.

He's not my dog, he's Greg's, I'm thinking, but I will never let that happen.

I can't really say Newt did nothing wrong. Most dogs would not bite a child pulling him under the fence, whether it hurt or not. Most dogs would also not bite a stranger who was towing my tenants' car. But Newt did. As became his *modus operandi* (M.O.), it was one bite of warning, never more.

The car incident made perfect sense to me, from a dog's perspective, and the tenants' daughters had left the gate open, without my knowledge. I also didn't know a strange man was going to drive up and "steal" my tenant's car that day. She wasn't home, and I was in my office working, when I heard Newt bark.

That sounds like he's out front! I registered, and I ran down the stairs and out, and found the tow truck driver standing on his truck, cursing, with Newt barking at him.

"Your dog bit me!" he yelled.

He's not my dog, I thought, grabbing Newt and putting him in the fence, as I tried to ascertain why this man was trying to steal my tenant's car. His boss later called and made Greg pay $500. That wasn't the only time Newt cost poor Greg, who struggled to make a living doing construction.

So there were incidents over the years. Most times he just snapped air, a few times he hit the mark.

But then there was the time that Newt didn't do it but got penalized anyway. This time made me angry, and I fought it. I felt animal control was wrong, and I was actually penalized for having dog licenses, which shocked me. At the same time that animal control was basically calling us bad pet owners by pinning a dog bite on Newt, the same agency had brought two starving horses to our heated barn, asking us to take care of them and bring them back to health.

Here's what happened: by this point, Newt was about 11 years old, and the back legs were going. He still went on my walks, but could no longer run, and getting up was probably the hardest part of his day. He had maybe a year or two left in life, I figured.

Every day I'd walk the dogs, behind my house directly to a beautiful, tough set of trails, and we'd do the two-mile loop and go home. We would take this walk about 10 or 11 a.m., before school was out, when the trail I used was almost always empty. (In summer, I'd sometimes add a second walk, at night, since Alaska stayed light past midnight.) Never did we change this routine. We went straight behind my house, never turned right down the power line to go toward houses.

But one night my tenant got a call from an angry father. His daughter had been jogging down the power line and a dog ran out and bit her on the rear and ran off. It was a black dog. He knew I had dogs because his other daughter had been to our house for a birthday party.

I said, "Invite him over. Have her come meet Newt [our only dog at the time with any black on him, as Buddy and Bailey had passed away by this time]. He couldn't have done it." He drove up, came angrily out of the truck, and said, "My daughter says that's the dog."

I couldn't see his daughter in the dim evening light, but he motioned to the truck and said she saw him out the window. Newt was lying on the dirt pile, where he spent most days when it wasn't too cold, and he struggled to stand up; he couldn't make it, and fell over.

"Look at him!" I said. "Tell your daughter to come out and meet him. It couldn't be him. He can't run anymore, and he doesn't go out of the fence unless he's walking with me."

"She said it's him, so it's him!" he yelled, and he argued some more with me, then jumped in his truck and punched it, angrily roaring away.

We were in trouble, no doubt. I didn't sleep that night.

Greg and I were gone when the animal control officer showed up, but my tenant let him in. He went upstairs and took pictures of all the dogs. They all sat obediently for the camera, and none of them barked at him or showed any aggression (I wouldn't have blamed them if they had though; you would think they'd be more protective of my house when I wasn't in it).

The animal control officer returned, interviewed me, recorded it (without my knowing). By now I was angry. I had found he had decided Newt was guilty even before he talked with me.

I said, "What do you base this on?"

"The girl identified him in the picture."

I said, "That's after she came to my house. My understanding is her report said it was a black dog, not black and white, and it ran at her, which Newt is clearly unable to do. What other pictures did you show her?"

"One," he said. "There are only two families with dogs licensed in this neighborhood."

"Are you kidding me?" I said, incredulous. "You are penalizing me for licensing my dogs? There are at least 25 families with dogs in this neighborhood, probably a lot more." I was thinking, I'm probably the only one with a fence; all he has to do is drive around and look and he'll see dogs on every lawn!

In fact, I admitted, I probably knew which dog did this, but I was not one to turn him in. Anyone in the neighborhood, if he had asked, would have the same suggestion. Unfortunately, this dog belonged to Greg's boss, who lived just up the hill and across from us. He was known to roam the neighborhood, to shy away from people, and to have aggressive tendencies. I didn't know the number of incidents, but I knew he was prone to biting. He was black.

I knew him well, although he never let me near him. My "girls," Blue-Chew, were in love with him. He'd pop over to see them on his daily rounds, and they'd excitedly run to the fence to visit with him.

"You girls, can't you see he's a bad boy?" I'd joke. "Believe me, I've known bad boys...you should stay away from them!" But my girls loved all dogs, especially the bad boys.

The animal control officer demanded, "If you know what dog it is, then you should tell me!"

I said, "I'm not doing your job for you. Just go investigate. Ask around. You'll find him."

But no, Newt had already been found guilty and sentenced and that was that. The officer had found a black (well, black and white, but close enough) dog in the neighborhood, and so he was the one.

Only that was not that.

I fought it, even though when I was paying the fees and filing the papers, the clerk told me she'd never heard of a decision by animal control being reversed.

I hired a lawyer (who was terrible and cost Greg $1,000 to about ruin our case, especially when he said, "This is an abortion of justice!"), I collected letters from many who knew Newt and had known him for years, I lined up witnesses, I got Newt's vet records to show his physical incapability of the bite-and-run description, I videotaped a teenage girl—my tenants' daughter Megan—of the same age as the accuser running and jumping over Newt while he ignored her. Indeed, while I was taping this, the other three children ran and jumped over and bumped Newt too. He did nothing.

We won. Newt was a free dog.

That night, Megan, the sweet teenage girl who had made the video with me, was sitting on the trundle bed I'd bought for Newt (because he hadn't been able to jump up on a bed or couch for a couple of years now) next to him, petting him, chattering away distractedly.

I was worried she'd hit his back, plus I figured he could use a brushing, so I handed her the metal horse brush I used on his stubborn malamute fur, thinking she'd pay more attention to what she was doing, and she began chattering away again, about school, about boys, about teachers.... Suddenly, she hit his back with the brush and he snapped.

Another $1,000 in medical bills for Megan's hand, which became infected. Worse, tears and mistrust from Megan, who had lived with us and my many dogs all these years without incident, and who had complete trust in them. She was even their caretaker when I went on vacation.

It was a horrible ending to what I thought was going to be, all in all, a good day. I can't tell you how badly I felt about it, and how ironic this dog, whom we had all fought so hard to save, was now absolutely guilty of the same damn crime, but with a different victim. But I still believe Newt was not guilty of the bite and run. As my friend Carolyn said, who'd known Newt for most of his years, "It's not his M.O."

The neighbor's dog roamed and terrorized a few more years before he passed away at last, mean and grumpy till the end, probably because he was never allowed inside by his owners and never, as far as I could tell, had been petted or touched in any affectionate way.

Newt lying on his favorite place in the yard: the dirt pile.

Some beasts are created, and some are born that way, I suppose. Overall, I think Newt was a kind old soul with a problem. His problem wasn't his back, which gave him some constant level of suffering. His problem was that his solution was to use his teeth to tell someone his back hurt. Even if most of the time those teeth landed in air, it is not a way dogs are allowed—by law—to notify humans of their complaints.

A good dog is one who will let someone in their house, even uninvited, without complaint, and who will let someone steal your car without punishment. A good dog will suffer all kinds of painful assaults by humans without fighting back. This is a "good dog" by law. This is how most dogs are.

(Sadly, this reminds me of a story I heard in Sacramento by someone who called Pets & Pals, mortified because his neighbor had beaten his own dog to death the night before. He said many nights he had heard the neighbor go outside and beat his dog, but this time it went all the way to the end, and although he had previously called animal control, nothing had been done. He said the dog cried out in agony till it was over. I never forgot this. It happens too often. And that was a "good" dog. The animal control and the neighborhood let that good dog down, that poor dog, helpless on a chain to the very end. A good dog, like that one, doesn't "bite the hand that feeds it," but licks the hand that beats it. I am not a fan of many dog laws, as you can perhaps tell. Dog laws are written to punish dogs and their owners more often than to protect the dogs and punish the bad owners for such abuse.)

Newt then, was not necessarily a good dog although he was always kind to me. He had his few bites over the years, and most of them made some sort of dog-sense. But one certainly did not. This one was a few years before the power line fiasco, when he greeted an elderly lady and her daughter as they got out of their car, and the dogs and I came outside to say hello. I say "greeted," because Newt's tail was wagging, and he seemed to happily be saying hello to the poor old lady by trying to jump up (not much of a possibility for him, and perhaps that cricked his back just so) and snapping some skin on her arm. I was horrified, but the dear old lady just said, "It happens," and I loved her forever for that.

Newt

For the bite of the elderly lady, and for the bite of poor teenaged Megan, Newt probably should have received some sort of punishment (house arrest, not death, but dog laws are not always written that way). But ironically, perhaps, he was *not* guilty of the crime he was charged with, then sentenced as guilty for by animal control, which we had to fight to get overturned. I am quite sure he did not do the power line bite, and I often wondered if what the girl's family really had in mind was a civil lawsuit as step two, after accomplishing the animal control guilty verdict of step one. ("Don't you want to find the dog who actually did this, so it doesn't happen to someone else?" I asked the father, and later the animal control officer. "Don't you want to find out if that dog has had his rabies vaccination?" No, they weren't interested. They wanted Newt to have done it, to solve their dilemma, to have a person to fine...to sue...and a dog to punish or kill.)

The final three years of his life, Newt gave me no trouble and no more bites. But poor Megan never trusted him again.

I started giving Newt Rimadyl and aspirin occasionally, which I should have started sooner. It stopped all problems. I suppose since Rimadyl is such an expensive drug, and Greg was not big on taking his dogs to the vet for prescriptions or buying such prescriptions, I didn't push it. But I had received Rimadyl for Blue's hip and elbow dysplasia, and quickly learned it turned Newt into a new, happier, more peaceful dog. Perhaps, all this time, the poor guy was suffering and simply needed medication. Dogs don't complain like we do when they hurt, but maybe they snap out their frustration.

I know after an editing client hit me in the neck to show me how "easy" it is for "women to protect themselves," and caused three herniated disks, I lived in agonizing pain for seven years (the first seven years of my son's life, unfortunately).[6] Especially bad was the one disk that pinched a nerve which ran down my back and left arm. I still worked, walked the dogs, and raised my child...but the pain was always there, spasming my brain like a dentist drilling into a nerve. Finally, I found a surgeon (my hero!) who replaced the disks. But until then, I was in the kind of pain that made me want to cry or scream almost all the time; twice I drove to the hospital in the middle of the night begging for a shot in the neck of something, anything, to make the pain go away so I could live another day.

What if Newt was in that kind of pain but couldn't tell us? As pet "owners," maybe we are responsible for being more proactive in treating their pain. I have never liked pain medication, including for myself, but thinking back on Newt's generally sweet disposition but sometimes snapping, I think he was suffering a great deal. If I could go back, I would happily pay for the expensive Rimadyl and give it to him daily. I should have started the minute I heard the vet's diagnosis that Newt's spine was breaking.

Another sign that perhaps the pain was too great for him was that once we moved to Anchorage, instead of taking him on grueling, several-mile long walks on steep trails as I did in Palmer, we went on an easy, flat, one-mile stroll around University Lake Dog Park, where Newt was always a sweet gentleman to everyone, despite their paws and pats. There were no more problems with him. Other than our short daily walks, he just rested, and he was much more at peace. I had not realized, until then, that the difficult terrain of the Crevasse-Moraine Trails had been too much for him.

So Newt gentled down and passed away, after saying goodbye to Greg one night, softly putting his head on Greg's lap while they sat on the stairs together, Newt staring long and hard in Greg's eyes, which struck Greg as important enough that he got up in the middle of the night to check on him and saw Newt had passed on.

I was traveling and sorry I didn't get to say goodbye to the dog who was never mine, but who somehow thought perhaps he was. Still, I was glad Greg and Newt had their final moments together.

So maybe Newt knew, finally, at the end, that he wasn't my dog after all, but Greg's. You sure couldn't tell it by the way he followed me around and lay by my side of the bed and caused me a lot of trouble.

---

[6] The client, when I asked him to check if his insurance would help out since it happened in his office, looked me straight in the eye and said, "It never happened."

A full, happy family back in Anchorage in 2008: Winston, me, and Greg and our dogs (from left): Schatzy, Blue, Newt, and Chewie (Photo by David Jensen).

Newt in his last year (Photo by David Jensen).

Lessons Learned from Newt

Even if you're in pain, don't lash out at others. Try to explain that you need medications when you are suffering. Nothing feels as good on a warm day as lying on a dirt pile. Snapping at someone is the wrong way to handle problems.

12 Blue-Chew

There is no psychiatrist in the world like a puppy licking your face.
—Ben Williams

Neither knew it at the time, but a line had been crossed that could not be uncrossed—a running leap over a chasm of ignorance and misunderstanding between species and worlds...and a baby step taken into life's endless possibilities for wonder and joy and surprise that could no more be reversed than one's first taste of chocolate. A dog kiss.
—Berkeley Breathed, Flawed Dogs: The Shocking Raid on Westminster

"Blue-Chew," Greg would call them, no matter how much it irritated me.

"They are individuals. This one is Blue," I knelt down and cuddled the soft mass of yellow fur, the softest fur I'd ever felt on a dog. "See her Paul Newman blue eyes?"

"And this one is Chewie," I cuddled Blue's sister, who was licking and biting on my ears. "See her Batman mask? That's Chewie."

It didn't matter. Greg kept calling them Blue-Chew for the rest of their lives, and the name stuck.

Now, when I'm walking in the woods, if they get too far in front of me, I yell, "Blue-Chew!" and they both turn and run back to me, both eager and sorry they got out of my vision.

They know better, as I need them, and I need them close, like I've needed all my dogs.

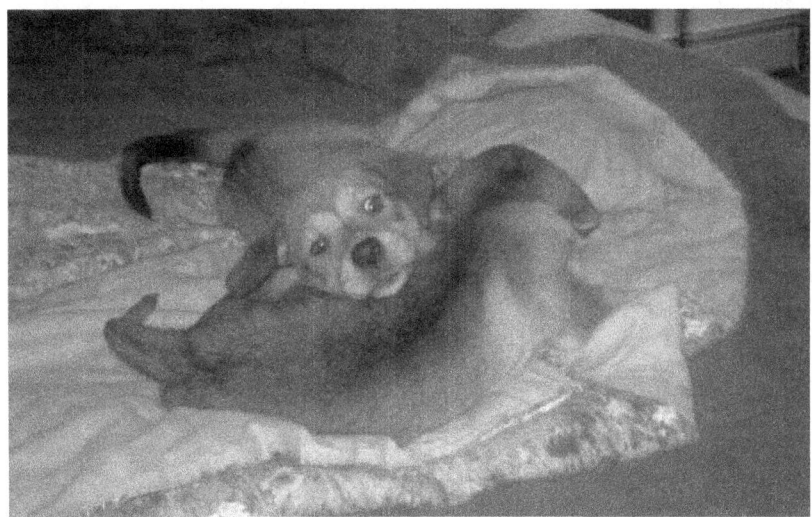

Blue facing camera, and Chewie, puppies.

Fostering

Blue-Chew tumbled into my life together soon after Buddy died, in January 2006.

What happened was, I told my little boy, "We can go foster a puppy for the dog rescue"; I figured this would help him (and me) with our pain of losing Buddy.

And maybe, in the back of mind, was the thought, maybe I will adopt that puppy, even though I have Schatzy and Greg's dogs...Bailey and Newt. A full household of dogs already.

That Saturday, we went to the puppy rescue. I was surprised to see cages just like at an animal control; I was hoping for something different, I suppose.

My eyes were drawn to two puppies, two little girls, mutts as can be. They were sisters, the last left over from a litter of five. Their brothers, already adopted, were black. These two were golden and black. They looked to me to be shepherd-lab-husky, and in the littlest one, the one with the black Batman mask face, a little beagle. (I'd been told, a few years earlier, that the local animal control received many of their dogs from mushers. It seems to be a "no-no" in Alaska to say anything negative about mushers, but I assure you not all of them give their dogs good homes, many of their dogs live most of their lives on chains, and often puppies are born and abandoned or "culled" that are not mushing material. I have often wondered whether Blue-Chew's mother was one of those staked-out huskies, and the sire [or sires; litters can have multiple fathers] was whatever dog happened by.)

That one was in the arms of a man, and I instantly felt jealous and possessive. Memories of my beagles Poochie and Snoopy popped up when I looked at that little black masked face.

Her sister, though, looked just like Woody, ah dear Woody, killed by a car in Washington, my fault, my fault. My love. My Woodhead, always an emptiness in my heart. (And of course, Buddy kind of looked like Woody too, only he got fat and was all black, while Woody's black puppy color turned to golden tan as he left his first year. Forever I will try, I suppose, to find Woody again, to make some other dog replace what cannot be replaced.)

I don't want that man to take that puppy, I thought, watching him. I want that puppy.

He didn't. He stuck her back in the cage with her sister.

So now which one do we foster? I couldn't decide. I held them both. They kissed me, of course, as puppies are always so generous and loving.

I told the puppy rescue we'd foster them both.

They said good, now bring them back next Saturday for the next adoption fair.

I had a week to foster and decide.

Chewie as a puppy.

It was fun shopping with them for supplies.

It was fun having two puppies in my bed, kissing on me, chewing on me, so quickly falling in love with me. It was fun watching my son and my tenants' children playing with the puppies.

But kids go to bed, and moms are left, on a cold dark January night, trying to save their house from puppy stuff.

It was not fun trying to make it downstairs on the cold, dark, icy outside staircase in time for them to "do their duty," and when I finally got down there with them, they wouldn't go, just shivered, looked at me, and whined. So I'd carry them back upstairs, and they'd go.

The kids are happily sleeping away, tired out from playing with the puppies, and mom is still awake, cleaning up vomit and pee and puppy poo...so much came out of those tiny little six-week-old things you would think I was fostering two elephants.

When I finally slept a little, the smell of puppy poo or the sounds of their wails woke me. The sounds of their peeing on my carpet, my beautiful expensive carpet, or on my bed, my very expensive mattress, ruined any chance of enjoying sleep.

The next morning I was back at the puppy rescue.

"I'm sorry," I truly was. "I'm just too old. I need my sleep. I guess I can only foster older dogs."

The lady seemed to be scowling at me. I didn't blame her. I had failed as a foster parent.

As she led me to the building where they were to go, into a cage just like at an animal control, little Batman-face started wailing. She didn't want to leave me. Little golden-hair cried right along with her sister, and both of them shivered much worse than if they were in the snow.

This is so unjust; this is so wrong, they seemed to cry. We had a night together. We trusted you; we thought you were the one! They wouldn't stop crying. I put them in the cage, and left, now trembling myself.

I drove home, smoked cigarettes nervously, thought of them the rest of the night, so sorry and so ashamed for leaving them there.

The next morning, at 9 a.m., I was in a college class. I was taking some extra computer classes to get my skills up to par, and it turned out I was close to another (fifth!) degree, so I was going for it.

But I couldn't focus on what the teacher was saying. All I could think of was those wails.

I left class and drove right back to the Dog & Puppy Rescue.

"I'm here for the puppies," I told the same lady.

She looked at me sternly over her glasses. "You said they were too much for you to foster," she reminded me.

"Foster? No, I'm here to adopt them!"

An hour later, as I was playing with puppies in my home office, getting wet, happy, forgiving kisses all over my face and neck, I thought of Greg, who'd left at 6:30 a.m. to work in Anchorage.

I decided to do something I'd never done with Greg, or any man, for that matter. I asked him permission.

"Greg," I said when he answered his cell phone, "I really miss those puppies."

Brief silence.

"Do you mind if I adopt them?"

Greg was stunned. I couldn't see his face, but I knew he had a shocked expression, that I would even consider asking him before adopting them.

"We'll have five dogs," he reminded me, but then he said (as if he had a choice), "Yes, you can adopt them." He tried to sound gruff, but actually sounded very pleased, because he had suddenly somehow become "Master of the House," which he had never been before.

But Greg isn't stupid. That's one thing I'll say for all the men I've dated...I don't like them stupid. And he's definitely the smartest.

He walked in from work that evening, came right into my office, as I was lying on the floor being pounced on by my little babies, and said, "I *know* you already *had* those puppies when you called me!"

I just smiled and said, "Aren't they cute?"

Chewie (left) and Blue as puppies, asleep.

The tenants' oldest daughter Megan kept coming up with names for them, but naming is personal and serious to me. I named golden-hair with the bright blue eyes, "Blue," I think just because I always wanted a dog named Blue after reading about such a dog in the animal novels I loved as a child. (I didn't know, since she was still a puppy, that those eyes would turn golden and her name would be absolutely ridiculous within a few months.)

Everyone agreed it was a dumb name, but she had a name. (It seemed especially stupid years later when I would call her at the dog park. "Blue!" I'd call, and big ole yeller dog would come running up to me.)

Batface was named Chewie by my son because she loved to chew things. I didn't tell him that all puppies chewed things.

And anyway, I figured I'd get away easy with these puppies. Unlike Woody and Buddy (Eb was the only other dog I got as a puppy, and he was too smart to destroy things), these two wouldn't eat my furniture, my house, my car. They had each other to entertain and play with.

I didn't realize that two puppies actually meant double the damage. One day I came home from work and caught them playing tug-of-war with my couch.

Another day, I came in and they were ripping the trim off from around my doors.

"How cute they are!" I exclaimed, and asked my tenant, Kelly, if she had a camera. She just looked at me and said, "I would have killed them."

But I had made up my mind when I adopted them, and so I was never upset by the messes and destruction. I knew I'd have to get new carpet and new furniture, and it was time Winston learned to either pick up or lose his toys anyway. Once a dog is mine, it is mine for life, good or bad, and that's the way it was. My son was especially sad when the couches left, because he liked playing games on the half-circular blue sets, jumping from one to the other, and hiding toys and other things in their neat little cup holders that opened up. I felt badly as I didn't know how much the couch set meant to him, and if I'd realized, I would have kept those couches till the dogs ate them to the ground.

Chewie, left, Blue, middle, and Schatzy.

Veterinarians

My old black mare, Dusty, was requiring frequent vet visits. Although I took my dogs to the vet regularly, it was my horse vet who pointed out Blue's problem when she was about 6 months old.

"See how she's walking splay-toed?" I motioned toward her when the dogs all came over to say hello as he got out of his truck. Blue's front feet turned outward, the opposite of pigeon-toed; she walked oddly and hopped instead of ran. "That just started, and I've never seen a dog walk like that before."

It was a question. He had an answer.

"She has elbow dysplasia," he said.

I'd never heard of elbow dysplasia, but I'd heard of hip dysplasia, and that was bad. I assumed this was too.

So began the trips to vets, just like I had done with Buddy, to find out what was wrong with my puppy—by now the size of a miniature horse—and what could be done to fix it.

My regular vet performed a surgery on one elbow. He insisted she had to stay in a cast and I had to keep it "dry" for the next two months.

It was an early winter in Alaska, probably late September, and the cast was wet and ruined within a few days. Also, he said she needed to keep still, which was a ridiculous demand for a puppy, especially one with an equally energetic sister.

Blue as a puppy, before her elbow dysplasia was noticeable.

So I waited a few months, and took Blue to a specialist in Anchorage. I brought her x-rays, but they insisted I had to leave her there and come back.

I waited all day, anxiously.

When it was time for our follow-up appointment, I came back, excited to see her.

"I'm here to get Blue," I said.

"You can't have her until you pay," said the receptionist.

"Okay," I thought this was odd, as usually you pay after the appointment. But I paid, in full, $700, and then asked for my dog.

"Just a minute," she said.

Minutes ticked and ticked. My appointment time passed.

I heard Blue crying in pain in the back.

I marched to the desk. "I want my dog. Now."

"That's not our policy. You have to see the vet first."

"What are you worried about? I already paid! Let me have her now! I can hear her crying."

(It turns out they were cutting her nails, right then, and just about every one bled the rest of the night. She *was* in pain! I heard her, and I knew it.)

Blue, showing her odd elbows; the right hand had surgery.

More receptionists or whatevers showed up and told me I couldn't have my dog till after I saw the doctor. I insisted I wanted her now.

The doctor showed up in the reception area and practically shouted at me, "Do you not want to see me? We have an appointment."

"I know, and you're half an hour late. I just want my dog while I wait," I said, frightened and shocked by all their behavior. What the hell!

Finally, I got my dog, after I was led back to a room. The vet came in with his diagnoses: she had elbow and hip dysplasia, the surgery done by the Palmer vet made the one elbow worse, he would do a different kind of surgery, the hips, there was not much to do but he suggested some kind of breaking them and then trying this or that or the other thing and maybe....

I listened and left and knew I would never go back there.

I tried to get copies of her x-rays, and they refused to give them to me. I said, "I already paid for them. They are mine." They said, "No, they are not yours."

When I tried to get them sent to my vet in Palmer, I was told they "couldn't find" Blue's x-rays.

I drove home, humiliated and crying, and I promised Blue that she would not have to go through those tortuous surgeries, she would never go back to that place, and I would give her the greatest life possible, even if it was a short one.

"Quality over quantity," I told her. "You will not suffer any more surgeries."

I started looking on the Internet for extra large strollers, because after all the vet had said, it sounded like she wouldn't be walking in a year.

Blue will turn nine years old soon, and she still goes on daily walks with me in the woods. The only real trouble she has is with the one elbow that surgery was performed on. If it seems she's having a rough day, I give her a Rimadyl. But my best decision, based entirely on my gut feelings and not on what the vet said, was to choose a quality life for her.

Chewie had a bad vet experience too. The only good thing that came out of it was I found a good vet, at last, one I could trust, near my home.

It was Friday night, and she started vomiting. Vomiting is not a normal thing for a dog. It is a bad thing. I've only seen it a very few times...with parvo in a rescue dog, with Blue and Chewie when they were puppies the first night in my home.

But Chewie was by this time about three years old, healthy and strong and sweet.

I had picked up dog food, horse chow, and cat litter at Walmart® that day and had thrown in my cart the usual supply of dog treats. One was a bag of Old Roy's peanut butter dog cookies. I put them in the doggie treat drawer, which Chewie later opened, and munched on a few.

I didn't know how many, but she couldn't reach all.

However, I was up with her most of the night. Winston had someone spending the night, so I couldn't drive to Pet Emergency in Anchorage 50 miles away. I kept monitoring her. Mainly she just lay on the couch, so sick, staring at me helplessly.

Dr. T's office was closed on Saturdays, but there was a new clinic right near my house, not 5 minutes away, and I was going to be there right when they opened. But one thing I saw on the Internet just before I left was about some dog treats from China having something toxic to dogs in them, and dogs were getting sick and dying.

I ran Chewie to the new vet, and she lay in the corner of the room. Her belly hurt, I told him. He reached down to touch it, and she growled.

He jumped up, angry, it seemed.

"She's just a growl-talker," I explained. "She doesn't bite, never has." It was true. Chewie talked by growling. Sometimes it was hilarious, as her entire conversation would be growls and moans. She'd try to communicate with people that way. I had never had such a talkative dog, and I really respected her attempts to say something people could understand. Chewie was the first "growl-talker" I'd ever had, but I later met people who said they had had such a dog too. A couple times it got me yelled at by people who said, "Your dog just growled at me!" and I tried to explain that was how she said hello, but they just stomped off disbelievingly.

(Chewie especially growl talks when I ask her questions, like "Do you love mama, Chewie?" or "Do you want a treat, Chewie?" Her response is a long and throaty, "Grrrrrrrrr!" I love this amazing attempt by a dog to speak with me; it makes me happy.)

Chewie, the "growl-talker" (Photo by David Jensen).

Well, clearly the vet had never heard of growl-talkers either, because he stormed out wordlessly and came back with a muzzle, and put it on her. It was so tight her skin hung around it. She stared at me, sick and dejected, but still not moving from her spot on the floor in the corner.

Then the vet felt her belly, and said, "Well, I don't know what it is, but we're busy today. You'll have to leave her here and I'll do an x-ray when I have time."

"What? Leave her here? In a cage?"

"Yes," he said firmly.

"With a muzzle on?"

"Definitely!"

"I can't do that," I said. "Look, I only live 5 minutes away. When you have time, just call me, and I promise I'll be right here."

"Absolutely not," he roared at me. "I will fit her x-rays in when I have *time*!"

My God! No, I said, and took off the muzzle off poor humiliated Chewie with some difficulty as I'd never used one before, trying not to cry in front of him, but so angry and upset I couldn't talk.

They forced me to pay them $70 before I could leave.

Typical bullshit, I thought, paying them for fucking nothing. Typical arrogant asshole vet bullshit! It reminded me of all the know-it-all vets who insisted poor Buddy go through their various (expensive and repetitive) tests just done by other vets, and how all insisted their diagnosis was the correct one, and they were all wrong. I wanted to scream at them, "Why can't just *one* of you admit you *don't know*!" as my poor Buddy got worse and worse.

I was beyond upset as I took Chewie home.

I drove down to Palmer to another new vet clinic, right downtown, and walked in, pissed off and ready to fight.

"Does your vet actually *like* dogs?" I demanded of the receptionist. It was not really a question. I was furious.

"Sure, they both love dogs."

"How am I supposed to believe that?" I wanted to know. "I want proof." I am thinking that there is no way any person can get through vet school and its damned vivisection and still love dogs. I had heard and read too many stories about what goes on in vet school. Everyone assumed I would become a veterinarian, but I knew better, even as a child. When I lived in Sacramento, a fellow told our humane society about finding a still-live cut-up beagle in a dumpster behind the vet school. Plus I worked at a vet clinic once. As a mere receptionist, they were outraged when I barged into a room once where I heard puppies screaming in agony. "What are you doing?" I wanted to know. They were chopping their tails off, all for the American Kennel Club, which wants certain breeds with bobbed tails. All for so-called beauty. No dog of mine would ever have cropped ears or tails, I knew that. "It doesn't hurt them," a vet tech later told me. "They are just puppies."

As if in answer to my demand for proof that there might be a vet in this new Palmer clinic who actually likes dogs, a dog came up behind the receptionist, wagging its tail. He looked happy and loved and normal.

"That's Dr. H's dog," the receptionist said.

"Well, I want to meet her. Now. Before I bring my dog in. I need a vet who actually loves dogs, understands that they are part of my family, that they are like my children."

She went in back, and vet came right out, and not to the receptionist area, but right to the lobby, and shook my hand and asked what I needed.

I told her what just happened at the other vet's.

"No, no," she shook her head, when I said how they wanted me to leave her there all day with a muzzle on in a cage. "you can *never* muzzle a vomiting dog! She could die!"

Now I really was crying, and so grateful she understood, and I ran home and got Chewie and brought her in.

And when she was lying on this new vet's floor, and the vet came up to feel her belly, and Chewie growled, she just said, "Oh, do you have a tummy ache, poor baby!" and Chewie's thin whip tail tapped the floor in answer. And she felt Chewie's belly just fine.

Chewie was very sick.

She had to stay there, on fluids, and other medications, for a few days, but she pulled through.

And in the meantime, the lawyers for the dog food companies put out public service announcements that they would cover all vet bills. I called and signed up. It was all bullshit.

I never received any response, any form, any money, despite my numerous calls. Their 800 number they had set up for pet owners disappeared as quickly as it appeared. It was all a ploy to get the media on their side.

I never bought Old Roy food again. And I always check to see if dog food is "made in China," so I can avoid it.

Dog Parks

Blue-Chew at University Lake Dog Park in Anchorage.

After we moved to Anchorage and were therefore relegated to dog parks instead of wild empty trails, Chewie was the best behaved of my little pack. Blue would go running into a group of dogs, joyously, happily, but scattering them miserably as she can't stop properly (her elbow and hip dysplasia present themselves in odd hops instead), and probably didn't want to. She wanted to throw herself into the party, not approach it delicately. She thinks all dogs love her and want her gloriousness, and she is so happy to join the party, but sometimes she's treated like an embarrassing drunk that tumbles in, and everyone turns away from her.

Schatzy, when she still lived, was gentle and slow, and meandered into the dog park near-blind and all-deaf. Sometimes I would lose her there, as she started following some blur that she thought was me. I was always insulted that it was a fat lady.

Newt did surprisingly well at the dog park when he was alive. No problems at all. No barking, no biting, no concerns. But he didn't live long after we moved to Anchorage to enjoy them too many years. Miza, as discussed later, was nothing but problems at the dog park, the kind of dog who elicited anger from other dog owners.

But Chewie, always gentle, always happy, was popular with people and their dogs, still running into a crowd with her sister, but never scattering the crowd, but joining it. She never barked. She never met a dog she didn't like. Because she is such a large dog, though, and typically for large dogs completely fascinated by tiny dogs, her attention was usually drawn to them, and she went to the tiny breeds to say hello first. Often their owners feared the giant coming toward them, but it always worked out well, as she said hello, tail wagging, to the little schnauzers, pugs, terriers, dachshunds, shih tzus, miniature Dobermans, and various other odd, tiny breeds that I have never owned.

Chewie at the dog park in Anchorage.

(Sometimes I have wanted to get a "little" dog just as a toy for Blue and Chewie, since they are so fascinated by them, but I end up with what comes to me or touches me or needs me, and they are always large dogs.)

One April I was at the dog park with Blue and Chewie only, as Schatzy was struggling with walking that day, and it was a glorious spring day, temperatures above freezing, wind not bad.

I was talking to a regular I saw there often, Tammy. A seagull came and dive-bombed Blue, which she took to be a fun game, and the seagull led her across University Lake.

"Oh my god!" Tammy screamed.

"What's wrong?" I asked, as I enjoyed watching Blue happily run to the island and back.

"My dog fell through last weekend, near shore; it's bad out there."

"Well, she made it okay, thankfully," I said, not worried, as Blue was now next to me. Suddenly, she spun around and ran out on the lake again.

"Blue!" I called, worried now, especially at Tammy's expression.

Blue turned to come back and fell through the ice.

Oh my god oh my god oh my god what do I do what do I do oh my god. I'm screaming and yelling and in complete panic.

Before I even say anything out loud, Chewie looks at her sister, out splashing in the water, and runs out to join her, and falls through too.

They splash desperately for a moment, and the ice just breaks around them when they try to get on. So then they stop, float, and just stare at me, with happy dog smiles.

Come save us, mom.

This is the absolute worst of all. They are calm and know I will save them. They aren't worried a bit.

Now I really am vocally hysterical, and I keep asking Tammy what to do, and all she does is call her dogs and run for her car and leave. She doesn't want to be here.

I'm calling 911 and reporting it and asking them to send help (which they never do), and I'm calling Greg to come help, and in the meantime, I am walking straight into the water toward them, coming from a side where the ice has melted, figuring I'll break through to them.

When the water reaches my chest height, I realize I am not going to make it. I am freezing, and I am going to die, and that is not going to save my dogs. I reluctantly turn around and go back.

I can still run, somehow, and I do, the adrenaline driving me, to a hotel that is being built (right in my park, which I've always been irritated by, especially since it's a hotel that doesn't allow dogs). Some workers are breaking for lunch, and I'm running at them hysterically, begging for help.

Four of them come with me, and we all stand on the shore, looking at my calm, peaceful dogs, who just stare at me: Okay, mom, you can come get us now.

"What do I do? What do I do? What do I do?" I just keep saying, over, and over, in panic and stupidity. I am mindless; all thought is gone but that my beloved dogs are going to die.

Chewie, suddenly, to all our amazement, tires of waiting for me to come get her, and somehow finds a way to pull herself out on the ice. Blue, I know, with her elbows, will not be able to do this, but then a wonderful miracle happens.

A man, who is early 20s and fearless as such young men are (I'm told this is why they make great soldiers), takes off his coat, and begins crawling. I suppose seeing fat Chewie do it, he knew he could make it. He crawls out to Blue, reaches down and drags her up on the ice, and crawls back. Blue runs happily back to me.

I follow my hero to the car, forcing money on him for pizza.

"I don't need your money," he smiles.

"Look," I said. "You don't understand. What they mean to me...." I am crying.

He looks at me and nods. "I understand." And he gets in his car.

I feel like the $20 I threw at him is not enough, so I write a letter to the editor thanking him. A few weeks later I see him again (I didn't recognize him because I was so panicked the day it happened, but he heard me call "Blue" to the car and came up and talked to me). Turns out he never saw the letter. Perhaps another thing about young men is they don't read the newspaper, but I forever have a hero. Someone who risked it all to save some crazy lady's beloved dog. Forever grateful.

My son, Winston, and Blue, resting.

Another danger lurks at the dog park, this one an issue in summer only. Surprisingly, it's beavers.

Dogs are attacked by beavers in the water, on land, going into the water, chasing balls. Sometimes it even leads to death. I hear rumors, see flyers, and don't believe it. Beavers? Seriously?

One day the dogs and I are walking on a trail near the lake, and down the hill I see a beaver on top of its house. He turns and looks at us.

We look at him. Silently, for a second.

Then he charges.

I had no idea beavers could run, and run so fast. He was up that hill in a few seconds, and the dogs and I have scattered and are running for our lives.

We meet at the trailhead. Blue seems to be laughing. We look at each other, both thinking: Beavers! Who knew!

My sweet misnamed "Blue" (Photo by David Jensen).

Cars and Communication

Chewie was hit by a car. Well, not really hit by a car, but she ran into a moving car. After, she was upset, ran off, got lost, and it took me two frantic days and numerous posters and several visits to animal control to find her.

I had just moved to a new house on the hillside of Anchorage, and Blue-Chew didn't know their way around yet.

The neighbor who hit her came up apologetic and concerned, and he helped me look for her.

"It's not your fault," I said. Blue-Chew had a history of chasing cars, one I couldn't seem to train out of them, no matter how much I had tried over the six years they had shared my life.

But an amazing thing happened after Chewie's frightening experience.

I picked her up from animal control (they brought her in, recognized her from my flyers, and kindly didn't officially check her in but called me to come get her). I brought her home to Blue, who had spent her first and only night without her sister, quite concerned.

The two touched noses, made no sounds, but I watched them, fascinated.

Chewie was telling Blue something.

I don't know how dogs communicate. Is it smells? Osmosis? Meeting of minds?

In any case, in those few moments, Chewie explained to Blue that they were never, ever to chase a car again.

And they never did.

Sisters, in love always.

Weighty Issues

As Chewie ages, there is something similar to Dane in her, but not the saint part. No, Dane was special that way.

But like Dane, Chewie waits on her couch for me to come pet her, instead of shoveling her head into my arms or jumping next to me on the bed and snuggling with me like Blue does—she simply watches and waits for my attention.

Unlike Dane, if she doesn't get it, she pouts terribly and is angry about it. Chewie's solution to anger, to happiness, to all emotions (and I have the same problem) is one thing—food.

Food is Chewie's mantra, her meaning, her purpose. Blue and I are important too, of course, but Chewie will do dastardly things to obtain the fruits of her obsession, including standing up and reaching for what is on a counter, following my son to see if he drops something, sneak food when we're not looking (or pretending not to see).

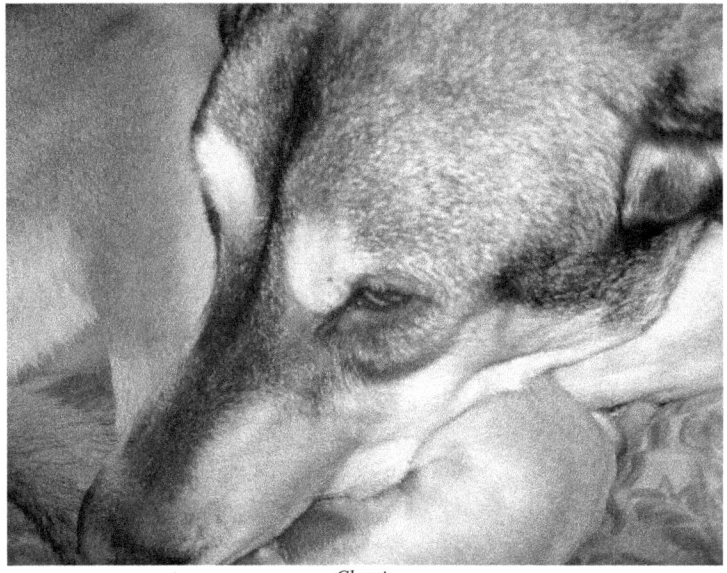

Chewie

But she eats slowly and carefully. She is always the last one done with breakfast and dinner, savoring every bite carefully and thoughtfully, while Blue literally licks her bowl clean in less than 30 seconds and then follows Miza around while he carries his bowl, growing and spilling dog food throughout the house, which Blue happily cleans up behind him.

Oddly, Blue then eats more than Chewie, but has never had a weight problem. They go on the same walks, eat the same meals, and are from the same litter, but Chewie is 50 pounds heavier. I wonder if Chewie's sire is different from Blue's, and therefore that side of her genetics causes her to be fat. But I take comfort in her size, as I struggle with my own weight, because I can see there is no fairness to it, no cause. Her own sister is lithe while Chewie is obese, and she cannot be blamed. She gets the smallest bowl of dog food, the fewest treats, but still she grows.

So next time someone criticizes your weight, just think of Chewie. It's not your fault. It's the Great Gods of Metabolism. So enjoy that candy bar.

Winston and Chewie (Photo by David Jensen).

Satisfaction

Life with Blue-Chew has been good, all good (at least after that first night, when I had to accept that the destruction of my house was inevitable). They are kind souls, loving and fun. They are great with children, kind to other animals, easy dogs.

They are how most dogs are.

I don't know that the next dog to come into my life will be the opposite of them and, for the first time, make my life dog hell. His name is Miza, but he is about four years away, after Greg's dogs Newt and Bailey pass on. But before Miza comes to ruin our lives, another dog stops by for a few days. I call her "Dog."

Blue at the vet, asking me if we can leave. Please!

Chew and Blue, in the shape of a heart (Photo by Jennifer Huntting)

Lessons Learned from Blue and Chewie

Your sister is your best friend. Adopting two puppies does not mean your house will be less damaged. Just because two dogs are bonded with each other doesn't mean they won't fully bond with their human. Beds, couches, and cars are all glorious places to be. Don't walk on thin ice.

13 "Dog": The Seeker

You can tell a lot about a man by the way he treats his dog....
—*Peary Perry, Manuel Muldoon*

Twelve separate studies have reported that between 18 and 48 percent of battered women, and their children, delay leaving abusive situations in fear for what might happen to their animals. Women who do seek safety at shelters are nearly 11 times more likely to report that their partner has hurt or killed their animals than women who have not experienced domestic abuse.
—*American Society for the Prevention of Cruelty to Animals*

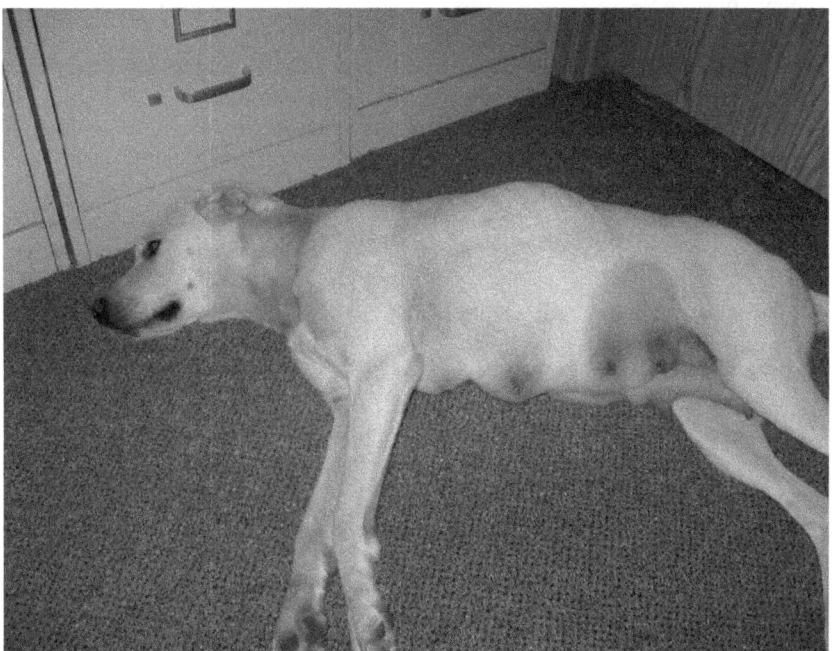

"There's a Schatzy-looking dog standing on the doorstep," Greg announces one evening in August 2007.

I run down and open the door and there she is, a yellow lab, skinny with swollen teats, and I immediately want to know where the puppies are. I search everywhere, all around the woods near my house and down the road. My tenant's daughter, Megan, helps me.

We find nothing.

But we bring in "Dog," as I call her, of course knowing I can't keep her, with a five-dog household already, and I feed her and water her and she fits right in.

The next day I run down to animal control and fill out the "FOUND DOG" sheet. I place advertisements in all the newspapers. I list her on Web sites.

Dog comes along on our daily walks on the trails and is well-behaved (indeed, she knows more tricks than any dog I've ever met) in every respect except one: she barks at bicyclists. It angers them to no end, and more than one tried to kick her as he sails by us. (I was always taught to stop and say hi to the dog, letting it sniff the bike. But I never rode bicycles anymore, so my dogs weren't familiar with them. A couple years later, when I moved to Anchorage, Blue-Chew started running alongside bicyclists at the dog park, which infuriated the riders. So I put a bicycle in the living room for a week. Forever after, they ignored bicycles.)

"She's not my dog," I apologize, but they are long-gone already.

Jesus H. Christ, I am thinking, how do I end up in these situations, and now another dog? I've already got Blue, Chewie, Schatzy, and Greg's dogs Newt and Bailey, plus three cats, two horses, a bird room of rescued parakeets and cockatiels, and now this dog?

I am still worried about the puppies, and I keep looking for them, even driving her around to see if she acts like anything is familiar.

Dog seems to be searching for something too, looking at me wistfully and eagerly sometimes, trying to tell me something. She stares intently in my blue orbs with her brown ones, waiting to see if I understand. I never cared that dogs and I don't speak the same oral language before, but suddenly I wish she could tell me what happened. Why is she here? Where is her home? Where are her puppies?

The answer comes about ten days later.

A girl—she sounds like a teenager—is calling me from animal control, where she is looking at my FOUND DOG flyer.

"I just want to know that she's all right," she says, tearfully.

"Is she your dog?"

"Yes, but my boyfriend wouldn't let me keep her. He took her away. I can't keep her. He hates her."

"Well, just come say hi to her. She misses you and has been looking for you. I live just two blocks from animal control."

She hesitates, saying no, she doesn't want to see her, just wanted to be sure she's all right. I work harder to convince her.

When she shows up, I guess she is about 20 years old, yet she has a quiet little toddler, not much younger than my own son, with her. He never says a thing, just sits quietly in the truck and stares at the dashboard. I feel very sorry for him, and I don't yet even know why.

Dog runs up to the truck and jumps happily in as soon as the girl opens the door. The girl is crying, and Dog is ecstatic. They hug each other happily.

I have no doubt they love each other.

What I do have doubts about is the stupid-ass boyfriend.

I know, because I've had stupid-ass boyfriends. But I'm not 20 years old anymore; I'm in my 40s, and blessedly, years do bring wisdom.

So I impart it.

First I have her tell me what happened.

When the boyfriend moved in, the dog moved out. He insisted she be on a chain out front all the time. Then he got crazy mad when Dog barked. He said was going to "fucking get rid of her."

Yes, she had puppies too, but they were "okay," the girl said. He didn't hate them like he hated Dog.

The night Dog showed up at my house, the boyfriend had had enough, grabbed the dog, threw her in the car, and drove her to animal control, which was closed. So he kicked her out of the car and drove home.

Dog must have run until she found my house, up a hill. Perhaps she could smell that dogs lived there.

Now for the wisdom imparting. By this time, having lived so many years with Brock in Oregon, I had a pretty good idea of what was going on.

"Does your boyfriend hit you?" I asked.

"Yes," she started crying.

"Listen, I've been there. You have a good dog here. A smart dog. Your dog has clearly been loved and well-trained."

"Yes," she sniffed. "Before he came, I trained her a lot."

"Right, well, you need to get rid of him and keep your dog. He's no good. He will never change. You will never fix him. And you not only have one of the best dogs I've ever met, but you have a wonderful little boy there. You need to get out now."

I let this sit for a minute, while she stared at me, shocked and nodding.

"Do you have a place to stay?"

"Yes, well, my mother's."

"You need to move in with your mother. Will you mother take your dog?"

"Yes, she'll take her." This she says with much more confidence. "I am going to take her there right now."

I realize that she's made a decision. She is keeping her dog, but at her mother's house. Sadly, I also realize she can't quite fathom leaving her boyfriend.

"I want you to think about what I said," I continued. "I know you love him. But a man like that, who would take away your beloved pet, and would treat her like he did, is going to go after whatever you love." I look pointedly at her son. "You need to be very careful, but you need to get out."

"I will," she says, half-heartedly.

Ah, to be young, and in love. It can be terrifying.

And yet, in her car were two little beings who loved her more than anyone else in the world. Two beings who depended on her to find strength. Two beings whose very lives depended on her.

What happened to that little boy, who never said a word, or smiled, or looked up? His life must have been already a little hell in the house with the monster his mommy brought home to live with them. Or maybe the monster was his daddy?

What happened to Dog, and her puppies?

What happened to that girl-woman, whom I tried to give a tough-love lecture to in the prayer that she would survive her bad relationship and go on to a good, rich, kind one, as I was able to do.

I will never know.

"Dog" on a walk with me and my pack.

Lessons Learned from Dog

Women sometimes make the wrong choices for lovers, and choose them over a good dog. If you're lost, keep searching until you find help. Bicyclists want to be left alone.

14 Lessons from Louisiana Puppies

Pictures of "Louisiana cur dogs" from the Internet, that look similar to the puppies. Since my camera was stolen in an IHOP in Louisiana, I have no photos of the puppies.

Charm, Tick-Tick, Blackie, and Terk—the names my son, who had just turned six a few days before, gave to four Louisiana "cur dogs" we found abandoned in the woods when we went to visit a friend in May 2006. For days, we struggled to save them. My friend Pam taught us how to twist the never-ending supply of humongous, blood-engorged ticks out of their ears and bodies, since we don't have ticks (or fleas) in Alaska, fortunately, at least where I live. (My sweet animal-loving son refused to stomp on the ticks. "I can't believe you'd ask me to kill an animal," he said.) We gave them food, love, and attention...all things they'd clearly never had. When we parted their fur, I was horrified to see their skin was moving with thousands of fleas. The poor things were miserably under attack.

Most importantly, we tried to find them homes, all to no avail.

The humane societies and animal controls I called all said they were overrun; even my offer of donating as much money as needed to care for them and to pay for spaying and neutering was useless. Money, it turns out, cannot buy happiness. Or life.

Pam said they had to go, and so she put them in the back of her truck, Winston and I climbed inside. The entire drive, my son tried to convince us that we couldn't take them there.

"We have to take them home with us," he said.

"We can't," I said, thinking of the four dogs we had at home, as well as the thousands of dogs in Alaska's animal controls that needed homes. Eight dogs! I could not fathom it. I reminded him our neighborhood covenants only allowed "two pets," so even my aquarium was in violation. Plus one of the puppies (ironically, the one named "Charm") was very food-aggressive, and would get in fights with the other puppies. Of course, he was starving to death, so he had a reason, and would have sweetened in time.

I then probably lied to my son; I wasn't sure if it was true or not: "The airlines won't let us fly that many, and they won't let us take any from Louisiana this time of year because its too hot, and they could die in the cargo hold."

As we spotted animal control, my son saw a used car lot.

"Just buy a car, and we'll drive them," he insisted.

"To Alaska? That would take too long, and you'd have to repeat all of first grade." This last part was probably a lie too. It was near the end of the school year. Surely they wouldn't make him repeat it, especially since he was acing everything.

He thought about this for a few seconds. He did not enjoy school. "That's okay," he said, with finality. "I will repeat first grade. I don't care. You *have* to save them." I wish I had.

While Pam talked with personnel, Winston and I visited and talked to as many dogs as we could. I had the same feeling I'd had visiting Anchorage, Sacramento, and Mat-Su animal controls in the "old days," when such places were designed to collect and cheaply kill as many pets as fast as possible. I sensed that none of these dogs would make it out of here alive. They seemed to know it too, desperately pushing against the cages, begging us to release them. Certainly, dogs, with their powerful senses of smell, know the odor of death at animal controls and humane societies and understand their fate, although they, like I, cannot comprehend the reason for their death penalties.

Fortunately, there is a no-kill movement spreading across the country. I don't think it has reached most of the south yet, though. Even today, the Web site for the animal control where we took the puppies starts its mission statement with: *"Monroe County Animal Control endeavors to protect people from the perils that result from their interaction with domestic animals."*

The next day, Arkansas Humane Society called back and agreed to take the four puppies. I immediately called the animal control to say I was coming back for them.

"We don't hold dogs that are abandoned or owner drop-offs," I was told.

"They're dead?" I couldn't believe it, even though I knew it was true. I didn't know they'd be killed immediately, before even having a chance at life or finding a home.

"Yes. We don't have room or money to keep them. If it's a stray, we have to keep it three days, but otherwise, we euthanize them right away. We kill 700 a week here, ma'am."

Seven hundred souls every week, in a little town in rural Louisiana. I am overwhelmed by the number. At the same time I'm telling myself, "I know, I know, it's not animal control's fault," I am also thinking, "There's got to be a way they could try harder, do better, instead of just kill." Much better. They are burned out and just doing a "problem elimination" job instead of working hard on finding solutions.

I am so sad for those puppies.

"Winston," I said after I hung up, looking at his eager face, waiting to hear that we can go back and get them, "the puppies are dead."

I should have thought about it and taken that moment to lie to him.

It was a life-changing moment for me, for my son, for my friend. We were all devastated. Pam drove us to Shreveport next day, a day early, and left us at a hotel. There was nothing more to say to each other. Perhaps deep inside I partly blamed her, but it wasn't her fault, of course. It wasn't even animal control's fault. But it still felt very wrong, so unfair, and we all regretted the drive down the dirt road (we were looking for turtles, as we don't have them in Alaska) where we found those poor, four souls.

We had a final lunch together at an empty IHOP before Pam drove away, and I left my camera on the table. When we came back 15 minutes later, the camera—and our waitress—had disappeared. All my pictures of our Louisiana trip, including my son's birthday, and probably the previous six months since I'd done a backup, were gone. I sometimes wondered if it was a blessing, though, because also missing were the dozens of pictures my son and I took of Charm, Tick-Tick, Blackie, and Terk, pictures which would have haunted me.

Sometimes people ask me why I donate so much of my time and money to saving animals and spay/neuter programs. You have only to look into the eyes of those trusting puppies, so eager to be loved; so grateful to have food in their starving bodies; so sick, alone, and desperate for help.

And then, you see their eyes when they realize where they are being left and why. You hear their wails as you leave. You say nothing during the drive back to your friend's house. You go to bed early, and you don't sleep. Your son tries not to cry.

Coming home to Alaska, my heart broken and my mind flooded with guilt, I walked in the door to be greeted with pure love by four rescued dogs—Blue, Chewie, Schatzy, and Newt—and my cats.

My four dogs live a different kind of life than the Louisiana four had. They sleep on my bed; they walk every day in the woods with me, not dumped there. They are surrounded by their choices of chew toys, fluffy toys, rope toys, squeaky toys, and balls. They get petted and scratched and loved every day. They gave me so much love and joy when I came home that I had to remind myself of the lives I had saved instead of the four I had failed to save.

In some way, my son has never forgiven me. I think back to my first dog, Poochie, and how disappointed I was in my mother when she made Poochie disappear. For years after, I experienced the same thing from my son.

"Why couldn't you have brought them with us to Alaska?" he demands, over and over, and finally, one night in the car, three years later, I scream at him to never mention it again, and he never does. I regret this in some fundamental way. I don't miss his accusations, but I miss how he talked to me about everything, afraid to say nothing.

I silenced him, at least about the puppies. "It's not my fault!" I said. "It's the fault of the idiots who are too cheap to spay and neuter and then abandoned those puppies in the woods. You *have* to stop blaming me!"

But something changed in my son that day we found out the puppies were no more, a kind of sadness he'd never had before was implanted in him. He grieved terribly for them. I saw him lose faith in me, always the rescuer, the one who helped all animals. I couldn't save the puppies, let alone my child from the hurt. And, like my sweet son, I can't forget the four puppies who were tragically killed for one reason: they were born.

Just before we'd left for our Louisiana trip, a friend had us over and showed Winston and me four cute wiggly puppies before I left. I was shocked she had her dog bred, especially after knowing me and my mission for the last 30 years. Have I reached no one? Have I accomplished, then, nothing, saved no lives? How could my own friend, who knew better, become a breeder?

"Oh, I have homes for them all," she said proudly.

I bit my lip and didn't say, because it was too late, and because I was so upset with her for doing this, "I would have happily adopted four puppies from the pound for you to find homes for if you're so damn good at it."

Or: "You just denied four dogs homes."

Of course, after I returned to Alaska, I never went back to look at her four puppies again. I could only think of the four who just died so needlessly back in Louisiana.

Over the years, I've had to forgive myself because trying to save dogs when there are no homes for them can drive one crazy, and I have a son to raise and other dogs to rescue, humane societies to volunteer for, and spay/neuter vouchers to fill out. I want to believe that Charm, Terk, Tick-Tick, and Blackie are in puppy heaven now, living the life they deserved and never got a chance to live here, just because someone wouldn't spay his dog.

Lessons Learned from Louisiana Puppies

Life is sometimes short, and unfair. Enjoy the food and baths while you have them. Take pleasure in the little kindnesses you receive. Forgive us our sins, for we know not what we do. People should spay and neuter their pets. In many places, it's cheaper than a case of beer. And even if it's not, it's worth it. Don't leave your problems at the end of a road. Sometimes its better not to be born at all.

INTO THE FIFTIES IN ALASKA (2009-2014): MIZA & THE FOSTER PUPS

15 Miza: A Very Bad Dog

Dogs feel very strongly that they should always go with you in the car, in case the need should arise for them to bark violently at nothing right in your ear.

—Dave Barry

Let me preface this by saying I believe all dogs should be rescues from animal shelters and humane societies. And some of the best dogs you can get are already grown, influenced by others, even by bad owners, such as Bobbie, Dane, and Schatzy were.

All three were adults when I found them, and each was a beautiful soul, although each was unique: Bobbie was insecure and needy; Dane was saintly and mature; and Schatzy was at first a little terrifying, then playful and loving, and finally, matronly.

In all my experiences, I have never had what I would consider a "bad" dog. Oh, Newt and Bailey, who weren't actually mine, but Greg's, weren't the best behaved, I will admit. Bailey at first wanted to tree people we ran into on the trails, and Newt had his occasional biting issues. But in their hearts, they were good, and tried to be good. They both mellowed into fine friends.

But Miza, now. Miza is different. He is what I would call a bad dog. I sometimes expect the Dog Whisperer to show up and chastise me: "He needs to know you're the pack leader!"

How I Chose This Particular Piece of Trouble

I certainly didn't need another dog. I was living in Anchorage then, in the spring of 2009, back in the old neighborhood, with a small fenced yard and next-door-neighbors on the right who feared dogs (they own a fur store, so perhaps it was guilt?) and on the left, people who left their poor lonely Rottweiler outside, winter or summer (I'd sneak him chew toys through the fence). Greg, Winston, and I had moved from our four acres in Palmer to a tiny lot in the city with four large dogs: Schatzy, Blue, Chewie, and Newt.

Old age took Newt while I was on my first and only trip to Europe, stuck in the LaGuardia Airport trying to get home when the news came from Greg. So I suppose I was thinking of Greg, and how he now didn't have a dog, and how Schatzy was now at least 14 and showing signs of nearing the end, when I agreed with my niece Rachel and my son to go to animal control to see a dog she liked; Rachel had been taking a camp that day and had met a really sweet gray dog she had taken to, and she decided Aunt Jory should adopt her. Generally, I don't go to animal controls because I always adopt someone or try to rescue and find a home for someone.

She was a pit bull, as most of the dogs in the Anchorage shelter were that day, most abandoned there after some latest news story about a pit bull attack.

They all seemed sweet and kind and gentle enough, but I never had any intention of getting a pit bull. I had multiple dogs, walked in the dog parks every day, and didn't need the risk or the headache of fearing whether my dog would suddenly attack or people would scream at me.

But I saw a little black and white boy, I guessed about a year old, and the sign on his cage said "pointer-lab."

I liked him. He seemed happy and smaller than any dog I'd had, probably the size of a boxer. He was a boy like Newt, and mainly black with white like Newt, although certainly the breed was entirely different than Newt. To me he was just simply cute. And he needed a good home, and that was one thing I never doubted I could provide.

Winston and Rachel argued for her favorite pit bull, but I went home, then went back within the hour, and I adopted little black and white Miza.

Of course, I didn't know his name was Miza then. I didn't know what anyone had called him before; he was a stray that no one claimed. He earned his name, more than any dog I've ever had. Before I tell you how, let me tell you about his personality.

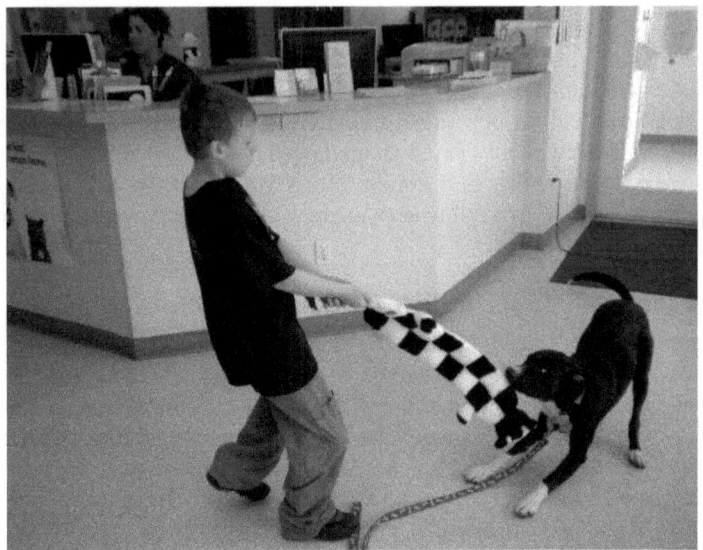

Miza at animal control seemingly normal and fun.

He's Got Personality...

From the day we pulled him out of Anchorage Animal Control, now some six years ago, he has been a black and white pile of trouble.

I think of all the dogs I've rescued, from animal controls, humane societies, or the streets. All have been tossed away by someone somewhere, but found their way to me. Every single one of them over the last three decades of my life has showed nothing but gratitude. Miza is different. He confronts the world that threw him away with That Bark.

By the time I got home from the miserably loud two-mile ride home from animal control that day I adopted him, I knew this was bad. I had my first of what were to become many Miza-caused headaches (previously, I had only suffered from migraines while I was pregnant), and this pain was right in the frontal lobes, my ears hurt and hearing loss had begun, my hair was turning gray, and I had taken on a new and permanent personality of constant seething irritation. I knew I desperately needed a prescription for Xanax or to take up drinking again, neither of which I did but which probably would have helped, and I had only shared my life with this dog for about 20 minutes.

When I looked at him in the light of my house, I thought, "Pointer-lab my ass, animal control!" and told him, "You're a pit!" Jesus, I got myself a pit, I thought, but here's me, adopt for life and all. And I thought it was actually touching of them to try to find him a home by leaving off "pit" on his description, in a way. But if anything happens, I thought, I'll blame them, but silent, as I do, seething inside, being so angry that I eat M&Ms all day long.

That's how I settle my accounts with the unfair world.

(He wasn't full pit, if any, but he had those brindle colors sneaked into the inside of the legs and a little blockiness to his head that made me wonder. Plus his personality was so damned obnoxious and different than anything I'd experienced in a dog before. Years later I fostered six puppies whose mother was a pointer [according to a different animal control], and indeed they had the same shaped heads and two were brindle, so I suppose it's possible. Or it's possible that "pointer" is the breed used by desperate animal controls to get pit-mixes adopted.)

So I'm stuck with you, I think, looking at him, watching him...worse, listening to him.

His bark is one of the worst sounds I've ever heard in my life. It is not a gentle "woof" saying hello. It is loud, both roaring and piercing at the same time, challenging, and maddening. Some think he is threatening an attack. At first, I wondered that too. He has a throaty, fierce, and terribly long growl that he blends into the end of each terrible bark. He used this to run my beloved Blue and Chewie and both my cats off my bed the minute he walked into my bedroom for the first time. Schatzy was already on the floor, unable to get on the bed anymore. He laid claim to the bed, immediately informed the entire four levels of our house (and probably the whole neighborhood block) of this new rule, and never gave it up, although after some months, or maybe years, Blue began to ignore him and climbed up anyway, and just recently, after only six years, Chewie did the same, once in a while.

Miza playing piano and barking away.

Miza's spot is mom's side of the bed, on my legs, usually, or where I want my legs to be, as I try to kick him over. He usually crawls back on top of them during the night. I love sleeping with dogs, but I've never had a dog literally take my spot. Dane, who'd lie right next to me, would suddenly stretch her long legs in joy when I'd say, "Good morning, Dane!" sometimes rolling me off the mattress if I wasn't ready. Woody took to sleeping behind me, his own head curled next to mine, separating me from my abusive then-boyfriend, Brock. I thought it was a sweet way to protect me, in Woody's gentle nonconfrontational way. The rest of my dogs would find their spots on the bed, always in the area where "mom" didn't sleep. But that was different than losing part of your very own sleeping space to a dog, and your legs going numb because he is on top of them. Particularly because by then my lower legs were about all that was left of me undestroyed by falls and other atrocities: three herniated disks in my neck, two torn rotator cuffs, fibromyalgia ravaging my joints, and oh yes, Buddy's gift of a torn ACL and meniscus.

Often at the dog park, Miza was the only dog barking in an entire park of 30 dogs. He would bark his way the entire mile walk around the lake. One man, Gerald, whom I walked with there many times, actually tried to kick Miza one day because he was so overcome with irritation and anger at Miza's bark of greeting. "I HATE Miza!" he screamed. Winston and I looked at each other in surprise and slight shock until Gerald, panting, gave up his failed attempts to kick our dog. Miza just barked louder every time he saw Gerald's boot coming toward him, but he easily dodged the ridiculous kicks. As much as I liked Gerald before that, I never walked with him again. And Miza never saw him again without greeting him with that horrendous bark, even as the years mellowed Miza and he now just (usually, except for Gerald) barked when he first got out of the car.

Chewie (middle), Blue (front), and Miza (top right) at the dog park.

I even, for the only time in my life, tried a bark collar. Well, about five bark collars, as they broke soon after I bought them, probably overloaded by Miza's insane sounds. Miza, not dumb, learned to just growl, loudly, when a bark collar was on, and I immediately removed it when he behaved (I do, after all, want him to warn me about moose, bears, and bad guys), but then the insane barks resumed as soon as he was bark-collar free. He learned nothing, except to change the volume of his output when the collar was on.

The $10,000 Accident

Then there's the expense. Two weeks after he came to make our lives miserable and ruin our feeling of "home," he decided to challenge a car in front of my house as I opened the door to put the dogs in the van and head to the dog park. Miza didn't quite get the rule yet...no streets. It was my fault; I just assumed he knew, after two weeks of the daily schedule...house to car, car to park, dog walk, car to house, nothing else. He ran right in the street just as a young woman, who seemed to be looking down (perhaps at her phone?) drove onto our street, and the crunch and bang were horrendously loud.

"What the hell!" Greg screamed at me, as he was outside working on the lawn. His first reaction was to blame me, as he should have, at least partially. Still, it could have been a child who ran in the street, and then would the driver hold any blame?

"Winston," I said, still and shocked, to my eight-year-old child who was behind me, getting ready to go to the park with me, "Miza's dead."

But amazingly, he wasn't.

Instead, he stood—still stood!—on the lawn across from our house, not moving, waiting for us to come get him. The bone on his left leg was somehow not broken, but all the skin and flesh and tendons had been ripped away.

So Miza, just a couple weeks from adoption, became a $10,000 dog. The leg was saved, but not without angry lectures from the vet about never having seen a dog break a cast before. They didn't understand Miza. Just because his leg was encased in a thick plastic case did not mean he wouldn't run—barking—at other dogs, or jump on the bed to run off the other dogs, or chase the cat down the stairs.

This was the same vet office that wouldn't give me my Blue back after x-raying her, and who never could "find" her x-rays. I was told by Pet Emergency that they were the only ones who could help a dog with a leg this bad.

Before transferring Miza from Pet Emergency to this vet, I called my friend Dave and explained what happened there with Blue. He knew everyone in town who had anything to do with dogs, due to his pet-related business and amazing years of volunteering. He was also, unlike me, a political animal, and managed to keep most people as friends instead of enemies.

After he talked with the office manager, my x-rays of Blue, which had been missing for years, suddenly appeared and were given to me, and we were promised that Miza would have the best treatment possible.

There was a lot of discussion over whether this leg could be saved, and the vet said we needed to bring him back every week to get anesthetized and the leg cleaned and checked and a new cast put on. This went on for about three months. Hence, the $10,000.

Looking back, I would have asked them to take the leg.

Not because of the money. I understand that, as a pet owner, things happen, and pets cost money, and what else is money for, but your family? But if I could go back, I would tell them to take the leg because a three-legged barking-growling monster hopping toward other dogs instead of running full force would draw pity from people, and not screams and kicks and glares. People would blame his personality on the sorry state of his being, instead of realizing that he's just a very bad dog.

People at the dog park would have stayed my friends instead of shunning me. For the next two years, after Cindy moved away, no one ever walked with me around the lake. It's true, Cindy drew the people in, but Miza chased them away, out of my life forever. I could tell when I greeted them and they scowled at Miza, and then me.

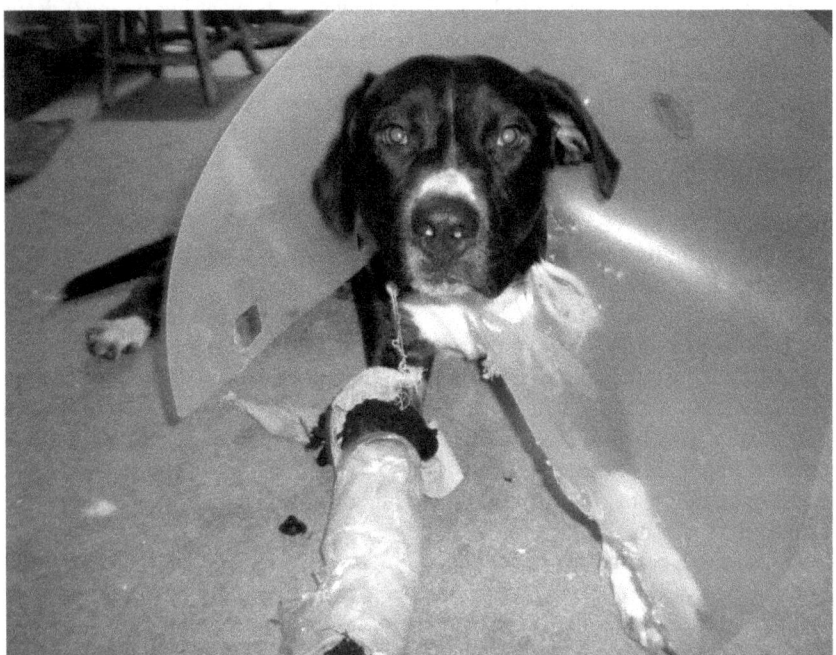

Miza would rip his cone and tear up his cast every week after the accident.

Car Rides

I've never had a dog who was bad in the car. Snoopy (and for a time, Blue) got car sick; Bobbie and Dane were a little too eager to see what was going on, but they were quiet about it; and the rest of them have just relaxed and enjoyed the ride. One of my favorite things to do, until I got Miza, was tell my dogs, "Let's go for a ride!" and then go drive somewhere far away to explore some new wilderness trails to hike. Such rides have always been peaceful and fun.

Before.

But here's how Miza rides in a car: Jumping from the front seat to the back, barking at the other dogs, jumping on the other dogs, pacing, whining, growling, vocalizing every second of the ride at full volume—that's Miza. For the first time in my life, I bought a car separator to block a dog from the front seat. I figured it was a safety as well as a sanity issue. Miza ripped it apart, even somehow destroying the metal grates.

My beautiful van, which had transported numerous children and up to five dogs at a time for two years yet still looked brand new, suddenly looked like it had been dragged from a junk heap as soon as you peaked inside. Miza nervously and frantically tried to make a nest in all the seats, scratching them to shreds.

Per people's advice, also for the first time in my life with dogs, I tried to put the beast in a crate while in the car (I never believed in crate training, and still don't, as so many people misunderstand it and actually leave their grown dogs in a crate all day). He barked louder than ever, and when we got to the dog park, jumped out and ran at the first dog he could see, barking so furiously that the owner ran away, and he knocked that dog over in his frustrating dash to escape that damned crate and to tell me what the hell you'd better never put me in that again! (Was he, perhaps, one of those dogs left in a crate all day while his "owner" was at work, driven mad from anxiety?) I had to grab him as the owner screamed hysterically at me, and take him back to the car, embarrassed and crying. We didn't get our walk that day.

About His Name

Back to Miza's name, now that you have the picture. The little boy with his new dog couldn't decide on a name for him. Over the first week or so, my son changed the new dog's name from Midnight to Inky to Zebra. By the end of the second week, we had arrived at Zebra, and that's what the vet's chart said. But we picked up Rachel one day, and I heard the two cousins in the back of the car, arguing about which name was better. She preferred Midnight.

"Why don't you just combine the names and call him MIZA?" I said. "It's an acronym. M for Midnight, I for Inky, and Z for Zebra."

"What's the A for?" they asked, chiming.

I know I shouldn't have said it in front of two little children, and I've never thought of a dog and this word in the same breath, but I said it, exhausted and irritated after a mere two weeks of living with the little monster: "Asshole."

The children giggled happily, and so decided that was indeed his name.

Miza, Blue, and Chewie in my van.

The Trauma of Life with Miza

Miza aged me, and he ruined my life. I have no doubt about it. I have been blessed to know many good dogs. I am sorry that my 50s had to be destroyed by this fiend. But that's the way it is.

And anyway, I could only hope he would mellow with age, as dogs tend to do.

Of course, he's not just any dog.

I don't know what makes him so much trouble. Maybe there's some insecurity, like Bobbie had, but Bobbie was sweet while Miza is furious. Maybe there was some abuse in his past, like Bobbie, and I suspected Schatzy, and maybe being a male, instead of taking it internally, he lets the world know externally through that awful bark and those terrible body slams he still does to Blue-Chew when we get out of the car.

Sometimes when I read about how neutering is supposed to make a male dog gentler, I think, what a bunch of bullshit. When I had got Buddy, I was actually full-on into reading animal rights philosophers at the time, and although certainly still pro-spay-neutering, I called various vets around Seattle asking if they could give Buddy a vasectomy instead of neuter him. Every clinic said no, ridiculous, why would we?

Because I don't want to change his personality, I said.

But of course, it didn't. Buddy was sweet before, and sweet after, and nothing changed at all. What neutering does do is stop the desperate hunt for a female in heat. That is comforting to both genders, no doubt.

What neutering did for Miza, I don't know. I assume he was probably about the same level of asshole before as he was after. Maybe it helped a little. It's hard to believe he could have been any worse.

I can't say he's a "dumb" dog, as he is bright, curious, and learns tricks as fast as a magician. But he is definitely mentally challenged in some way.

"Were you dropped on your head?" I ask him sometimes, half-joking and scratching his neck and ears. But what I'm really wondering is, "Were you kicked in the head, hard, when you were a puppy? Were you thrown off a balcony and landed on that beautiful little dog brain, and things got mixed up in there? Did someone think it was funny to feed to you marijuana-laced brownies?" (The latter was a tragedy I walked into at a high school party, as a poor husky puppy sat sick and confused and frightened, while everyone but me laughed at him.)

I think maybe some terrible tragedy befell Miza in his youth; why else would he be so obnoxious? Especially after moving in with the most loving dog-mom in the world?

Or could it be he was just born this way, trying and wanting to please but unable to control himself?

Take the ball for instance. Miza wants me to throw his ball more than any dog ever has wanted a ball thrown. Or, in the summer, at the lakes, he wants me throw him sticks. He brings them to me desperately, but then begins the battle. He can't let go of the stick, or the ball, or anything he has grabbed with his wolf-teeth. Here's how it plays out:

He growls ferociously if you try to take it. He pulls and tugs, and the sounds emanating from him are so frightening that you think he doesn't want you to throw it or touch it at all. So you let go, and he drops it, and wags his tail, and barks happily, asking you to throw it. So you bend over to throw it, and he furiously grabs it away. Over and over. I sicken of this game, of his sickness.

Years and years have gone by, and training, and he still can't get this, but he improves slightly. He has learned to let go of the giant ball, for example, with his teeth, eventually, if I'll stay and agree to throw it, but then he holds on to it tightly with his paws and arms, so tight that I can't remove it, growling and barking at me as I reach my precious fingers to grab it. So I ignore him, saying, no more, that's it, and finally, desperately, he drops it, his teeth only an inch from it, begging, please throw it, I promise I won't grab it. Most of the time he still does though. When I do get to throw the ball, you never saw a happier dog go running through the woods to fetch it and proudly bring it back to me, then once again refusing to drop it and leave it.

In their younger years, my dogs Bobbie and Schatzy both loved chasing Frisbees, leaping up into the air to catch them and bring them back to me, gently placing them at my feet for another toss. Not Miza. No Frisbee has survived one throw, even the $20 "nonbreakable" ones. Miza runs and catches a Frisbee, smooth as water, then stands and tears it into a dozen pieces, maybe bringing back the largest piece, then refusing to drop it for me. Every single time.

Yet he's smart. He's the gentlest dog I've ever seen on a leash. He breezed through dog training classes without a hitch, except that inane barking.

"Oh, just squirt Binaca Blast toward his mouth, and that'll stop the barking," the elderly teacher smiled.

Yeah, right. All it did was teach him to dodge breath spray and bark louder in complaint. Week after week we went to obedience classes, where Miza easily performed every trick, but I could see the dog trainer developing nervous ticks as his bark began to drive her slightly mad.

I know exactly how you feel, I thought. And you only see him an hour a week, lady!

Even with his tendonless leg, Miza is the fastest dog at the dog park, zigzagging happily around them all, making friends with none.

Miza with a stick at the dog park.

He picked up on the rules of flyball quickly...the ball, the jumps, the tug...got it (and he only crossed the room to grab some other dog's much bigger, better tug three times).

At flyball, we were told dogs had to be in crates when not training, and I tried to explain, but they didn't believe me. "Just cover the crate with a blanket; he'll be quiet."

"Have you actually met Miza?" I grumbled. The covered, crated dog's insane barking drove the flyball team to actually carry him and his crate out to a truck during one flyball demonstration, as they couldn't stand the noise anymore, after just a few minutes. I'm thinking, I've lived with that noise for years. I'm thinking, my dog will never be able to compete in flyball, and I was right (although probably some of it was due to his $10,000 forever-damaged leg, with which he couldn't make the turn correctly). (The flyball club, Alaska Dogs Gone Wild, was incredibly patient with Miza, Winston, and me, and I admire all their members for giving us two years of their lives even though our crazy dog was clearly not going to make it.)

Winston and Miza at a flyball demonstration (Photo by Jim Haga).

Miza loves his toys, and loves to play with them, throwing them, chasing them, rolling on his back and holding them in the air with his two paws (something I'd only seen Bobbie do...using her paws like human hands). Yet he's toy aggressive and possessive, terribly insecure about having none, just as he is about losing me.

I have an entire drawerful of toys and chew toys for the dogs, but for the first few years, Miza wants the one he can't have, the one Blue or Chewie might be enjoying. This latter problem, he did finally overcome, but it seemed so unnecessary, so selfish, so...so *undog* of him!

Since 1979, when I was 19, I have always had at least two dogs at a time, and I'm always surprised to see this greed in Miza, since I've never witnessed a speck of such behavior in any other dog. If I'm petting Blue, Miza shoves in to be petted, for example. And he doesn't just push in to be petted too; no, he has to run Blue off with his barks and growls at the same time.

If it's Schatzy's time for attention and grooming, Miza barks his complaints. (These things will ease off with time, but a long time. Years. Years in which I age as fast as a dog.)

Is it possible for dogs to be bipolar? I have wondered. All kinds of questions have come into my life since he threw himself barking into my pack of peaceful, older, female dogs, making us all regretful. Sometimes we look each other in the eye, Blue and Chewie and me in particular. What do we do? How do we get our life back? Chewie in particular looks at me and tells me, quite firmly, he doesn't belong here. Why did you bring him here? Blue, ever cheerful, accepts him as part of the pack, and ignores his misbehaviors. As long as it doesn't affect her breakfast and dinner, which it doesn't, she tolerates everything else just fine.

Schatzy, whose last few years were not lucid, since she suffered senility, blindness, deafness, and hip problems, but stubbornly refused to reach the point of death (or more accurately, died for about three years), mostly ignored him. She had that happy type of senility, only wrecked by her nighttime barks ("seeing ghosts," as my vet called it), but even blind, her tail wagged happily when I knelt to pet her or help her out the door, and being deaf, she had no idea the hellish sounds that drove the rest of the household—except Winston, I suppose—crazy.

Miza certainly had no desire—ever—to leave my side once I claimed him. He follows me up and down the stairs, into my office, into my car, out of my car, and never leaves me, not for a moment, not ever, unless he knows I'm safe and Winston wants to play ball or trampoline in the yard. I am possessed by this dog; I am owned by this dog. I don't believe in ownership; I believe in companionship, but Miza, dear desperate fool, believes in ownership. He's got it completely backwards; the way I always heard it, people own dogs, but that's not happening here.

I have never been so sure in my life that I, my son, and my partner Greg are safe from other people, dogs, wild animals, or anything else that might threaten us. This dog owns us, and will stand between us and danger.

But fortunately, few threats come my way, except by people who can't stand my dog.

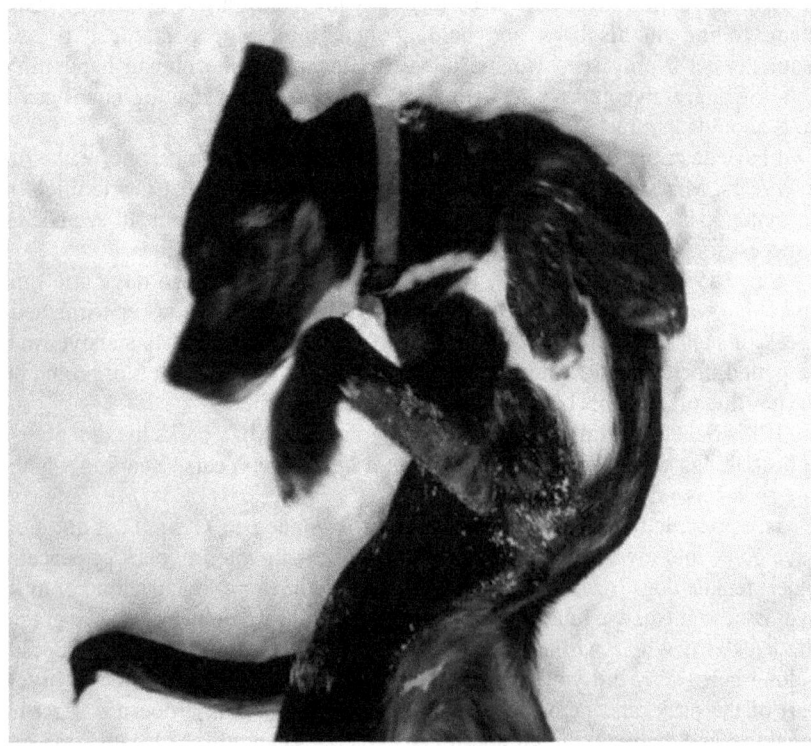

Miza rolling happily in the snow, pretending he doesn't ruin my life.

Marked for Death

I do know—relief, relief—Miza doesn't intend to fight other dogs; he just seems to want to inform the world—particularly anything he sees out the window of my car and any other dogs, not their people—that he is king, he is mighty, he is in charge.

But his bark caused one dog to hate him so much she targeted him for death. By this time I had moved to a different house than Greg, up to the hillside of Anchorage, with acreage for my dogs. It is possible that Miza's incredibly irritating personality helped ruin our little home life; in any case, our relationship needed a temporary break, so I moved away, with the source of my irritation right there barking all the way to our new abode, of course.

I thought we'd be happy with our acre and our creek, but I quickly found out that the next-door-neighbors on one side hated all my dogs, and the next-door-neighbors on the other, after six months, got a full-on white satanic pit bull, let's call her "She-devil," who hated Miza.

After I saved the screaming other neighbor from the maybe six-month-old She-devil one night, with Miza jealously watching out my window as I played with her and walked her home, I suppose I helped create the mess. The pit bull seemed nice enough, and yes she was tormenting the neighbor, but just attacking her shoes, I assumed, in the way puppies do. I petted her and convinced her to follow me to her home. Staring out my window, his body trembling, those terrible growls and barks building up in his throat, was Miza, watching the entire show.

Never since my childhood dog Snoopy had I had a dog consumed with jealousy over me, unwilling to share me.

But, for whatever reason, the next time we saw the pit bull, she was headed toward my yard when I was out playing with my dogs one day, Miza ran toward her, barking, as is his way, announcing his authority over everything and everyone, and in turn she burst forward and grabbed him by the throat, pulled him to the ground, and began chewing, carefully, with sure commitment, to ensure his death. In the meantime, the neighbor's sweet other dogs, who for those six months had been fine with Miza's dominance, gleefully attacked all other parts of him, the Great Dane biting his back, the tiny terrier attacking his face, the bloodhound going for everything he could find.

My dog was being killed right in front of me! I was screaming for help, trying to pull her off him, but pit bulls don't let go. It took my neighbors and me about 5 minutes to get She-devil's jaws open, and in that time I was watching my Miza's life ebb away, slowly, his eyes rolling desperately at me.

I loved him, madly, purely, completely, I knew then, despite his being an asshole. I would do anything to save him.

So I built a $12,000 fence to keep She-devil out. Still, she found her way over the deep snow banks or followed us into my garage, terrorizing us always, hunting, hunting him, to finish the kill.

I bought mace. I talked with animal control about what they do (they use a stick to get the jaws open). I built more fences. I complained to my neighbors that they had to build a fence too, that she was dangerous.

They wouldn't; they always blamed Miza, and later, the other neighbors' Labrador retriever. They leashed her, but they were too elderly and frail to hold her back when she spied my boy, my asshole, my Miza.

Chewie, Miza (being good!), and Blue at the dog park in Anchorage.

I even took Miza to doggie day care, 12 times, just to be sure he wasn't at fault in this matter. He had never got in a fight at the dog parks, and had met hundreds of dogs on our various walks there, but I wanted to be sure. Every time I came back for him (and Blue and Chewie, since I didn't want Miza to think I was abandoning only him), after 4 to 6 hours, I'd always ask, "How did he do?"

"He did fine," they said.

"Are you *sure*?" I'd demand.

"Absolutely, he's no trouble at all!"

(All my dogs were unhappy that I left them at doggie daycare, though. We always walked together, including at dog parks with numerous other dogs. Why would I put them in a group of 15 to 30 dogs, and then just leave? It confused them. Our daily routine was to always go places together, not for me to leave them in a pack and disappear, and honestly, it was no fun for me either. I missed them and worried about them. But I wanted to be sure that Miza was fine with other dogs and was not creating the very-serious and dangerous situation with the neighbor dog. I wanted to be able to tell my neighbors, "He not only goes to dog parks every day, but he also goes to doggie daycare, and he's never gotten in a fight with another dog." This was true, but they still blamed him.)

Miza is no trouble at all when he's sleeping with his teddy bear.

So Winston and I lived in our house on the Anchorage hillside, stalked by She-devil, and I, at least, was terrified. My son said the pit bull was friendly and nice when he was at the neighbor's house, although she did turn and attack their other dogs once in a while. I don't know what went on there. I just know the more I read about pits, the less safe I felt. It seemed that Miza was her "mark," and it was therefore over for him. She would never forgive him, never let up until he was dead.

Miza was stupid about it, of course. He had to have known he couldn't beat her. He wasn't a fighter, just a barker, and every time She-devil got him, she did the same thing...an instant grab by the throat, chewing carefully toward the jugular, as pits are bred to do. Once I opened my window to say hi to my neighbor lady, who was walking down the road, looking for her runaway pit, it turns out. Miza saw the pit running toward us, having heard his horrible Miza-bark from ¼ mile away, and my fool dog literally jumped out the partially rolled-down window toward his death. She-devil was on him in a few seconds. Miza never once got a bite in; I don't know why he kept trying. That's the day I tried the mace out, but I had to use the whole can (on both dogs and the neighbor lady, it turns out) before her pit bull would let go long enough for me to throw Miza in the car.

I couldn't report She-devil to animal control; I couldn't give them the address and names. I didn't have the heart to cause her death. It turned out I didn't have to report her. My other neighbor, who hated my dogs, and actually called animal control and complained about them after the surveyors came out and marked my fence (which clarified some of which she called her yard was mine, and was therefore the real reason for her call), had the pleasure of having her Labrador attacked by the white pit bull from hell twice, both times when her teenage daughter was walking him, and she—finally, the second time—called animal control. By the time, maybe an hour later, animal control showed up to collect her, the elderly couple said the pit was living with family members near

Fairbanks, 358 miles away,. All I knew was, she was gone, and I was happy. My dog would live.

One night, a few weeks later, I went outside with my dogs, and here She-devil came, running full toward Miza, who was fortunately behind my 6-foot fence. I called my neighbors and left a message: "If she ever comes to visit again, I want to know in advance." They never spoke to me again. But I knew I could still never walk my dog outside my house, throw a ball in my driveway, park the car and load and unload the dogs anywhere but the closed garage, as long as I lived there.

There was one other fight involving Miza, who had now lived with me about four years. I rented a room in my house, and the tenant, Jim, brought his dog, a friendly setter mix "Red." Jim then almost immediately left for 6 weeks training in the "states," and I and my three dogs and his one got along fine. I took Red on our walks; Red slept on the bed, ignoring Miza's complaints, and even played with Miza. I was very happy about this, because only one dog had ever played with Miza, my friend Cindy's dog Cadence. When they met at the dog park, they played and rolled like crazy. Miza didn't know how to play gentle, but Cindy took it well, joking that Cadence was the kind of female who liked abusive males.

Miza (top) and his best friend Cadence wrestling at the dog park.

Cindy moved away from Alaska, not able to bear another winter, as many people do, and no other dog could stand to be near Miza.

It's kind of like having an unpopular child who can't make a friend. You feel so bad for him. You try to teach him proper manners, but he won't listen. You try to explain, "Look, if you don't charge at them and yell [bark] all the time, they'd know you're really a nice guy!" But Miza, even though his tail was wagging when he barked, did not give off the proper signals. So he had no friends.

Well, two years after Cadence moved away, Miza finally had found a dog—Red—who played with him, and we all did fine, for about six months.

Then, one night, I told Winston to go shovel the walkway in front of our door; our tenant always did it, and I thought it might be nice if my 12-year-old son did something around the house other than play Minecraft.

Now, Miza is very protective of me and Winston. One thing I do appreciate about him is how, on our walks, he stays close to me, and he stops in front of me and barks to warn me when a bear or moose is close by, while Blue and Chewie will just silently run to play with whatever beast is approaching us, and then run terrified to hide behind me when they are chased. I have to admit, I feel safer when Miza is with me on the trails than I did with just Blue-Chew and Schatzy.

But this personality trait of his—to protect his family—took a bad turn that night.

Red suddenly attacked the shovel that Winston was holding, in a playful way I'm sure, treating it as if it was a giant stick. So Miza attacked Red. And Red attacked back, and once again, Miza was losing, getting torn to pieces instead of chewed this time, his ear and head shredded, while Red had no marks at all. In the meantime, Jim ran out and started punching Miza into the wall, over and over, and Winston just stood there silently, and I was in my bedroom upstairs watching the news and heard none of it.

It lasted maybe a minute, if that.

But all consequences were bad.

My tenant ended up with a bite on his lip, which Winston said was from Jim's own dog because Miza was "holding Red's neck, like She-devil did to him." My tenant told the doctor and then animal control that Miza bit him, insisting that his dog never would.

Now Miza was legally categorized as a bad dog, and one more event and he could be killed. He was put on two weeks' quarantine, at my house, to be separated from Red, which meant that Red got the run of the place, but I had to call from upstairs and get my tenant to put his dog in his room so I could take Miza outside.

It was miserable and unfair. Miza was a bad dog, but I believe he was trying to do a good dog deed that night. In his perspective, Red was attacking Winston, and therefore, without thought, he jumped in. Would Blue or Chewie have done the same? Absolutely not. So maybe, back to the Preface of this book, and my friend Nick asking me, "Are boy and girl dogs different?" yes, maybe male and female dogs are different. Maybe the males can get more jealous and more protective, as well as fight (although Woody and Buddy had nothing in them to even consider a fight...they were so friendly and loving, so it could be a breed thing more than a male-female thing).

Should Miza have been punished by law? Absolutely not. I read Title 17. I wanted to throw the law back in the animal control officer's face. The "levels" shouldn't have applied in this case, with the dogs both in one household. There were also conflicting versions of who bit whom, Miza was the only dog left bleeding, Jim beat Miza, Jim jumped in between two dogs so the bite was not intended for a human but for each other, and Miza was protecting his boy. These are all factors that should have mattered and something we should and could have worked out ourselves, in the household. I, after all, lived and slept with both these dogs for six weeks and had walked them together every day while the owner was gone. But now, my dog was marked, and I was penalized.

For me, it was the end of my friendship with my tenant. And it was the end, at last, of Anchorage and its ridiculous dog laws forever. I walked away from my house on the hillside, still unsold two years later, happy to leave that place forever, and moved back to the Valley.

(The good thing is that my family was reunited again in Palmer, and Greg, Winston, and I live a happy existence together here. So in some small way, the terror Miza who perhaps helped separate Greg and me by creating an unbearably stressful household perhaps helped bring us together again.)

The whole Anchorage hillside experience left me a little bitter that the white terror who lived next door could stalk and attack for years yet escape any punishment, but now I was pegged the owner of a bad dog.

Okay, well, he *is* a bad dog. Or at least an asshole.

All God's Creatures

> *All things bright and beautiful,*
> *All creatures great and small,*
> *All things wise and wonderful,*
> *The Lord God made them all.*
>
> — Cecil Frances Alexander

I sometimes wonder if God created Miza, or if someone on the opposite end of the religious spectrum did.

I ponder, "Well, I had a dog (Dane) who was truly a saint, so perhaps I was due for a some kind of lesson by having another kind of nature's creature."

But if so, what is the lesson?

Was it like when I finally earned enough money to buy myself my first horse, Cherokee, and she ended up being the opposite of everything I expected in a horse? Her feelings toward humans were certainly bitter disrespect. The only time she was happy was when I was flying through the air after she'd bucked, reared, or suddenly turned and jumped a fence. During our winter rides, she took obvious pleasure in swinging her beautiful pinto hips into spruce trees so the boughs would drop their heavy snow right on my head, completely missing hers.

What did Cherokee teach me? What has Miza taught me?

Maybe that not all God's creatures are satisfied with their place in life as pets, with rules, with fences, with ownership? That love can't always be enough, even though it was with Bobbie, to cure a dog's insecurities? I don't know.

What I do know is that each of the dogs I have known is an individual, with unique interests, abilities, and personalities.

It's just that Miza's personality is oh so hard to live with.

He's the only dog where I've calculated what year he will leave me with a little bit of hope, instead of tears.

"I've made it six years, and he was a year old when I got him, so there should be about six or seven left," I struggle to do the math. "I will be about 60 or 61 years old when he goes to whatever place he's doomed—I mean blessed—to go to. I can make it that long. I can survive this."

I pat him and smile, thinking of the time ahead when I get to visit his grave, read a poem, and cry a little for missing him.

He gives me a dog smile, and then breaks my eardrums again with his hellhound bark, whacks me in the stomach with his giant, heavy red ball, and grabs it away when I reach for it.

"What did I do to deserve you, you little asshole?" I ask him. I feel a little guilty, as I've never called a dog a bad name before, no, not once, my entire life.

But Miza just wags his tail madly, knocking over my garbage can in the process, and barks happily at me in reply. I cover my ears and sigh.

"A" Stands for...

As the years go by, the poor beast tries so hard to be good that I can't help loving him, even if he does basically fail every attempt.

Now, instead of barking all day long, he just barks if someone drives up to my house (my "doorbell," I call him), as I go anywhere near the car, when he first gets in the car, as we near a park where we're going to walk, and when we first get out of the car for our walk. Those first few moments of our daily walks are horrible, for me, for Blue and for Chewie, especially, as he pounces on them barking hysterically, but also for anyone within earshot, but we are all glad the barking does come to an end, and then we can enjoy our walk.

For example, before we left Anchorage, and I still went every day to the dog park, a lady joked, "Did you get a new dog?" just ten minutes after she first saw him get out of my car. By then, we were passing each other with our numerous dogs, halfway around the lake, and Miza was now a gentle, sweet "normal" dog, wagging his tail, dog-smiling hello. He'd changed from Cujo to Lassie.

If he does bark during our walk, I know there is something in front of me I need to be aware of, and based on his stance, I often turn around, as I assume it's a moose. If it's a person or a bicycle, it is one bark, a warning and a greeting, as he runs forward. If it's a moose (or perhaps, at times, a bear), it is three or four barks, blocking my way firmly, unmoving.

As for car rides, the drives to a park are still infernal noisy anxious terrors, but the drives after our walk are fine, as long as he has the front passenger seat to lie on, his foot or head resting on my leg. If someone else dares to sit there, then Miza makes his dissatisfaction known by the jumping and whining and sometimes barking, even though I've just tried to wear him out with a rigorous walk through the woods.

And sleeping in a bed with him has changed slightly too. Now if my legs are sore or I want him to give me more room, I say, "Miza, move!" and he actually does, and he stays over there, just giving me enough room to stretch my legs out comfortably. Now when Chewie wants to get on the bed, he lets her, without argument or domination, and Blue has long ago learned he is all bark without consequence. He has never bitten Blue, Chewie, Schatzy, or the six foster puppies who came into our home, no matter how irritated he seems to be.

Miza is a bad dog, but I have no fear that he would ever hurt me or Greg or Winston, or any other person unless they were trying to harm one of us. He loves us intensely, possessively. If someone broke into my house or car, Miza would die to save us. He is probably the closest dog to "Old Yeller" than I've ever met. Old Yeller as a dog character was both cunningly wicked while at the same time heroically good. Until I met Miza, I didn't know such seemingly conflicting personality traits are possible in one dog, but I certainly now know they are.

The things that are unacceptable in a dog by neighbors and dog laws—barking concerns, running toward someone or something, and protective behavior—are the things that assure me that I have never been so safe in my life. Miza is a "bad" dog to the current way of thinking; however, perhaps—is it possible?—he is not so bad at all.

So these days, the "A" has changed from "Asshole" to "Annoying."

Most of all he is the dog every boy needs. Winston and Miza wrestle, play tug of war and Frisbee, did flyball together, and jump on a trampoline, always together. When my son explores the Alaska woods, I know he's safe as long as he has Miza with him.

It took a few years, but Miza somehow finally realized we are his forever family, and no matter how rotten he's been, we aren't abandoning him. This sweetened him up a lot. Now he tries his hardest to be good, and most of the time, he is.

I'm hoping, after another few years, maybe before he dies or I do, that "A" will stand for Angel.

But honestly, I doubt it.

Miza, Blue, and Chewie, all on my bed at last.

Miza starting to mellow after I got the foster puppies (next chapter). Photo by David Jensen.

Lessons Learned from Miza

Tell the world when you have complaints, but then stop talking about it. If you want to play with others, you have to share your toys. Don't piss off the neighbors, especially when one of them is a pit bull. A boy can be the best toy of all.

16 Foster Puppies

Whoever said you can't buy happiness forgot about puppies.
—Gene Hill

I suppose there's a time in practically every young boy's life when he's affected by that wonderful disease of puppy love.... I mean the real kind, the kind that has four small feet and a wiggly tail, and sharp little teeth than can gnaw on a boy's finger; the kind a boy can romp and play with, even eat and sleep with.
-Wilson Rawls, Where the Red Fern Grows

Kip (left) and Harper.

"If I ever say I will foster puppies again, please kill me," I post on Facebook.

At the time I write this, in November 2014, my friends know it's my typical sarcastic humor, but I'm not laughing. I have been crying straight for three days.

My Facebook friends justifiably don't have any pity for me. The "I told you so's" fill up my computer screen. Every time I mentioned the puppies the last few weeks, they asked me how many I was going to adopt. "Zero," I would always reply. "If I didn't have Miza, who equals ten dogs of work, I'd consider it, but how would I ever pick one? I will take them back as I'm required to, and that will be that."

First of all, here's how it happened: It is summer, and to encourage my son to get off the computer, I go with him through volunteer training at animal control. They have a dog walking program (as well as washing pet bowls, making Kong treats, doing laundry, watering pets, cleaning up dog poo, and lots of other jobs the staff appreciates volunteers doing).

During volunteer training, I tell the Public Relations (PR) director that I would be happy to foster puppies after she says they have some. It's late July, and the warmest, loveliest, longest summer we've ever had in Alaska, and I can leave them outside and won't have the issues of house destruction I had with Blue-Chew.

She starts listing rules for foster parents, and when one is that I have to keep them separate from any other dogs, I say, "Well, that's impossible. I have three."

"Well, we can't risk the puppies getting parvo."

"Okay," I say, although I assure her mine are older and have all their shots. So I think that's done, and I think that's a good thing.

I know one thing, I'll never foster in winter, or get a puppy in winter. That was hard enough with Blue-Chew nine years ago, and I've had surgeries on my neck, both shoulders, and knee since then, along with fibromyalgia and arthritis, so even walking can be a painful experience, let alone carrying puppies down the stairs to the outside every hour or so.

But somehow, in October, the PR director calls me and wants me to take four puppies, just for a week or two, to get them weaned and ready for spaying and neutering. As the week of waiting for animal control to release them turns to two, and I think of the poor little things in a cage, I am ready and actually excited about being around puppies again. Also, I figure with four of them I'll never be able to pick one so there's no risk of what happened with Blue-Chew.

By the time I am allowed to take them, there are suddenly six, as two more have been found out in the tire piles near Big Lake where these came from. And it's now late October, and the ground and sky have frozen (although thankfully, the snow is late this year). There will be no leaving them outside.

In any case, that is how six little puppies come to live at my house.

Two of the foster puppies; I called the one on the right Bella and would have adopted her if I could.

First of all, as much as I dearly and fully love Blue-Chew, I have to say these six puppies are Harvard material compared to my sweet dogs (and previous foster puppies).

They learn housetraining quickly (okay, after two weeks of constant cleanup), and walk with me in the cold but still snowless yard often. I work so hard cleaning and walking them that I lose 11 pounds in those three weeks. Speaking of weeks, it is supposed to be one or two, but because of a Halloween event animal control personnel and volunteers are decorating for, I am told to keep them another week.

"But I'm getting too attached," I warn several animal control personnel, but they just smile.

A week later, it is too late.

I am completely attached, and I love each of them. Winston is attached to them as well. They love us too. I have become their "mama" and my son is their playmate. I have the admiration of six little toddlers, but now it is time at last to take them back.

The six foster puppies. The two black ones in front were to become my newest dogs. The little girl in the top left, Bella, I never got to say goodbye to.

Perhaps I made a mistake that last week by sitting down with them in the evenings, four on my lap, two on each side of me, and reading them a novel. As I read the Dean Koontz book to them, they would happily snuggle up with me, some sighing contentedly, others chewing the hard covers of my novel as I read away. They'd watch me like adoring preschoolers stare at their beloved teacher during reading time. Life, they'd decided, was good, with this new mama, unlimited toys, lots of blankets, walks every two hours, cuddles and baby talk and books to listen to and eat. And life was good for me too. I felt blessed by their trust and adoration.

My kind animal-loving son with four of the foster puppies.

I can't think of a time I ever took a dog to animal control (except the Louisiana puppies, but that was not my decision or my car, but my friend's), but now I am taking my six babies and leaving them there.

After making sure they are two to a cage, have toys to play with and towels to lie on and newspapers to go potty on, I cuddle each one and say goodbye.

It is awful, but I am okay with it. My main concern is that they are spayed and neutered that day, as I was told they "probably" would be.

I e-mail the director twice, reminding her they've had no food or water; have they been spayed yet? Her answers are vague and a little belittling after all I've done, so at 4:30 I go by to check on them.

I can hear them wailing from the locked puppy room and their tiny cages right when I walk in the door. They have not been spayed or neutered. But I go into their room and comfort them, and immediately their cries turn to happy sounds.

I am back, and they are at peace. I brought their puppy chow from home, and I start to feed and water them. I can see someone tried, but all the bowls have been knocked over and their food is under their cages in a tray they can't reach.

"I promise I'll come visit every day," I tell them, "until you are adopted. I will come lots. It will be okay. *I promise.*" This will be hard on me, but I have seen how they calmed down when they saw me, and I know it's important that I'm here for their transition to their new homes.

Suddenly an animal control worker comes in, grabs their bowls out and tells me angrily, "I already fed them!"

"Their food and water is spilled under their cages," I said, stunned. "Look!"

She refuses to look, and repeats, "I already fed them."

I grab their bowls and start putting them back, saying, "Look, I have lived with these puppies and taken care of them and cleaned their poop and fed them for the last 3½ weeks, and I know when they are hungry and thirsty! I think you should be a little thankful for what I've done!" I'm angry and crying at the same time.

She grabs the bowls out again and slams them down and leaves, after saying a few more words to me which did not sound thankful at all. (At the time I thought she should be fired; looking back, I'm not sure; I was much too attached to be logical, certainly.) The puppies stare at me, confused and frightened. I give them their food back, trying to hide my tears and sound comforting to them.

After I returned home, I e-mailed my complaint about the employee to the manager. I also wanted to know why they were not spayed and neutered, and said that they should be allowed to come home with me until they were ready to do so.

"I worked hard housetraining them so they'll make good pets, and this will all be ruined if they spend days in a cage," I told her.

Her response, after several e-mails, was that my "fostering duties are over" and I was not to visit the puppies anymore.

Miza was amazingly gentle with all the foster puppies.

I was devastated. I had promised the puppies. I cried for days in guilt for not seeing them and in anger for my treatment and theirs.

I finally made an appointment with the borough manager, taking my complaint there, bringing my son along o he could learn about the power of politics. (I do understand that agencies have their rules, and that to work at an animal control one has to "harden" oneself, or how else would you manage what has to be done? I am clearly not cut out for fostering, which the director, no doubt, was trying to tell me by forbidding me to see them, but on the other hand, I had given them my full-time attention for nearly a month, so I was allowing me daily visits was too much to ask for.)

Still not welcomed to see the puppies, I faxed over a request to adopt two of them. I figured that was the only way I could see them. I don't know how this happened. I didn't want more dogs. Miza, as I told everyone, was too much trouble, it was hard to think of bringing in more. But if adopting was the only way I could go see them, then that is what I would do.

The next day, five of the six puppies were spayed and neutered. I was able to finally see them and adopt two and say goodbye to and hold and comfort the rest, except for dear Bella, whom they said would be "in recovery" for a few days as she'd just been spayed, and I couldn't see her. I would never see her again.

I noticed my posters were removed from their cages; I have no idea why. Maybe because I suggested adopting two, which was, it turns out, against their rules (although they did allow me, as the foster mom, to take home two instead of one). "Why?" I asked, when I was told about their "one-puppy" rule.

"So they'll bond with the adoptive family instead of each other."

"That's so ridiculous; two puppies can play with other, and of course they bond to each other as well as to their human family," I said, probably speaking before thinking, per usual, but giving as an example Blue and Chewie's love of me as well as each other. Here was what I wrote on the posters I had put up that were removed:

> *From the "Foster Mom":*
>
> *These are the **smartest** puppies I've ever been around! They were actually potty trained within a few days of coming to my house. I just had to take them out every 2 to 3 hours, and they would hold it. They will also hold the #2 all night if needed; some of them "had to go" during the night, but they used the newspapers I set out in a corner for them. At first, I kept them in a large pen (at night) with lots of blankets, and they didn't want to soil them. So they would hold it, as long as I didn't sleep in too late. (They might need to be retrained as once they are back at animal control, they won't be going outside.)*

> *They are sweet, friendly, loving, never barked, and didn't whine or cry (of course they had each other to sleep with)! They love to sleep on my soft "outdoor" furniture (which I brought indoors) with lots of blankets, cuddled together.*
>
> *They love to play with each other. (If you can adopt two, they will have each other to play with!)*
>
> *They were incredibly playful and sweet. They love toys, all kinds of toys. They are very trusting, and I am amazed by them all.*
>
> *They followed me on our walks around the yard, and almost always went off in the woods to "do their duty." They come when called. I just used the word "Puppies!" though I suggested names in honor of great dogs I have known and my loved ones have known, but you are welcome to give them your own. I am sure they will be wonderful hiking dogs as they grow up.*
>
> *They are very sweet with my son and adore him, and they were also sweet with his friends. They were even nice to my cat!*
>
> ***They will bring you a lot of love and be terrific companions, so please give these sweet guys and girls good forever homes. I know I will miss them terribly, but I can only pray they have loving, kind, happy homes. They will bring you so much joy too!***

So, my second time fostering, I ended up with two puppies, just like back with Blue-Chew. Now I have a five-dog house again.

I have the shy big boy, the largest of the litter, whom I named Kip. He was depressed for the first week I had him; I'm quite sure he missed his mother. I worked especially with him to build his trust in people and help him overcome his fears. I also have the runt, a little black and white sweet girl, whom I named Harper (both are named after writers). She is unafraid of anything; life is a party to her. As soon as I brought them home, the two tangled in happy wrestling, chasing each other madly through the house, then back to my bedroom where they climbed up past growling Chewie and barking Miza to shove themselves into my arms and kiss me.

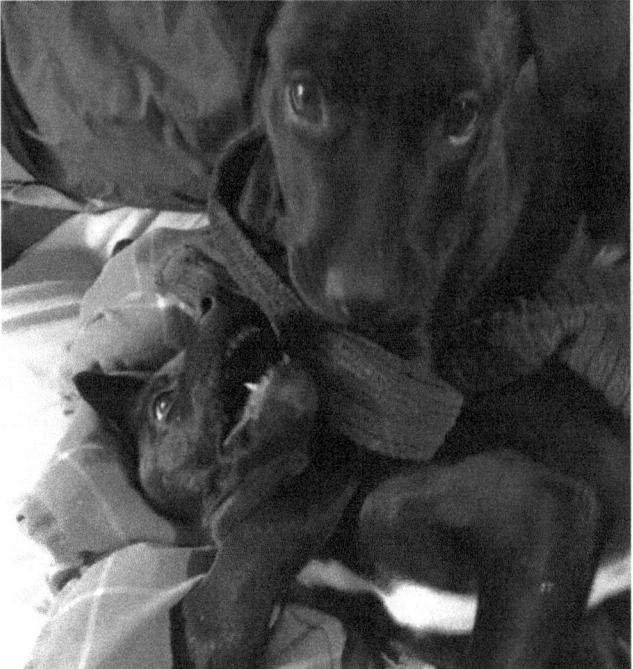

Harper, the runt, and Kip, the giant "shy guy."

Their love and affection for me, and each other, as well as their trust in me and enthusiasm for living brings me so much happiness and amazement, as dogs do.

I was, of course, worried about how Miza would react, especially since I brought home another male (I would have adopted the two females, Bella and Harper, just because of Miza, but I was also worried about the Kip's fears and shyness, so the decision was made for me by Bella not being made available yet).

Surprisingly, Miza has been gentle and relatively quiet about it. Little Harper actually kisses him right on the lips as he growls at her, and puts her little head inside his mouth. I watch them carefully of course. Miza actually seems to be enjoying the affection from her, and even has started playing with her a little. It seems to be calming him. I'm thinking of renaming her "Xanax." I sometimes daydream that the little Harper's love will calm Miza down, stop his insane barking and growling, and make my life peaceful again. A lot of pressure to put on one little puppy.

I already know that Kip and Harper and I will have a great life together. We will have lots of dog walks in the woods, and we will sleep on the bed and cuddle, and we will play tug-of-war with toys, and I will throw snowballs for them in the winter.

I will take care of them if they are sick or hurt, and they will take care of me always, in that kind, gentle way dogs do.

I didn't mean to have five dogs, but it happened, and I think of the times I used to walk Blue, Chewie, Schatzy, and Newt (and after Newt passed away, Miza) at the dog park in Anchorage.

"*How* many dogs do you *have*?" people would ask me, over and over, every day.

"Four," I'd reply, apologetically. I'd try to say they were all rescues, needed homes, something, but most would just give me an unpleasant look and walk on.

So I was expecting the "look" when a man with the acceptable two dogs asked me one day, "How many dogs do you have?"

"Four," I said, awaiting his disapproval.

"Well, aren't you blessed!" he said happily.

His sweet, enthusiastic reply made me smile the rest of the day.

I am blessed. I have been so blessed to know so many wonderful dogs. And so, Harper and Kip, on to our future adventures and eventual heartbreaking parting. I am ready if you are.

Shy Kip, coming out of hiding after we adopted him. (Photo by David Jensen).

Kip (top) and Harper's first vet visit. Kip, the "shy guy," hides behind Winston, while Harper happily eats her first leash.

Lessons Learned from Foster Puppies

Fostering is a great kindness. It builds trust and training and helps assure we will find good forever homes. But sometimes you have to let go and trust that we are happy. If you're really lucky, and blessed, you can keep one or two of us. We promise to be grateful to you always.

WHAT THE FUTURE HOLDS

> *Because of the dog's joyfulness, our own is increased. It is no small gift. It is not the least reason why we should honor as well as love the dog of our own life, and the dog down the street, and all the dogs not yet born. What would the world be like without music or rivers or the green and tender grass? What would this world be like without dogs?*
>
> —Mary Oliver, Dog Songs

What would my life have been like without dogs?

I can't picture it, to be honest, nor do I want to.

The one consistency I've had, through all the bad relationships, jobs that didn't work out, friendships that faltered, family members who passed away...is the love of my dogs.

I am overwhelmed with their love, and grateful, and sorry I couldn't see sometimes that it was enough. That it was better to be "alone" (but never really alone) with my dogs than to accept relationships with men that were not rich and real.

My life now is good.

I have a beautiful son, who is 14 years old as I complete this, and I have a man in my life who is stable and kind. I am also blessed to have my health, even after a few short years of five surgeries back to back. I am still able to walk my dogs every day, and I'm so thankful for that.

Walking with dogs has always been the happy, peaceful break of my day. Their joy in the car ride and as we embark into the wilderness—whether it was in Alaska, Oregon, Washington, or California—is nothing if not infectious, no matter how tired or busy I might be, or how much pain I am in.

As I write this ending, Blue and Chewie are nearing nine years old. Miza is probably six, although he still and will forever, I assume, act like a crazy half-grown pup. I fear their aging and eventual loss, but I have no regrets. It is true that every loss has been incredibly painful, so bad that at times I felt like I couldn't move or function, but I tell myself, "I gave them good homes and good quality lives when such things do not exist for many of this world's dogs." I promise them I will trudge onward, and do my part to rescue other dogs, like them, who need a loving home, and to continue working to end pet overpopulation.

And now suddenly, unexpectedly, I have the two foster puppies in my life, Kip and Harper. I calculate my age (54) and how, if I'm lucky, they'll live to be about 14, so I'll be 68 when they leave me. That sounds very old to me, whose parents died so young (60 and 63), and I wonder if they will be my last dogs. I tell myself I'll do my best to outlive them. I wouldn't want them to go through losing me, as I have had to experience losing my beloved dogs in each decade of my precious life with these wonderful animal companions.

For my life with dogs has been a treasure, and the future only holds more happy walks and hugs, and too...great grief. In a few short years, Blue, Chewie, and yes, even Miza, must leave me because their lives burn so much faster than mine.

Through it all, I know that I am a very lucky person...to have bonded so closely with dogs.

Schatzy, me, Woody, Chewie, Winston, and Greg (Photo by David Jensen).

Chewie in December 2014 (Photo by David Jensen).

ABOUT THE AUTHOR

Jory Ames writes and lives in Alaska. She has lived throughout the Northwest and taught English for 18 years. She enjoys her family, writing, reading, music, nature hikes, mountains, dogs, and cats but is not so much a fan of cold Alaskan winters. Jory has been volunteering for humane societies since 1977, particularly focusing on ending pet overpopulation and the killing of healthy, adoptable dogs and cats at animal control shelters. She has published hundreds of poems, short stories, articles, and essays in newspapers, literary journals, and magazines. She is especially grateful to her readers.

WORKS BY JORY AMES

NONFICTION
Birth 101
For the Love of Dogs: My Life in Dog Years
Poor Little Allison: The Struggle to Survive a Loved One's Murder

POETRY
Lucifer and Other Love Poems
Poems of Love, Loss, and Regret

CONTACT THE AUTHOR:

I appreciate your reading my book. Here is how you can contact me:

E-mail: joryames@gmail.com

www.ingramcontent.com/pod-product-compliance
Lightning Source LLC
Chambersburg PA
CBHW071310110426
42743CB00042B/1240